RESHAPING THE PUBLIC SECTOR VOLUME 8

Series Editors:
John Gretton and Anthony Harrison

EVALUATING THE NATIONAL HEALTH SERVICE REFORMS

Edited by

Ray Robinson
Julian Le Grand

POLICY JOURNALS

Transaction Books
New Brunswick (USA) and Oxford (UK)

Reshaping the Public Sector

Other volumes in the series include:

Reshaping Central Government
  edited by John Gretton and Anthony Harrison

Reshaping the National Health Service
  edited by Robert Maxwell

Reshaping Local Government
  edited by Michael Parkinson

Reshaping the Nationalised Industries
  edited by Christine Whitehead

The Control of Public Expenditure, 1979–1989
  Anthony Harrison

Not for Profit: Not for Sale
  Michael Starks

From Hierarchy to Contract
  edited by Anthony Harrison

Published and distributed in the UK by
POLICY JOURNALS, The Old Vicarage,
Marlston Road, Hermitage,
Nr Newbury, Berks RG16 9SU

Published and distributed in the USA by
TRANSACTION BOOKS
Rutgers University, New Brunswick,
New Jersey 08903

ISBN: 0-946967-42-3 (hardback)
ISBN: 0-946967-43-1 (paperback)

Design: David Cutting Graphics, Cambridge CB2 1DB

Typeset by Anneset, Weston-super-Mare, Avon, BS23 1RF

Printed by J W Arrowsmith Ltd, Winterstoke Road, Bristol BS3 2NT

CONTENTS

Introduction   *Ray Robinson*   1

1 Origins and Early Development
   John Butler   13

2 Monitoring Managed Competition
   John Appleby, Paula Smith, Wendy Ranade, Val Little,
   Ray Robinson   24

3 The Performance of Trusts
   Will Bartlett and Julian Le Grand   54

4 GP Fundholding: Wild Card or Winning Hand?
   Howard Glennerster, Manos Matsaganis, Pat Owens and
   Stephanie Hancock   74

5 Choice of Hospital for Elective Surgery Referrals: GPs'
   and Patients' Views
   Ann Mahon, David Wilkin and Carl Whitehouse   108

6 Monitoring Changes in Health Services for Older People
   Dee Jones, Carolyn Lester, Robert West   130

7 Monitoring Medical Audit
   Susan Kerrison, Tim Packwood and Martin Buxton   155

8 The Changing Role of the NHS Personnel Function
   Ian Seccombe and Jim Buchan   178

9 Is it Fair? Evaluating the equity implications of the
   NHS reforms
   Margaret Whitehead   208

10 Evaluating the NHS Reforms
   Julian Le Grand   243

   References   261

   Index   281

CONTRIBUTORS

Ray Robinson is Professor of Health Policy and Director of the Institute for Health Policy Studies at the University of Southampton. He was formerly Deputy Director of the King's Fund Institute.

John Butler is Professor of Health Services Studies and Director of the Centre for Health Services Studies at the University of Kent at Canterbury

John Appleby is Senior Research Fellow, Health Services Management Centre, University of Birmingham

Paula Smith is Research Fellow at the Institute for Local Government Studies Birmingham

Wendy Ranade is Senior Lecturer at the Department of Economics and Government at the University of Northumbria in Newcastle

Val Little is head of commissioning at Sandwell Health Authority

Will Bartlett is Research Fellow at the School for Advanced Urban Studies, University of Bristol

Julian Le Grand is Richard Titmuss Professor of Health Policy at the London School of Economics and Political Science and Professorial Fellow at the King's Fund Institute

Howard Glennerster is Professor of Social Administration at the London School of Economics and Political Science

Manos Matsaganis was a Research Officer at the Santory-Togota International Centre for Economics and Related Disciplines, London School of Economics

Stephanie Hancock was a Research Assistant at the Santory-Togota International Centre for Economics and Related Disciplines, London School of Economics

Pat Owens was a Research Assistant in the Department of Social Science and Administration, London School of Economics

Dee Jones is Research Fellow in the Research Team for the Care of Elderly People, University of Wales College of Medicine, Cardiff

Carolyn Lester is Director of the Research Team for the Care of Elderly People, University of Wales College of Medicine, Cardiff

Robert West is University of Wales Reader in epidemiology, Cardiff

Ann Mahon is Research Fellow in the Health Services Management Unit, University of Manchester

David Wilkin is Director, Centre for Primary Care Research, University of Manchester

Carl Whitehouse is Senior Lecturer in the Department of General Practice, University of Manchester

Susan Kerrison is Research Fellow with the Health Economics Research Group at Brunel University

Tim Packwood is Senior Lecturer in Public and Social Administration in the Department of Government, Brunel University

Martin Buxton is Professor of Health Economics and Director of the Health Economics Research Group at Brunel University

Ian Seccombe is Senior Research Fellow at the Institute for Manpower Studies, University of Sussex

Jim Buchan was Research Fellow at the Institute for Manpower Studies, University of Sussex and is now Senior Human Resources Specialist with the NHS Management Executive in Scotland

Margaret Whitehead is an independent health policy analyst and visiting Fellow at the King's Fund Institute

INTRODUCTION

Ray Robinson

Taken together, the proposals represent the most far-reaching reform of the National Health Service in its forty year history.

This was how Margaret Thatcher, when Prime Minister, described the NHS reforms in her foreword to the white paper, *Working for Patients* (Secretaries of State, 1989), in January 1989. Given the sweeping nature of the changes, there was, at the time, widespread criticism of the decision to press ahead with implementation without making any official provision for testing, monitoring or evaluating the impact of the reforms. But the Government was unmoved. Indeed, in his evidence to the House of Commons Select Committee, the then Secretary of State for Health, Kenneth Clarke, denied the need for formal monitoring and evaluation and expressed the view that calling on the advice of academics in this way was a sign of weakness (Health Services Journal, 1 June 1989).

It was against this background of official lack of interest in monitoring the reforms – and in the belief that this view was misguided – that the King's Fund decided to make such evaluative work the focus of a major grants programme. Consequently, during the summer of 1989, applications from interested researchers were invited through national advertisements in the specialist press. In the event, 72 applications were received and, after consideration, seven of these were selected for financial support. Each project was subsequently carried out over the period 1990 to 1993.

This book contains accounts of these seven research projects. Each chapter has been specially written for the book and describes the project in question, reports a number of its key findings and offers some thoughts about the likely course of future health policy in the relevant area as the NHS reforms develop over time.

Although detailed results from several of these studies have been published elsewhere in specialist journals and research reports, we feel that there is a strong case for bringing them together – in a format aimed at a more general readership – given the collective record they offer of a period of dramatic change within the NHS. Moreover, although inevitably they do not cover all aspects of the reforms we believe that taken together they represent the most wide-ranging and authoritative account of the change process yet to appear. This feature is of particular importance in an area where special pleading and polemic still sometimes dominate accounts of recent developments in the NHS.

The Reforms

The reforms embodied in the 1990 NHS and Community Care Act and introduced on 1 April 1991 represent the greatest change in the organisation and management of the NHS since it was established. In essence, an internal market has been created within the NHS in which the responsibility for purchasing, or commissioning, services has been separated from the responsibility for providing them.

On the demand side of this market, the key decision makers are district health authorities (DHAs) and general practice fundholders. DHAs now have major new responsibilities for assessing the health care needs of their resident populations and for commissioning a mix of secondary and community health services which best meets these needs. Over the last two years there have been a number of amalgamations among DHAs – as they have relinquished their previous provider functions – and several initiatives designed to integrate DHA functions with those of other agencies responsible for the commissioning of primary care (Family Health Services Authorities) and social care (local authority Social Service Departments). Operating alongside DHAs on the demand side of the market there are an increasing number of GP fundholders. These GPs receive budgets top-sliced from district allocations with which they can purchase a range of diagnostic, out-patient and minor inpatient procedures for patients registered with them. The rate of growth of fundholding has proved to be one of the more unexpected elements of the NHS reforms. From small beginnings, when it was widely regarded as something of a side-show to the main reform agenda, fundholding has now grown to the point where it constitutes an important part of the purchasing scene. By April 1993, fundholding practices covered more than one quarter of the population in England: it seems likely the proportion will rise to two-fifths by April 1994.

On the supply side of the internal market, the key change has been the establishment of NHS trusts. These are independent, non-governmental organisations providing secondary and community health services. They are directly accountable to the Secretary of State for Health although special NHS Management Executive Outposts have been set up to monitor trusts and to operationalise this accountability. Compared to units that were directly managed by DHAs, trusts have greater autonomy and freedom of action. This autonomy includes the ability to set the pay and conditions of service of their workforce; to decide upon the size and skill-mix of their staff; and to exercise some limited new freedoms in relation to capital expenditure. If present plans are realised, 95 per cent of hospital and community services in the UK will be provided by NHS trusts by April 1994. Table 1 summarises the main changes introduced as a result of the reforms and reflects the Government's own view as to their significance of the reforms.

The Chapters

The events leading up to the introduction of the reforms are described in the first chapter of this book. This has been prepared by John Butler of the University of Kent. In fact, Professor Butler's work did not form part of the original King's Fund major grants programme and so we are especially grateful to him for agreeing to draw on his own work in order to set the scene for the subsequent chapters.

In his review, Professor Butler highlights the political environment of the 1980s: an environment which he argues 'valued wealth above welfare, markets above bureaucracies, and competition above patronage'. This was the seed bed for the NHS internal market. The proximate cause was, however, the political crisis surrounding the NHS funding position which came to a head in the winter of 1987. This led to the setting-up of the Prime Ministerial Review and, subsequently, to *Working for Patients*.

At the outset of the reform programme, considerable emphasis was placed upon the internal market and the role of competition within it. Thereafter

Table 1: Comparison of Old and New NHS

Old system	New system

Role of District Health Authorities

Old system	New system
DHAs have confused responsibilities covering both the overall planning of services and the running of hospitals and other units.	DHAs' main responsibility becomes the health of local people. They will assess health needs and decide how best they can be met.

Funding of Health Services

Old system	New system
DHAs funded for the services which happen to lie within their boundaries, largely on the basis of historic patient flows.	DHAs will be funded to purchase services on behalf of their residents. Funding will, over time, reflect the size, age and relative health of DHA populations.
Hospitals and other units receive a budget from their DHA, often bearing little relation to the number of patients they are expected to treat in the coming year (inadequate funding arrangements for patients from other DHAs).	Hospitals and other units receive funding from those DHAs with which they agree NHS contracts (or service agreements). These contracts set out the quantity, quality and cost of services to be provided (through the year.) This links funding and the activity required to meet identified health needs.

Management of Health Services

Old system	New system
Too many tiers of bureaucracy controlling the activities of hospitals and other units.	All hospitals and other units take on greater responsibility for their own affairs, so the people providing services are the ones taking decisions. Some become self-governing NHS trusts, independent of DHAs but still firmly within the NHS.

Table 1: continued

Role of GPs

Few incentives for hospitals to respond to the needs and preferences of GPs and local people.	DHAs consult extensively with local GPs on preferred referral patterns and conduct surveys of local opinion as part of the process of agreeing contracts with hospitals on the services to be provided.
	Some GPs become GP fundholders, giving them the financial backing to purchase certain hospital services directly for their patients.

Integrating Health Services

Very little integration between primary and secondary care, and little attention focused on achieving the right balance of prevention and treatment. FPCs not under management of Regional Health Authorities.	DHAs (responsible for hospital and community health services) and FHSAs (responsible for primary health care services) both under the management of RHAs, ensuring effective joint working to improve the health of local residents. DHAs new role in focusing on health puts them in a better position, jointly with FHSAs, to achieve a balance of prevention and treatment.

Source: Department of Health, PN 91/138

official views about the role expected of competition started to shift and to soften. As Professor Butler points out, this created something of a paradox: a competitive market with winners and losers had been deemed necessary in order to improve economic performance, but on grounds of political sensitivity the Government was at pains to distance itself from a too pro-competitive stance on health care. Hence the concept of managed competition was adopted.

Managed competition is the focus of Chapter Two. In it John Appleby and colleagues report on a project based at the National Association of

Health Authorities and Trusts (NAHAT). This set out to monitor the introduction of managed competition in the West Midlands Region. Given the scope of the topic, a multi-disciplinary team of researchers used a variety of methodologies to analyse change over the three year period. These included surveys of managers' attitudes and activities in relation to the reforms, detailed case study interviews which revealed in-depth accounts of the way in which change did – and did not – occur at the district level, and an examination of managed competition through the use of an empirical measure of the degree of competition facing each of the acute general hospitals in the region.

The surveys and the case study findings provide a fascinating insight into the importance of local management cultures in the process of implementing change. In broad terms, these cultures can be characterised as pro-active or re-active, with the former emphasising clarity of purpose, willingness to prioritise, emphasis on learning-by-doing, and a strong corporate commit-ment. The measure of competition developed as part of the study offers an empirical perspective in an area where, to date, theoretical predictions and speculations have dominated discussion. Interestingly, and contrary to some of the early expectations surrounding the introduction of competition into the NHS, the findings of the NAHAT team suggest that hospital markets are far more competitive than is often supposed. For example, their results suggest that, in the case of general surgical services, around three-quarters of hospitals in the West Midlands operate in markets that can be designated competitive. Despite its early stage of development, this measure has already attracted widespread interest from Government and from other researchers with an interest in competition policy.

In Chapter Three, Will Bartlett and Julian Le Grand present an assess-ment of the performance of NHS trusts. In doing so, they identify two approaches to assessing performance: a direct approach which measures performance in terms of particular indicators such as the rate of return on capital employed or costs per patient day, and an indirect approach which identifies those market features that are necessary for a trust to operate successfully and then seeks to establish whether, in practice, these conditions are met.

As far as the direct approach is concerned, their own econometric study suggests that first wave trusts were a self-selecting group that already had lower unit costs than other hospitals before they acquired trust status. As such, their lower costs cannot be attributed to trust status. The indirect approach – which they feel has more potential for measuring performance in the future – suggests that market conditions may well be right for trusts to obtain greater efficiency, offer more choice and be more responsive, although concerns about equity persist.

Beyond these assessments, however, they argue that the lack of a well-defined theory of trusts' objectives and behaviour makes it difficult to predict exactly how they will behave in the future and, therefore, makes it difficult to derive mechanisms which will ensure that they meet pre-determined public policy objectives.

Chapter Four contains a report on GP fundholding by Howard Glennerster and his colleagues at the London School of Economics. As they point out, fundholding was seen only as a peripheral part of the NHS reform programme back in 1989. It was widely regarded as a 'bolt-on' to the more central features of the internal market. However, the role of fundholding has changed dramatically since then, producing more rapid change than elsewhere, with GPs changing their own practice styles and bringing about change in those hospitals and support services from whom they purchased services. Fundholding is now centre stage and posing serious questions about how it can be developed alongside a district-based purchasing approach.

In their study, Professor Glennerster and his colleagues offer an absorbing account of the development of fundholding, together with a balance sheet of emerging evidence on the efficiency and equity consequences of the scheme. Given the polarisation of views on fundholding, they conclude that its fortunes in the future could range from abolition – which they consider would be very foolhardy – to the development of purchasing arrangements which give even greater powers to fundholders with the roles of enlarged districts confined to strategic functions rather than day-to-day purchasing.

Throughout the 1980s, the introduction of market based systems of resource allocation in a range of economic and social policy areas was seen by the Government as a means of widening consumer choice and, thereby, increasing producer responsiveness to consumer preferences. The extent to which this objective has so far been met through the NHS reforms is examined by Ann Mahon and her colleagues from the Centre for Primary Care Research at the University of Manchester. Their work is reported in Chapter Five.

Through the use of postal questionnaires distributed to GPs and their patients, both before and after the introduction of the reforms, the researchers sought to examine any changes in the nature and extent of choice offered to patients by GPs when referring them to hospital. Their findings indicate that the level of patient involvement in the choice of hospital is low and that there was little change in this level during the first year of the reforms. Most patients reported that the choice of hospital was made by the GPs with less than one in ten claiming that they had chosen the hospital themselves. Most people seemed to be happy with this arrangement. The study also examined patients' willingness to travel for treatment and found that there was a good deal less willingness than suggested by some other studies.

Overall, the Manchester researchers concluded that there was little evidence of any major changes in patient or GP experiences of hospital choice following the introduction of the NHS reforms. More generally, they question whether the mechanism for empowering patients and extending choice, based upon the 'supermarket model' of consumerism, is appropriate in health care, and suggest that other mechanisms for increasing public participation may be more suitable.

The extent to which patients' interests have been accorded high priority following the introduction of the reforms is also the focus of the study carried out by Dee Jones, Carolyn Lester and Robert West and reported in Chapter Six. In this case, attention was concentrated on services for the elderly. As the researchers point out, services for elderly people account for the lion's share of health care expenditure in both community and hospital sectors and this proportion can be expected to increase in the future as the numbers of elderly and very elderly people increase.

Their study involved asking a random sample of around 1,500 elderly people in South Wales about their views and experiences of community health services in 1990, before the introduction of the NHS reforms, and asking the same questions of another random sample of the same size after implementation of the reforms in 1992. A similar approach and sample size was used to establish views and experiences in relation to hospital services. By using this approach, a detailed 'before' and 'after' picture was able to be built up about patients' views of, *inter alia*, services offered by primary care teams, community health services, experiences of waiting for and receiving hospital treatment, and discharge arrangements.

The overall conclusion of the project is that health service performance measured in terms of four main criteria – accessibility, choice, communication and quality – has so far shown little improvement following the reforms. Restricted patient choice between hospitals, problems with accessibility to GP services and complaints about catering, privacy and cleanliness in hospitals all remained more or less unchanged between the two survey periods. Of course, the authors concede that the timescale of the study was necessarily short and that large organisations such as the NHS clearly take time to adjust to new circumstances. Whether or not a longer term view will offer a more optimistic picture remains to be seen.

One aspect of the NHS reforms that received almost universal approval was the decision to implement systems for medical audit in all health authorities. Medical audit involves clinicians undertaking systematic review of their work with the aim of improving standards. As such, it offers clear scope for better quality and more effective care. Realising this potential, however, hinges crucially upon the successful implementation of audit systems. The implementation process was the focus of a study by Susan Kerrison and colleagues from Brunel University.

Their study, reported in Chapter Seven, provides an in-depth account of the implementation of audit systems in general medicine at four hospital sites. The sites were selected to offer contrasts in the extent to which, *inter alia*, doctors were involved in management, information technology was developed and systems for quality assurance were in place. Their results suggest that while there have been a number of audits displaying considerable depth and breadth, numerous problems have been encountered. They found that often audit was interpreted too narrowly and dominated by senior doctors, to the exclusion of other health professionals. Frequently, there was an absence of clear guidelines and standards were often based on implicit criteria or individual opinion. Indeed, many senior doctors seemed to question the need to standardise their practice. Management input was often minimal with the result that there was frequently uncertainty about what should happen as the result of audit.

To correct these deficiencies, Kerrison and colleagues make a number of recommendations for the more successful development of audit in the future. They argue for wider representation on audit committees – involving the inclusion of other professions besides doctors – and better planning. Better information systems need to be put in place and more attention should be given to following up the results of audit. At the moment, audit does not seem to be clearly integrated in the management systems of many hospitals. This problem needs to be addressed. They also raise the prospect that audit might be more usefully directed to the needs of commissioners within the internal market instead of its present focus on providers.

The need to address management issues surrounding the implementation of different aspects of the reforms is also the focus of attention in Chapter Eight. In this case, it is the impact of the reforms on management of the NHS workforce which is examined by James Buchan and Ian Seccombe of the Institute of Manpower Studies at the University of Sussex. With a workforce of around one million people accounting for approximately three quarters of total NHS revenue expenditure, efficient utilisation of the NHS workforce is obviously a key management objective.

As the Institute's study shows, the decentralisation of responsibilities following the reforms has had significant implications for the management of labour costs and NHS personnel. One example has been the increasing involvement of the personnel function in reviews of skill and grade mix. The changes affecting nursing, involving the introduction of health care assistants and the employment of proportionately fewer higher qualified nurses, is one consequence of this trend. To date there has been little evaluation of the cost-effectiveness of moves of this type. There are also some concerns that quality may have been compromised. Elsewhere the greater autonomy offered to trusts through the reforms has led towards systems of local pay bargaining. Interestingly, however, the move away from national rates of pay and conditions of service has not been particularly rapid.

From an overall perspective, Buchan and Seccombe suggest that workforce developments in the NHS are presently in a state of flux with changes such as the reconfiguration of services in London involving major consequences for the size and composition of the workforce and for its management.

Over the period when the seven research projects reported in Chapters Two to Eight were being undertaken, the King's Fund Institute organised a series of annual workshops for the research teams and was also able to keep in touch with emerging results through informal contacts with individual researchers. Among other things, this process revealed that the equity implications of the reforms were a recurring theme in several of the projects. At the same time, the Institute's own discussions suggested that equity, as a fundamental NHS objective, had been somewhat overshadowed in recent years as the pursuit of greater efficiency and value for money had become the dominant NHS policy objectives. Accordingly, in order to go some way towards redressing this imbalance, Margaret Whitehead was asked to review the evidence of the impact of the NHS reforms on the equity of the health care system. Her review is presented in Chapter Nine.

The very fact that equity issues have been neglected means that there is little systematic evidence in terms of which the reforms can be evaluated. Nonetheless, Margaret Whitehead has drawn on a range of sources in order to build up a picture of expectations and evidence relating to equity in three major areas; namely, GP fundholding, needs assessment and resource allocation and the provision of long term, continuing care. Her analysis indicates that despite clear improvements in performance in many instances, policies such as GP fundholding have undoubtedly created a two-tier system among patients in a number of areas; that *Health of the Nation* targets concentrating on health gain may sometimes generate greater inequality; and that policies towards long term care of the elderly have introduced major inequities. Many of these consequences have arisen because, as Whitehead points out, there are sometimes trade-offs between efficiency, effectiveness and equity. To avoid these dangers she suggests that careful monitoring, possibly through equity audits, will be necessary if longstanding, NHS equity aims are not to be jeopardised in the future.

Finally, in Chapter Ten, Julian Le Grand offers some reflections on evaluation and the NHS reforms. In doing so, he employs the distinction between direct and indirect evidence outlined in his and Bartlett's own study in Chapter Three and draws examples of both types of evidence from the King's Fund major grants projects and evaluative research conducted elsewhere.

Professor Le Grand argues that the impact of the reforms should be judged in terms of the fundamental objectives of quality, efficiency, choice, responsiveness and equity. However, he points to the considerable difficulty of isolating the precise effects in these areas, over what is only a three year period and when other major changes have been taking place at the same time. For this reason, he also discusses the indirect approach in which researchers seek to identify whether or not the prerequisites for an efficient and equitable market are met. But perhaps his main conclusion is to reinforce the message made by several of the research teams; namely that, for those who believe that sound policy should be based on firm information, the culmination of the King's Fund programme represents the first stage in the process of evaluative research and not the end of it.

These then are the contributions which have been brought together in this book. Taken together they offer an unrivalled account of major policy change across a broad spectrum of the NHS. Looking back, the King's Fund decision to concentrate a sizeable proportion of its annual grant allocation in this area appears to have been well judged and far-sighted. We hope that this view is shared by readers of this book. We also hope that it stimulates further work on the part of those who have responsibility for undertaking health service research and those responsible for funding it.

1

ORIGINS AND EARLY DEVELOPMENT

John Butler

Ostensibly, the reforms to the National Health Service that came into legislative force on 1 April 1991 began in January 1988 with the announcement by the then Prime Minister, Margaret Thatcher, that a Government working party had already been set up to review the operation of the service. The formal outcome of the review was known a year later, with the publication of *Working for Patients*. This was quickly followed by the slightly, but only slightly, more detailed working papers on specific aspects of the plan; then came the National Health Service and Community Care Act, which received royal assent in June 1990; and then followed a whole portfolio of regulations and guidelines to ensure that the reforms were implemented in ways acceptable to the Government.

In fact, however, the origins of the reforms went back much further than the Government's working group. In retrospect, a number of key changes to the NHS throughout the 1980s, which were designed to bring a distinctive set of political ideas to the public sector services, had laid many of the foundations of a central feature of the reforms, namely the internal market, long before the working group began its task. It is always dangerous to try to capture the political spirit of the times in a few impressionistic phrases, but it is worth recapturing the central tenets of Mrs Thatcher's philosophy, for they defined the broad goals towards which the NHS was moving before *Working for Patients* was even a twinkle in Ministers' eyes (Gamble, 1988).

Central to the philosophy was a belief in the paramount importance of a sound economy and a strong currency, the pursuit of which took precedence over other aims and objectives. Social policy had always to be subservient to economic policy, for the ultimate test of Government competence was seen to lie in its management of the economy, not of the social programmes. A sound economy was, in any case, seen as a necessary pre-condition if the country was to afford the luxury of a welfare state. Another core conviction was that nothing should be done in the public sector that could just as well be done in the private sector. In the case of health care, this led to an abiding tension for much of the 1980s between the Government's instinctive desire to control the flow of public funds into the NHS and its electoral need to proclaim the service safe in Conservative hands (Klein, 1989). And a third plank in the philosophy was an axiomatic assumption of the ubiquity of organisational inefficiency – an inefficiency that supposedly owed much to the dominant influence of corporate groups concerned more with preserving their privileges than with modernising their attitudes and activities. In shorthand language, the internal market in the NHS was the product of a political environment that valued wealth about welfare, markets above bureaucracies, and competition above patronage; and it was the steady application of these preferences to the NHS throughout the 1980s that made possible the introduction of the internal market in the 1990s.

Four developments of the 1980s can be seen in retrospect as harbingers of what was to come. The first was the growth of managerialism. It is perhaps surprising to recall that Mrs Thatcher came to power in 1979 on a broadly anti-managerial ticket. It was widely believed that British public administration was bedevilled by too much management and too many administrators. Indeed, in his first major pronouncement on the NHS, Patrick Jenkin, Mrs Thatcher's first Secretary of State for Social Services, explicitly rejected the notion of general management in the NHS on the grounds that it would not be compatible with professional independence (Department of Health and Social Security, 1979). Four years later all had changed, and by 1983 Mr Jenkin's successor, Norman Fowler, was unreservedly accepting Mr (later Sir) Roy Griffith's managerialistic diagnosis of the ills of the service and was enthusiastically implementing general management at all levels of the NHS (House of Commons, 1983). It was a move that, with hindsight, can be seen as an essential pre-condition to the implementation of the internal market by making the NHS more open to political influence through the creation of a management culture of command and obedience.

The second development of the 1980s that laid the foundations of the internal market was the introduction of schemes of income generation.

Though they never produced as much revenue as Ministers hoped they would, these schemes were of symbolic importance in signalling a new ethos of entrepreneurialism in the NHS, and they were of practical importance in releasing health authorities from the existing restrictions on their freedom to sell services for profit. A key event was the passage of the Health and Medicines Act in 1988, followed in 1989 by the Department of Health's guidelines on the scope for income generation (Department of Health, 1989). The result was swift if never spectacular. Shopping arcades were opened in unfilled corridors; health clubs were established in unused basements; mail order services were created selling everything from bandages to stretchers; wall space was sold for advertising; land space was sold for car parking; and fees were reportedly charged to undertakers for measuring the bodies of those who died in hospital (Pike, 1990). Marketing perspectives were beginning to permeate through to the very soul of the welfare state (Sheaff, 1991).

The third development of the 1980s was the policy of contracting out. For obvious reasons, contracting out was attractive to the incoming Conservative Government in 1979, and by 1983 a Department of Health circular was requiring health authorities to set up programmes of competitive tendering for their cleaning, catering and laundry requirements (Department of Health and Social Security, 1983). At the same time financial steps were being taken to ensure that private contractors could compete on equal terms with existing in-house services. By 1987 the process of competitive tendering had begun to spread beyond the domestic services to include other non-clinical services, such as portering, transport and computing, extending eventually to encompass clinical services, such as diagnostic and pathology services. The real importance of these developments, however, lay less in the financial gains that were achieved, though they were by no means negligible (Harrison, 1992), than in the principle that they established: the core responsibility of the health authorities is not to provide and manage services directly themselves, but rather to ensure that they are available when and where required at least cost to the authority and at zero cost to the patients using them. The separation of purchasing from providing had begun.

The fourth development of the 1980s was the growth of internal markets. It is worth recalling that the notion of an internal market in the NHS was well developed in theory, and to some extent in practice, long before it was adopted by the Government's working group in 1988/89. There had actually been a very extensive discussion of the idea in the academic and policy literature throughout much of the 1980s, most notably by Professor Enthoven, who in 1985 had mapped out the skeleton of an internal market for the NHS in which district general managers would be enabled to purchase services for their resident populations from private hospitals, from NHS hospitals in other districts, and from their own directly-managed hospitals (Enthoven, 1985). Not only that, the internal market had been discussed in a major report from the House of Commons Social Services Committee (1988); it had become a focal point of policy debate in other countries, most notably The Netherlands (Decker, 1987) and New Zealand (Davies, 1989); and simple elements of a market had been put in place in London by 1987, when some teaching hospitals began to charge directly for services to out-of-district patients rather than waiting to be compensated two years in arrears through adjustments to their districts' financial allocation. In fact by 1988, still before publication of *Working for Patients*, a fairly sophisticated competitive market was up and running in the East Anglian region, and the regional health authority actually offered itself to the Department of Health as a test-bed site to evaluate the working of the market before its widespread introduction (Timmins, 1988a).

It was, nevertheless, something of a surprise that the Government's working group eventually chose the internal market as its preferred solution to the ills of the NHS, not least because of the minimal relationship the market appeared to bear to the issues that had given rise to it in the first place. There had been no indication in the 1987 Conservative manifesto of any major changes to the NHS, and less than a week before Mrs Thatcher's revelation of the existence of the working group, the Secretary of State for Social Services, John Moore, had delivered a major speech in the House of Commons on the future of the NHS that made no reference to any such review (House of Commons, 1987). It appears, therefore, that Mrs Thatcher's announcement was a forced political response to the gathering storm over the funding of the service.

There was nothing particularly new about the threat of fiscal crisis in the NHS, for the growth in NHS funding in volume terms had been lower throughout most of the 1980s than in the previous two decades (Robinson and Judge, 1987). Indeed, the rhetoric of imminent disaster was almost as old as the service itself (Powell, 1966). Yet a number of events conspired together to create an irresistible perception of political crisis in the winter of 1987/88. There was extensive coverage in the media of stories of patients, especially young babies, suffering or even dying through the closure of facilities; there was a spate of early day motions and adjournment debates in the House of Commons about local failures of services; there was evidence of ward closures on an unprecedented scale; there was a gloomy editorial in the British Medical Journal declaring the NHS to be in terminal decline (Smith, 1988); and there was the rather naive, but nevertheless well publicised, lament from the Presidents of the three senior Royal Colleges calling on the Government 'to do something now to save our health service, once the envy of the world' (Hoffenberg, Todd and Pinker, 1987). And what the Government, or rather, Mrs Thatcher, did was to set up the working group, which was in effect a Cabinet committee barred to those outside the immediate bosom of Government.

Because the working group began its assignment in a climate of crisis over the funding of the NHS, it was widely assumed that this would be the central issue addressed by the group. For a while this did indeed appear to be the case. Most of the blueprints for change that were submitted by outside groups and organisations were concerned with alternative ways of funding the service, and it was clear from lobby briefings that the working group itself was thinking along these very lines. Mr Moore, who remained Secretary of State for the first half of 1988, presented at least two plans for switching from a tax-based to an insurance-based service, one of which would have allowed people with private health insurance to contract out of the public scheme. The whole thrust of the early deliberations of the working group was upon the financing of the NHS and how it could be changed in ways that would generate more resources.

By the late summer of 1988, however, the agenda had totally changed. The luckless John Moore had been side-lined; the wetter but more bullish Kenneth Clarke had taken over at the reconstituted Department of Health; and the focus of the group's concern had shifted from issues about the financing of the NHS to those about the efficient use of its resources. The shift occurred, it was suggested, partly because of Mrs Thatcher's continuing caution about the political consequences of tampering with the financing of the service, and partly because of the realisation that, for all its drawbacks, a tax-funded service is very good at controlling the overall level of spending. It was at this stage that all the background thought and experience about internal markets came heavily to bear upon the group – so much so, that by the autumn of 1988 the die was cast, and the commercial fate of the NHS was sealed.

Rather surprisingly, however, the intended structure of the market was still quite fluid at this stage. In particular, the identity of the purchasers in the market remained an open issue until surprisingly late in the group's deliberations. The model of the market proposed by Enthoven, who was widely regarded as the consultant architect to the market's design, had envisaged health authorities as the sole buyers. There was no allowance in Enthoven's plan for GPs to have their own budgets, and the speculative kites about budget-holding that had been flown by the likes of Marinker (1984) were not widely regarded as feasible. Yet towards the end of 1988, David Mellor, then Minister of State for Health, was talking quite openly about the merits of budgetary devolution to GPs as a way of curbing very high rates of referral and prescribing (Brown, 1988). Even later on the scene was the concept of self-governing hospitals, which, like fundholding general practices, had no part to play in Enthoven's vision of the internal market. Indeed, as late as December 1988, only six weeks prior to the publication of *Working for Patients*, the Government was reported to be still trying to interest some London teaching hospitals in the idea, albeit a version of self-government in which the fixed overhead cost of the hospitals would be met directly by the Department of Health and only the variable costs would be covered by contracts (Timmins, 1988b). It was not until the white paper actually appeared that the true extent of the Government's commitment to self-government for hospitals became apparent, and it was not until May 1990 that the full scope of self-government became clear: not only would the larger acute hospitals be encouraged to opt out of control by the health authorities, so too would all other hospital and community health services.

Working for Patients was published on 31 January 1989 and was launched amidst a blaze of show-business publicity. It sparked off a propaganda battle of truly spectacular proportions that threatened at one time to deal a mortal blow to the Government's plans for the NHS, if not to the Government itself (Butler, 1992). Yet it proved to be a battle that, although never really won by the Government and its allies, was finally unable to hinder the implementation of almost all the key elements of the internal market it outlined.

At the heart of the white paper was the idea of separating out the functions of purchasing and providing, and giving responsibility for them to different agencies. On the purchasing side were the district health authorities and their equivalents in Scotland and Northern Ireland, and the larger general practices that voluntarily held their own budgets. On the providing side, the new self-governing hospitals would be competing with each other, with independent, *ie* private sector, hospitals, and with directly-managed hospitals for the custom of the purchasers. The transactions between purchasers and providers would be regulated by contracts which would vary in their specificity and in their subjection to legal determination, but which would specify the normal parameters of commercial intercourse – cost, volume, quality, timeliness, and so forth.

Around these central features of the internal market, a number of buttresses were erected in the white paper to hold it all in place and make it work. First, there would be the consolidation of a clear and effective line of management command and obedience to ensure that the NHS would be responsive to political pressures from Ministers. Second, the mechanism for funding the health authorities would be changed to reflect the size and composition of their resident populations rather than the volume of work done in their hospitals. Third, capital assets in the NHS would be charged for in similar ways to private capital to ensure that the commercial competition between public and private sectors would take place on the famed level playing-field. Fourth, the modern information and costing systems needed to drive the market would be introduced. Fifth, the systematic use of medical audit would be promoted to protect the market against the politically damaging charge of placing profitability before the quality of care. And sixth, the clinical freedom of the hospital consultants would be subjugated to a greater extent than hitherto to the business needs of the hospitals, by changing their contracts in ways that would make them more accountable to local managers. In short, there was a logical and even elegant coherence in the white paper's proposals for tightening the management structure of the service, revising the method of allocating resources to the purchasers, charging the providers for the use of public capital, creating better information and costing systems, formalising medical audit, and reshaping the consultants' contract.

Yet what was it all for? What were the goals or purposes or objectives of the white paper? In what ways was it intended that the future should be different from the past, given that the one thing that would not change would be the level or method of funding for the NHS? What was the theory underlying the Government's belief in the capacity of the internal market to enhance the efficient use of resources? What criteria could, or should, be used to judge the success or otherwise of what has happened to the NHS over the last four years? These are huge questions. Space permits no more than some general observations that will be taken up and expanded in the subsequent chapters of this book.

One approach is to tease out the purposes or objectives that *Working for Patients* proclaimed on its behalf. In fact there are a great many statements in the white paper and its associated working papers that can reasonably be regarded as internal statements of intent; but they are not uniformly helpful in setting up benchmarks for evaluative purposes, for they vary considerably in their level of specificity. Some are so general or so vague as to be little more than political slogans: the best value will be obtained for the resources available, patients will be treated as people, the performance of all hospitals and GPs will be raised to that of the best, the quality of health care will improve, and so forth. Such declarations offer nothing of substance by which to evaluate the changes that have engulfed the NHS.

Other objectives in *Working for Patients*, however, are more precisely formulated and might perhaps be open to empirical investigation. Examples can be given from the sections on general practice, though they are by no means the only ones. The white paper, and the subsequent working papers, prophesied that, as a result of the proposed changes in primary care, patients would have fuller information about their practices, a greater range of services would be offered in primary care, practice staff would enjoy greater job satisfaction, patients would be able to change practices more easily, drug expenditures would fall, levels of financial investment in general practice would rise, and doctors would have much better information about their activities and costs.

Between these extremes of generality and relative precision, *Working for Patients* identified a number of middle-range promises that might also be open to empirical investigation. Waiting times for hospital admissions would fall; the huge variability in referral rates and prescribing costs would diminish; more power and responsibility would be delegated down the management chain; doctors and nurses would become more intimately involved in service management; and a closer partnership would develop between the NHS and the private sector.

So much for the promises that the white paper made on its own behalf. Other purposes or objectives were enunciated or elaborated by Ministers in the weeks and months that followed its publication. Both Mr Clarke and Mr Mellor were enormously energetic in spelling out the aims and objectives of the proposed reforms to journalists, to the Commons Social Services Committee, and to the House itself. A number of themes recurred in these ministerial expositions. One was the better use that would be made of the resources of the NHS as money began to follow patients to the most efficient providers. Another was the greater accountability that clinicians would have for the way they used the resources under their control. A third theme was the freeing of the health authorities from their current responsibilities for providing and managing services, thus releasing them to concentrate on measuring needs and determining service requirements. And a fourth was the benefit that the self-governing hospitals would derive from the greater responsibility they would have for their affairs and from their exposure to the bracing breezes of competition. In particular, Ministers emphasised that by controlling their own staffing and capital, the self-governing hospitals would acquire direct incentives to manage their production processes more efficiently. As Mr Clarke put it in a memorable illustration, although medicine is more important that baked beans, most baked bean factories run more efficiently than most hospitals (Roberts, 1990).

This list of promised outcomes is by no means the totality of the Government's justifications for its reforms, but it does reflect many of the more important themes that Ministers and their allies used to defend the white paper against its critics. It may also provide some relevant criteria against which to judge the impact of the changes that have been, and still are, occurring in the NHS, for if few of the outcomes promised in the white paper or by Ministers are actually materialising, then it has to be wondered how successful the changes have been.

What neither the white paper nor Ministers defined, however, was the level of competitiveness at which the market would be allowed to work. The proposals in *Working for Patients*, taken together, could clearly be seen as a blueprint for a highly commercial and competitive market in health care. It was a market in which there could be genuinely free choice for the purchasers, genuine freedoms for the providers to organise their affairs in their own best interests, genuine competition among the providers for the custom of the purchasers, genuine rewards for those who were successful, and genuine penalties for those who failed.

At the same time, however, enough controls were built into the design of the market to give the Secretary of State fairly precise control over the degree of competitive behaviour that would be permitted. These controls could be exercised in many ways. Restrictions could be imposed, and to some extent have been, on the freedom of the self-governing hospitals to enter the private capital market or to employ staff on locally negotiated terms and conditions of service. Controls could be placed upon the freedom of the fundholding general practices to pursue their own unilateral purchasing strategies with the providers of their own choice. The corporate purchasers, the health authorities, could be held directly accountable to the Secretary of State through regional health authorities or whatever intermediate tier might replace or supplement them. Local providers might be constrained in their business plans by the requirements of central government. The logic of the market may be frustrated for political purposes through the use of public subsidies to prevent the closure of uncompetitive hospitals. And so on.

It seems fairly clear that the Government's working group originally intended the internal market to operate at a fairly high level of competitiveness (Butler, 1992). The evidence is to be seen in the Prime Minister's introduction to *Working for Patients*, in the jubilant reception accorded the white paper from the right wing of the Conservative party, in the hawkish early documentation produced by the NHS Management Executive on how the market would work, and in statements of ministerial intention to allow the market to produce its benign effects with minimal interference from the Government. The stance was ostensibly maintained by Ministers for quite some time – certainly until the summer of 1990. In retrospect, however, it is clear that as Mrs Thatcher's grip on her office began to weaken, so Ministers and their officials began to distance themselves from the stance they had been taking.

The shifting use of language was perhaps the clearest public sign of the sea-change taking place behind the scenes at the Department of Health. For as 1990 progressed, the words and phrases that smacked most clearly of things commercial were gradually squeezed out of the canon of acceptable terminology (Sheldon, 1990). 'Buyers' in the white paper became, with the passage of time, 'purchasers' and then 'commissioners'. 'Sellers' became 'providers'. General practice 'budgets' became 'funds'. Drug 'budgets' became 'amounts'. 'Marketing' became 'needs assessment'. Most telling of all, the introduction in April 1991 of what had originally been trumpeted as the most radical changes ever engineered in the NHS became known as a time of 'steady state' – a phrase that means nothing if not a smooth continuation of existing ways of doing things. As if to confirm the shift, the new Secretary of State for Health, William Waldegrave, candidly admitted in a speech to the Royal College of Surgeons in December 1990 that the Government had been carried away in its application of business language to the NHS, causing alarm to many people who 'think that we do not know the difference between a hospital and a supermarket' (Brindle, 1990). By February 1991 The Economist, which had generally taken a supportive editorial line on the NHS reforms, was informing its readers that 'in order to avoid an election-losing shake-up the new market will be strictly controlled from the centre . . . The Government is terrified that the idea at the heart of the reforms — making money follow the patient — might increase efficiency but lose votes' (Anon, 1991).

By April 1991, when the first part of the National Health Service and Community Care Act came into force, a paradox was thus emerging which, if left unattended, was threatening to produce serious strains and contradictions in the system. On the one hand, the structure of a potentially highly competitive market was being created, with buyers and sellers, prices and contracts, winners and losers. At the same time, however, the Government was strenuously denying that any such thing was happening, and was taking steps to ensure that, at least in the short run, the market would not be allowed to work in accordance with its creator's instructions. It is with the implications of this paradox that the NHS has struggled to come to terms over the last two years, and it is a paradox that the remaining chapters of this book explore in their varied ways.

2

MONITORING MANAGED COMPETITION

John Appleby, Paula Smith, Wendy Ranade, Val Little, Ray Robinson

A consistent theme of Government policy during the 1980s was a belief in the superior efficiency of the private sector. A major part of this belief was that it is the competitive environment within which private sector organisations operate which provides the necessary incentives for achieving greater efficiency. This provided the stated rationale for successive privatisation programmes in different sectors of the economy.

For most of the period, however, the National Health Service was not greatly affected by these policies. Certainly, there were a number of initiatives designed to improve management through the emulation of private sector models (Griffiths, 1983), and the introduction of competition at the margins through tendering for ancillary services (Ascher, 1987). But mainstream clinical services were largely unaffected by these changes.

The NHS and Community Care Act, 1990, of course, changed this situation fundamentally. Through the introduction of an internal market, in which the responsibility for purchasing services is separated from the responsibility for providing them, hospitals and other providers are now expected to compete for service contracts from purchasers. The Government's expectations of this system were set out in *Working for Patients* as follows:

> *A funding system in which successful hospitals can flourish . . . will encourage local initiative and greater competition. All this in turn will ensure a better deal for the public, improving the choice and quality of services offered and the efficiency with which these services are delivered* (p. 22).

Thus, the internal market and supply side competition were expected to increase efficiency, widen choice and improve quality. Although some relevant evidence from the USA was drawn on when these plans were prepared (Robinson, 1990; Appleby, 1992a), these expectations were largely *a priori*. In view of the general absence of appropriate empirical information, the research project described in this chapter set out to monitor the introduction of the internal market in the largest English regional health authority, the West Midlands.

As will become clear, the magnitude and complexity of the changes – undoubtedly the largest with which the NHS has had to cope during its 40 year history – led us to adopt a range of research methodologies. Moreover, over the course of the project, it became evident that many aspects of the reforms were subject to a shifting and evolving agenda. Among other things, this complication affected the role expected of competition. As such, some preliminary remarks on the form that competition was, and is, expected to take are offered before the discussion of the study itself.

The Changing Face of Competition

In the period of debate preceding publication of the white paper, there were many calls from right wing think-tanks and others committed to private market models of resource allocation for the introduction of a rigorous form of supply side competition into the NHS. And, certainly, ministerial statements during the early period of the reforms seemed to support this approach. There was, however, always a school of thought which argued that the NHS has to pursue multiple objectives and that excessive dependence on the market could threaten goals such as equity and, possibly, quality. As a result, a number of instruments were introduced, or strengthened, in order to regulate the market. The term 'managed competition' was coined to refer to this process.

At the same time, a number of commentators questioned whether markets and hospital services could ever be truly competitive. The existence of local monopolies outside of the main urban conurbations was cited as a barrier to competition. As our empirical work reported later shows, this claim may well have been exaggerated. Nonetheless, the NHS Management Executive responded by saying that enhanced efficiency did not necessarily require the existence of competitive hospitals, only that markets should be *contestable*. A contestable market is one in which potential entrants can be relied upon to ensure that existing firms operate efficiently. For this mechanism to work, however, certain conditions need to apply, notably the absence of barriers to new entrants. Whether hospital markets actually display these features is questionable. Nonetheless, Government policy seems to assume that contestability exists.

Another aspect of competition policy that has been questioned since the early period of the reforms is the claim that net efficiency gains will result from the internal market, despite the considerable transaction costs involved in buying and selling services. This line of argument draws on the work of Williamson (1975) which identifies the conditions in which transaction costs will be substantial because contracts are expensive to write, complicated to execute and difficult to enforce. These conditions, Bartlett (1990) has argued, apply in the NHS. The significance of this for the internal market is that it points to the desirability of long term stable contractual relationships between purchasers and providers. If long term contracts exist, competition is likely to take place *for* markets at periodic stages of contract negotiation, rather than *in* markets on a day-to-day basis.

In summary, then, it is important to point out that the form of competition that is being implemented in the NHS has changed over time and is now rather different to that which was originally set out at the outset of the reforms. In particular, the degree of central regulation is far stronger. Our research has sought to identify and monitor this change.

The Project

The study began in December 1989, before the implementation of the reforms, and covered the succeeding three years up until December 1992. Given the scope of this task, some selectivity was essential. In the event, the study centred on four main objectives namely,

- Monitoring changes in the scale and pattern of service provision, tracking variations in the structure, volume and location of health services offered by providers.
- Subjecting the theory of managed competition to empirical testing by studying both the economics and management of the new health care market in order to understand its impact on dynamic efficiency, cost-effectiveness, patient/purchaser choice and access to services.

- Contributing to management learning and the management of change.
- Identifying and using 'indicators' of change to develop a framework for monitoring managed competition in the longer term.

The study focussed on one region, the West Midlands, which has a population of over five million and an annual health care expenditure of about £2 billion. It comprised 22 district health authorities in 1989, reduced to 18 by 1992 as a result of mergers, and 33 major acute provider units, also reduced in number following planned rationalisation of services by the end of the study period.

Within the region, four case study districts were selected to provide more detailed data. These districts varied in size – budget, population, area; their rural/urban mix; degree of competition as measured by distance between competing providers; cross boundary flow patterns; teaching/non-teaching status; socio-economic composition; and management style and history.

Finally, four specialties were selected for detailed analysis. The specialties were chosen mainly on the *a priori* basis that they were more likely than others to be subject to change due to competition within the internal market. These were: general surgery, orthopaedics, ophthalmology and gynaecology.

Data and information were collected in a number of ways and from a variety of sources. These included national and local, West Midlands, postal questionnaires; interviews with key managerial and clinical staff; routine and *ad hoc* statistical data from the region and case study districts; district, regional and national papers; and, guidance and other internal documents relating to the implementation of the reforms.

As Figure 1 shows, the survey and interview timetable was structured around 1 April 1991, the implementation date of the reforms, in order to try and capture a sense of 'before and after'.

The first, 'before', surveys gathered a wide range of information including details of business plans (or provider intentions in relation to their 'product' range); composition of contracting teams; type of contracts and contract negotiations; reform implementation arrangements; issues concerning staffing, skills and expertise demanded by the reforms and joint purchasing/provision. The survey of purchasers covered all district health authorities in England and Wales, and the survey of providers covered major acute units in the West Midlands region. The surveys did not just

Figure 1 Project Timetable

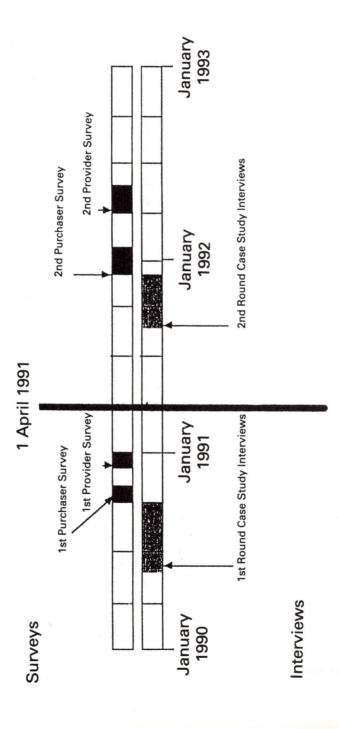

concentrate on measurable items, but also explored managers' views and opinions of various aspects of the reforms. These were seen as crucial to the development, interpretation and hence direction and outcome of the reforms themselves.

The initial first-round case study interviews were held with managers and clinicians at health authority headquarters and in one acute unit within each district. General practitioner and Community Health Council representatives and all other unit general managers were also interviewed, some 86 interviews in total. Relevant documentation including agendas and minutes from major co-ordinating and commissioning groups was also collected.

Through the case studies, the project sought to establish the attitudes of key players towards the reforms in general and the internal market in particular. They were also designed to examine intensively specific aspects of implementation and how these were developed, managed and perceived by key actors: the 'how' and 'why' of change.

Having established a baseline, follow-up purchaser and provider surveys were carried out after the implementation of the reforms. These surveys sought to establish data about purchaser and provider actions in comparison with previously stated intentions. They also examined future intentions in relation to the factors identified in the first round. Follow-up case study interviews were also carried out in the case study districts between October and November 1991.

Methodological Issues

Before reporting the project's key findings it is important to be clear about some of the methodological issues involved in studying the implementation of the NHS reforms.

The first problem to note, from a research point of view, is that the reforms were not the subject of any pre-testing: they were not randomised; there were no controls and there were no trials. Although certain aspects of the reforms were to be introduced gradually, for example trust status and GP fundholding, these were not set up with a view to testing the new policy. Indeed, to pursue these examples, units approved to become trusts were first self-selected and then selected again by the Secretary of State using various criteria such as managerial competence, the level of computerisation and the credibility of their business plans. Similarly, GP practices were only allowed to become fundholders if they expressed an interest in the scheme and if they fulfilled a number of criteria set out by the Department of Health. Other aspects of the reforms, such as the split between purchasers and providers, were introduced everywhere and at once.

There are two main options for evaluating change of this nature: monitoring of change over time, in particular, comparison between the before and after stages of change; and, comparison of the *predicted* effects of the change with the *actual* effects.

Isolating the effect of a specific social change ideally requires all other things to remain equal or unchanged. The problem is that all things are hardly ever equal. Economic and social systems are in constant flux; evolving, growing or shrinking in response to many endogenous and exogenous factors. In practice it is extremely difficult if not impossible to control for all of these variables.

Over the period studied by this project there were numerous changes occurring, changes which sometimes predated and/or were unrelated to the reforms. These often had a significant impact on the way the NHS functioned. Of particular note were the large real rises in funding received by the NHS in the first two years of the reforms; the continuation of the waiting list initiative (sometimes conflated with the reforms, even by health service managers); continuation and expansion of general management, first introduced in the early 1980s; the introduction of the Patient's Charter and the ever-evolving changes in medical practice, such as moves to day care rather than inpatient treatment.

In short, the picture we observe of the NHS at any one time reflects a multitude of interacting factors. Isolating the impact of any one of these – such as the introduction of managed competition – is riddled with interpretive pitfalls.

Both before and after studies and comparisons of actual with predicted changes suffer from a particular problem when it comes to the NHS reforms: namely, that change was deliberately constrained. On the one hand, a limited form of market competition was introduced, but on the other, the NHS was subjected to a 'steady state' during the first year of the reforms. This set limits on, for instance, district health authorities' ability to move contracts from one provider to another or substantially alter the content and scope of their existing contracts. Such restraints came on top of the general inertia any large and complex organisation suffers from, and which tends to slow down change. In this respect, it is clear that a three-year study of the reforms, taking in one and a half years of the reform period, cannot hope to monitor and map out all the resulting changes.

These problems were clear at the start of the study, and so one important strand of the work was simply to record and monitor changes during the implementation of the reforms. Another aspect was to identify indicators – such as the empirical measure of competition – which could be used to track the future development of the reforms. The rest of this chapter contains three sections which report on the project's key findings: namely, the effect of local cultures and contexts on the implementation of the internal market; the contracting process and measuring competition. The chapter ends with a view of the possible future for managed competition in the NHS.

Local Contexts, Local Cultures

Since the mid-1980s, the Government has tried to deal with the simultaneous desire for central control and local autonomy in the NHS by creating a powerful cadre of general managers at every level of the service, but at the same time making them more tightly accountable upwards by a variety of mechanisms. By 1989 the Department of Health was claiming the success of this strategy in *Working for Patients*. After the organisational changes to the NHS Policy Board and NHS Management Executive it would have for the first time:

> *a clear and effective chain of management command running from Districts through Regions to the Chief Executive and from there to the Secretary of State.*

However, although the Government had created the means for implementing its reforms, it could not dictate the precise form they should take. By definition it is impossible to prescribe exactly how a market should work, since inherently it is a dynamic process. Government uncertainty about how the market would develop as well as the diversity of local market situations meant that local managers had to be given considerable discretion in implementation. Much depended, therefore, on how managers perceived the reforms and moulded them to local circumstances. Given the lead implementation role of district general managers (DGMs) their attitudes assumed critical importance.

Our first surveys revealed a high level of general support for the NHS and Community Care Act 1980, with 85 per cent of DGMs saying they 'mainly approved with some reservations' and 88 per cent believing it would make the NHS more business-like, which was a 'good thing'. Six per cent had no reservations at all.

Approximately half had changed their attitudes over time with many becoming more supportive as the implications of the reforms became clearer and, in the words of one respondent:

> The scope for radical improvement in the NHS is much wider than I first thought.

But for others, changed attitudes reflected a more pragmatic acceptance of the inevitable and relief that some of the more 'ideological' aspects of the reforms had been pruned. The most popular aspect of the reforms was the separation of purchasers and providers, approved of by 87 per cent of DGMs. But there was greater ambivalence about the introduction of market concepts into the NHS. Over half thought a market could work successfully in health care, although one quarter disagreed and 17 per cent were not sure.

The reforms were not seen as a panacea for problems of funding or long waiting lists either. Eighty six per cent believed that underfunding was still a major problem, and 79 per cent that the reforms would not solve it. On waiting lists, 40 per cent thought that the new separation of purchaser and providers would simply shunt waiting lists around the system rather than reduce them, although 48 per cent disagreed with this view. Most criticism and disquiet was voiced at the scope and pace of change in so short a time. Over three-quarters felt that the pace of implementation was far too fast; 84 per cent believed it was causing considerable stress in their district and 62 per cent felt the quality of their work had been detrimentally affected by its sheer volume.

The general picture was very similar for the acute unit general managers (UGMs) surveyed in the West Midlands. However, they appeared to be suffering even more stress from the pace of implementation since they had the responsibility for the day-to-day running of services as well.

Yet in spite of this disquiet, levels of confidence were surprisingly high. Nearly 60 per cent of DGMs agreed that management was 'generally confident about their futures in this District' and three-quarters of UGMs 'were confident that this Unit can take on the competition'.

The case studies allowed us to probe these views further. In general, managers approved of the main features of the reforms in three districts but were more pessimistic and cynical in the other. There were no significant differences of view between district and unit managers in each authority. The main aspects approved of were: money following patients; the purchaser/provider separation; medical audit; and the potential use of contracts in clarifying and enforcing accountability on providers. Attitudes were divided on self-governing trusts; least liked was the GP fundholding scheme.

Behind this general picture, however, there were distinct differences in emphasis and approach. Two sets of factors appear to account for this. First the 'fit' between the national change agenda and their local situation (Pettigrew *et al*, 1992). The potential impact of the NHS changes varied greatly at local level. The choices available to purchasers, the scale of competition faced by providers, factors such as potential trust and GP fundholder applications, cross-boundary flows, the implications of capitation funding, and the relationships between units of management all posed different opportunities and threats for the different districts. All these affected local perceptions of the NHS reforms and the workloads involved in implementation. For example, the complexity of contracting was much greater for a purchaser which had 40 per cent of its patients treated outside its district in over 30 provider units, than one dealing almost solely with its own district general hospital. Similarly, a teaching hospital in the sample received referrals from 120 districts, whereas another dealt almost exclusively with its own district purchaser.

The second set of factors concerns aspects of the local management culture and what might be described as a pro-active or reactive approach to change. Pro-active authorities had a stronger record in managing previous large scale changes, and a more efficient management process for doing so. This usually meant they were better placed to benefit from the reforms and were more confident in their ability to handle them. For example, one of our districts clearly had a head start because of the work they had already carried out on clinical management, costing, rationalisation of facilities and both internal and external contracting for clinical services. Performance targets for managers were demanding, and the management style was characterised as 'highly corporate' internally, but 'very competitive' externally, with UGMs given a lot of entrepreneurial freedom.

By contrast, another district was fairly resistant to change, and its management style was characterised by many respondents as reactive and lacking a clear sense of purpose. Generally negative perceptions of the reforms meant that the district could see only threats, not opportunities, and had adopted a passive, almost fatalistic acceptance that these threats would materialise. Culture and perceptions explain these different approaches more than the objective levels of competition faced (for example, this latter district's general hospital had a stronger monopoly than any of the other acute units studied).

Nonetheless, whether leaders or laggards, all managers shared the common problem of deciding how to approach what appeared to be an immense volume of work, given:

- a general climate of professional and public hostility;
- the information required was limited, non-existent, inaccurate or late;
- guidance from the Department of Health, NHS Management Executive and RHA was often experienced as too little, too late or insufficiently precise to be of much help;
- existing services had to be maintained, and when authorities were often in the middle of other major developments;
- they lacked experience in many of the new tasks and skills required, including, for example, contract specification and negotiation.

Faced with these difficulties, key aspects of a pro-active approach to implementation involved:

Clarification: understanding and getting agreement within the management team on what the main features of the reforms were, and how they translated to their own local context.

Prioritisation: giving priority to those aspects which they felt to be of most significance in their district, either in guaranteeing their security or maximising potential opportunities.

Communication: at least two authorities had well thought out communication strategies with staff and the public, and worked hard to defuse anxieties and misunderstandings.

Simplification: cutting through to the essentials, and not being too ambitious in the first year was imperative for even the keenest district, given the information difficulties faced.

Corporate commitment: ensuring a corporate approach to implementation was a high priority for DGMs in these districts. This was probably most successfully achieved in a district which took the earlier stages most seriously and acted quickly to resolve personal uncertainties about future leadership roles. In these districts, shadow executive directors were appointed early, ensuring committed 'champions' for change. In contrast, a reactive approach in another district meant the implementation, far from being a corporate affair, was largely left to one individual who quickly became demoralised and overwhelmed by the size of the task.

Learning-by-doing: pro-active authorities took every opportunity to learn by attending relevant conferences, getting copies of contracts from districts thought to be pioneers (although they were often disappointed by what they found), visits abroad, particularly to health maintenance organisations and hospitals in the USA, and judicious consultancy inputs.

But if pro-active authorities stamped the reforms with their own local flavour, what aspects did they emphasise? Three merit special mention; namely, strategic purchasing, local bargaining in purchasing, and contracting.

First, there was strong enthusiasm for the new strategic role of the purchaser, with its consumerist and public health orientation. The role of 'champion of the people' was an appealing one. These authorities voiced aspirations to change their health care priorities in line with the needs-assessment process and consumer research, and assumed they would be shifting resources in favour of community health services, the priority services and health promotion. Translating aspirations into reality however may be another question since district health authorities faced the same difficulties they have always faced in shifting a service, shaped by powerful providers, to one led by needs. Progress on needs-assessment was also slow and fitful. Nevertheless, by the second year, there were several examples of innovatory forms of consumer research and more permanent consultative mechanisms, such as the Health Partnership Forums established in one district, plus pilot projects in locality needs-assessment and commissioning.

Second, pro-active districts were anxious to use their bargaining leverage to improve services for their residents but within a context of maintaining local services. By year two, as districts adapted to the purchaser role, a more detached and sometimes hard-nosed attitude to their own units was noticeable. This sense of detachment was observed in the hospitals too. As one respondent observed, 'I'm surprised at how quickly the district had dropped out of the frame'. Nevertheless at Board level there was a realistic acceptance on both sides of the interdependency between a purchaser and its main local supplier and the need of close collaboration to work on quality of products, service development and restructuring issues. The relationship between Marks and Spencer or Toyota and their suppliers were often cited as models.

There was also a consistent view in the way three districts conceptualised the role of competition in this relationship, as these quotations, taken from three different authorities, illustrate:

> *Competition at the margin . . . to tweak the unit's tail.*

> *. . . the creation of an environment of contestability . . . you will have preferred providers because people need services locally but you have to create some kind of tension.*

> *a win-win situation with incentives both ways but where there is a constructive tension that keeps people on their toes.*

Third, there was genuine enthusiasm in all the case study districts to use contracts to improve quality standards. The emphasis on quality was also one way of gaining support for the reforms from medical and nursing staff in the units. The surveys confirmed that additional emphasis on quality was widely seen as a major benefit of the reforms, with 81 per cent of DGMs agreeing that quality improvements had already occurred. Providers agreed strongly, but emphasised the need to translate the emphasis on quality into practical action by defining meaningful standards, establishing adequate monitoring systems and ensuring that quality influenced purchasing decisions.

Contracting

Although the NHS has for many years engaged in contracting – not just through competitive tendering for ancillary services, but also for health care (Ranade and Appleby, 1989) – the reforms dramatically increased its significance and scope. The process became central to the purchaser/provider split, while the contracts themselves embodied details of service provision (volumes, levels of quality, etc), prices, contractual periods, clauses on dispute resolution and action to be taken in the event of contract failure.

Clearly then, the contracting process and the resulting contracts are key elements in the market. They not only provide a bridge between purchasers and providers, but reveal many different aspects of how demands and other intentions are expressed, clarify the information needs of the market and show how risk is to be shared. As such, finding out how purchasers and providers were dealing with the process of contracting – from the setting up of contracting teams to placing contracts with providers – was an important part of monitoring managed competition.

Through surveys and interviews our study examined the process of contracting and the form of contracts being negotiated and placed in the first two years of the reforms.

In all cases, contracts were formulated and negotiated by teams established for this purpose by both purchasers and providers. Purchasing teams included representatives from planning, public health and finance and, less frequently, the DGM and nursing and medical staff. Provider teams tended to be established later than their purchasing counterparts and comprised the unit general manager, director of finance, and information officer. Medical and nursing representatives were included to a lesser extent. A quarter of provider teams included the DGM.

A number of factors were revealed as important in the contracting process. These included:

Expertise: Prior experience of contracting gained through compulsory competitive tendering, negotiations over regional specialties and the waiting list initiative meant that there existed some contracting expertise among providers. Nevertheless both providers and purchasers were seeking to improve their expertise in this area, the latter to a greater extent, by in-service training or buying in external advice.

Information: Lack of information was perceived to be a major area of difficulty. There were problems with information systems; a lack of data about the services currently being provided and doubts about the accuracy of available data; poor information on health needs; only crude information on costs and activity; and, uncertainty about demands expressed through GPs and GP fundholders.

Timetable: Only a quarter of DGMs surveyed in England and Wales believed that the reform timetable would give them enough time to implement contracting satisfactorily. Indeed, six months prior to the reforms there was a huge disparity between the number of contracts purchasers and providers intended to operate from 1 April 1991 and the number of draft contracts and contracts actually under active negotiation (NAHAT, 1991 & 1992).

Provider-purchaser relationships: although less than a quarter of DGMs surveyed in England and Wales (and none in the West Midlands) reported difficulties coping with the new unit (provider)/district (purchaser) relationship, in the case study districts there was wide reporting of the problems of wearing two hats – purchasing/providing – where districts retained managerial responsibility for units not opting for trust status. In contrast, half of the UGMs surveyed cited problems coping with the new relationship and, as Figure 2 shows, this is reflected in different perceptions about the way in which contract negotiations were carried out.

Quality: One particular topic of disagreement between purchasers and providers was quality. The debate about quality hinged on different emphases by managers and clinicians – the former favoured throughput, the latter mortality and morbidity measures; on the perception that purchasers were being too prescriptive and intruding into areas – for example staffing and beds – which were not their responsibility; and a belief that purchasers were unrealistic in their aspirations about quality given that they were unwilling or not able to match these aspirations with the necessary funding.

During the first year of contracting, block contracts or block contracts with ceilings and floors on activity dominated throughout the NHS nationally. This pattern was replicated in the West Midlands as is shown by the distribution of acute provider contracts for 1991/92 in Figure 3. This broad-brush approach to the form and type of contracts probably owed a lot to the very tight timetable for implementing the reforms. By the second year, however, the proportion of simple block contracts taken out by acute providers in the West Midlands was planned to fall in value terms from 52 per cent to 28 per cent, whereas block contracts with ceilings and floors and cost and volume contracts were both planned to become more important: see Figure 4. It remains to be seen to what extent providers' plans for contracts were achieved, however.

Table 1 at the end of this chapter shows the main factors influencing districts' purchasing decisions. The requirement to maintain a 'steady

Figure 2 Conduct of Contract Negotiations

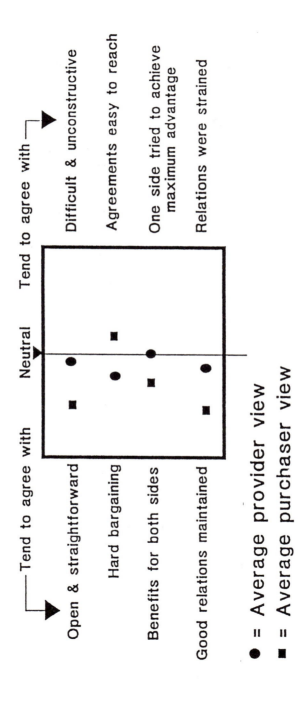

● = Average provider view
■ = Average purchaser view

Figure 3   Type of Contract: Providers: 1991/2

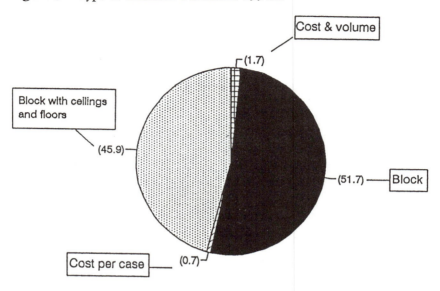

NB: Figures are percentages

Figure 4   Type of Contract: Providers: 1992/3

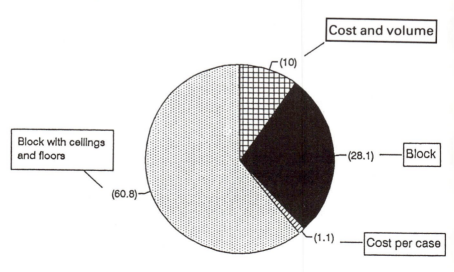

NB: Figures are percentages

state' in the transition to the new economic environment of the market meant that existing patient flows were a major factor influencing decisions about where to place contracts. Other aspects of importance to purchasers were GP preferences, previous experience of providers and ease of travel for residents.

Tables 2 and 3 list contractual partners for purchasers and providers respectively for 1991/92 and 1992/93.

Given the early stage of the reforms, and the adherence to the policy of 'steady state', it is perhaps not surprising that needs assessment was not a major principle guiding the contracting process. Nonetheless, it appears to be having a growing impact.

In our national survey of districts carried out in December 1991, nearly all – 116 out of 117 surveyed – had held meetings with their local GPs as part of their needs assessment programmes. In addition, around a third had sought the views of their populations directly, through postal questionnaires and public meetings.

Possibly more importantly, nearly three quarters of districts indicated that they would be changing their purchasing behaviour for the second year of the reforms, 1992/93, as a direct result of their needs assessment exercises. Over 60 per cent planned to cease a contract; 70 per cent to contract with a new provider; and 50 per cent to reduce contract activity by more than 10 per cent. However, with no indication of the financial aspects of these planned contractual changes, these figures should be treated with caution. Indeed, evidence from our case study districts revealed that by and large contractual changes in the first two years of the reforms were small even though a high proportion of contracts were affected.

As we pointed out earlier, a full evaluation of the impact of contracting in the NHS is difficult given the timescale of our project and various methodological problems. Nevertheless, it is possible to identify some trends in the refinement of the contracting process over time.

The key change on purchasing teams was increased involvement by Family Health Service Authority representatives and, on provider teams, the disappearance of the district general manager. Medical representation decreased slightly on both purchaser and provider sides. However, core membership of purchaser and provider contracting teams changed minimally.

The first year's experience of contracting led to a striking increase in the perceived expertise among purchasers, but a reduction in perceived expertise among providers. This appears to be consistent with the latter's more negative perceptions of contract negotiations.

Figures 5 and 6 show changes in the problems experienced by purchasers and providers between 1991/92 and 1992/93. Among purchasers, obtaining comparative cost data and the tight timetable were the most frequently cited problems in both years, although the number of districts citing them fell over time. In the case of providers, the major problems of the tight timetable and obtaining reliable data on patient flows were both cited far less in the second year of contracting. For both purchasers and providers, coping with the unit/district contracting relationship worsened slightly.

Monitoring contracts has emerged as a new area of difficulty. Ninety two per cent of purchasers surveyed in England and Wales were experiencing problems related to monitoring: chiefly the late arrival of monitoring data;

Figure 5 Problems Experienced by Purchasers with their 1991/2 and 1992/3 Contracts

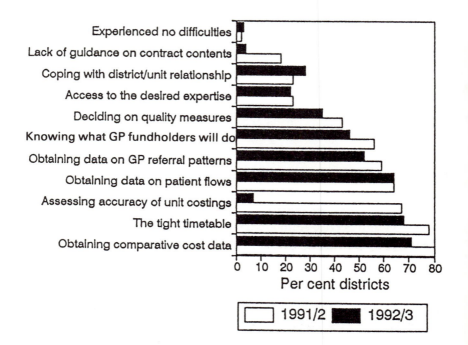

Figure 6   Problems Experienced by Providers with their 1991/2 and 1992/3 Contracts

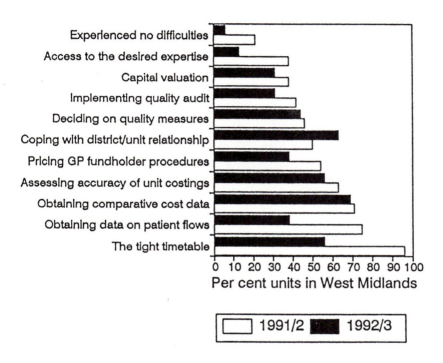

its poor quality when it did arrive; and difficulties with computer software used to monitor contracts. The sheer size of the task for both parties should not be underestimated:

> *the shock to the system for some providers in having to produce regular returns to us has been quite great.*

Measuring Competition

The debate leading up to, and indeed following, the introduction of the internal market into the NHS has been conducted almost entirely in terms of *a priori* theoretical expectations about the benefits and costs of competitive markets. Fundamental questions and issues about competition remain to be answered empirically, such as the extent of competition; inter-regional variations in competition; and the effects of competition on hospitals' pricing policies and efficiency. Recognition of these gaps in knowledge prompted us to investigate one particular quantifiable measure of competition – the Hirschman-Herfindahl index (see Melnick and Zwanziger, 1988; Miller, 1982).

Constructing the index for 39 West Midlands acute hospitals using patient flow data for one particular specialty, general surgery, involved three main stages:

- Identification of each hospital's market area.
- Identification of each hospital's competitors within each market area.
- Production of an overall index of competition for each hospital, based upon the number of competitors in its market area(s) and their market shares.

The index, ranging from 0 – perfect competition, to 10,000 – total monopoly, was calculated for each of three years leading up to the implementation of the reforms (1988/89–1990/91) plus the first year of the reforms. Table 4 details the value of the index for each acute hospital over these four years: gaps in the table arose as a result of mergers and other planned rationalisation. Local knowledge of the region, its history and hospital development plans is clearly essential for any interpretation of trends in individual hospitals' index values (as revealed by Table 4). For example, the run-down of Walsall General Hospital and the consequent increase in general surgical referrals to Walsall Manor in 1990/91 explains the increased monopoly position of the latter as reflected by an increase in Walsall Manor's index value in 1990/91.

Another way of presenting this information is to plot index values on a graph in order to, literally, give an indication of the shape of the market: see Figure 7. In general the flatter the curve, the greater the degree of competition in the market. Although there have been some small changes in the rank order of hospitals between 1988/89 and 1991/92, the change in the shape of the HHI curve overall for the West Midlands is statistically insignificant.

In the United States, where the Department of Justice uses the index in its assessment of anti-trust cases, a more formal measure of the state of the market is used: individual firms with values in excess of 1,800 are considered to be in potentially monopolistic positions, and, again potentially, able to exploit their situation by raising prices to excessive levels, restricting output, etc.

Applying this cut-off point to our group of West Midlands hospitals suggests that only around a quarter are in monopoly positions. If attention is focussed on the number of patients treated by these hospitals, rather than simply the hospitals themselves, the degree of concentration becomes somewhat higher, with 38 per cent of patients receiving treatment in hospitals with an index in excess of 1800.

Overall, however, these results seem to indicate that market concentration is low enough in most of the West Midlands, *ie* covering 75 per cent of hospitals and 60 per cent of general surgery patients, for effective competition to take place. However, the segment of the market in which concentration is high is sizable enough to merit attention. Moreover, there are two reasons to suggest that we may have overstated the true level of competition. First, the unit of market area used was the district health authority. Using smaller spatial units, such as electoral wards or even

Figure 7   The Changing 'Shape' of the Market

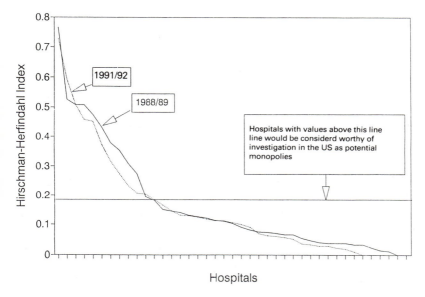

Hospitals

Note: Numbers on vertical scale reflect those g. Table 4 divided by 10,000.

enumeration districts, produces greater levels of concentration, *ie* more monopolistic hospitals and less competition. Second, the index is sensitive to the definition of the 'product'. We defined the product as general surgery, but this is very broad, including as it does procedures as diverse as hernia repairs and kidney transplants. If patient flows were to be disaggregated below the specialty level, a higher degree of concentration would almost certainly be found.

A further cautionary interpretive point is worth making: firms – in this case, hospitals – who are technically in possession of monopoly powers do not always act as monopolists. Indeed, as we pointed out at the beginning of this chapter, the theory of market contestability suggests that markets may appear monopolistic but in fact display the characteristics of competitive markets. This is due to the fact that entry into the market by new providers is relatively easy. In other words, providers are sensitive to potential and not just actual competition.

Despite the various caveats outlined above, it would seem essential for some quantitative approach to competition to be adopted in order to track changes in the competitive environment over time, and to provide empirical data to judge the effects of competition on hospitals' unit costs, quality of service and other dimensions of hospital performance.

Future Prospects

Any assessment of the future development of managed competition is bound to be fraught with uncertainty. Nonetheless, it is possible to identify two major determinants that are likely to play an influential role in the future progress of competition in the NHS: namely, government policy and the reaction of the major actors in the NHS itself towards the evolving health care market.

Government policy towards the NHS is influenced partly by internal issues specific to the NHS and partly by external factors in the economy at large. On the former, clues to current Government thinking on the future direction of the NHS, and in particular managed competition, can be gleaned from the most recent business plans issued by the Department of Health and the NHS Management Executive. These outline the Government's key priorities for the NHS up to 1996/97 (Department of Health 1993 and NHS Management Executive, 1993).

These plans reveal a new emphasis in policy, with a shift towards the promotion of purchasing in the internal market. But more than this, the plans stress the central importance of the internal market (and within this, purchasing), as the main engine driving changes in the way health care is provided and the type of health care that will be delivered in the future. The Management Executive recognise that if this is to be done, then purchasers '. . . must be free and encouraged to use the opportunities of the internal market freely to innovate . . . to drive this change.'

If the reforms are to bring about change, 'steady state' must give way to a version of 'unsteady state' in which purchasers are freer to use their purchasing power leverage to increase all aspects of provider performance.

Despite the Department of Health's and the Management Executive's commitment to the market, their progress in resolving some of the inherent tensions which lay behind the original policy of 'steady state' seem less clear. This raises doubts about the extent to which purchasers and providers can ever be truly free to pursue locally-based health care objectives. In turn, this raises questions about the extent to which the more general freedoms implied by the notion of a market will be allowed to develop and how a balance can be struck between current freedoms and other objectives, such as accountability and equity. In short, it is unclear how much stress is to be laid on managing the market.

Apart from these value-based issues, there are many practical questions identified by our project, which suggest that the internal market has a long way to go before it can be said to be operating effectively on its own terms. Although some of the early difficulties and confusions surrounding the separation of purchasers and providers will be resolved as the number of trust units increases, one longer term issue is worth highlighting: namely, the need for reliable and accurate information, particularly that required by health authorities and GP fundholders to operate as effective and efficient purchasers.

Evidence from our project over the last three years suggests that purchasers were still trying to get to grips with the basic information they required to assess health care needs and make rational decisions concerning the choice of provider — based on quantifiable measures of quality, reliable data on prices, and, importantly, local opinion. But in addition, purchasers are only just beginning to grapple with the underlying methodologies of priority setting, the construction of contracts and the information implications of monitoring contract performance.

In summary, then, the Department's and the Executive's policies emphasise the importance of purchasing, the freedoms of the internal market and consequently the power of purchasing to bring about change. However, these aims may not be fully realised due to a failure to get to grips with underlying tensions between market ideology and other desirable objectives such as equity and accountability, on the one hand, and practical problems involving such factors as well as extensive and continuing informational problems, on the other. These are not new issues for the NHS, but equally they are not issues which are naturally solved by the internal market.

In addition to these internal policy issues, there are external factors influencing future government policy towards the NHS which cannot be ignored. Two issues stand out: the Government's current and short term borrowing problem and the general policy on competitive tendering, recently revamped, broadened in scope and renamed 'market testing', which affects the whole of the public sector.

The former issue inevitably means a less generous financial settlement for the NHS over the next few years. Although underfunding was overwhelmingly identified in our surveys of purchasers and providers as a problem for the NHS, and one not solved by the internal market, the effects of future parsimonious funding on the development of managed competition are difficult to judge. On the one hand, limited growth in funding may induce greater levels of efficiency and quality as providers attempt to compete in order to maintain their market shares of business from public sector purchasers. On the other hand, providers may increasingly seek out private sector business to maintain their income levels. One long term consequence of this reaction could be to 'crowd out' public sector purchasers.

The other initiative – market testing – may have important repercussions for the management of NHS trusts, and the level of contestability in the internal market. One of the problems that a number of commentators identified with the internal market was the potential lack of competition. Market testing in the form of competitive tendering for the management of trusts could introduce a significant additional element of competition to the internal market, overcoming some of the barriers to entry to this market.

Finally, the future course of managed competition will depend on the NHS itself: how purchasers, providers, managers, clinicians and others interpret and react to the pressures, incentives and changes in the policies noted above. Crucially, however, the future scope, shape and success of the internal market will depend on a resolution of the central dilemma of managed competition – when, where and how to 'manage' competition when the market fails to deliver a satisfactory outcome in terms of the key goals for the NHS.

Significantly, the Management Executive has admitted in its most recent business plan (NHS Management Executive, 1993) that the policy of 'steady state', and large real increases in NHS funding in the first two years of the reforms, paralysed and distorted the effects of the internal market. In short, the management of competition was maximised whilst actual competition was minimised. What effects were observable at least in terms of patient activity, were due to other things, principally, increased funding.

In the light of this experience, the Department and the Executive are now committed to properly operationalising the internal market by increasing the power and abilities of purchasers. With this official commitment, and yet a continued absence, over two years into the reforms, of conclusive empirical evidence on its costs and benefits so far, it would seem that the need for evaluative research of the NHS reforms is now just starting rather than finishing.

Table 1: Factors Influencing District Purchasing Decisions

	High				Ranking				Low	
	1	2	3	4	5	6	7	8	9	10
					No. of Districts					
GPs expressed preference	38	43	15	8	6	2	1	0	0	0
Ease of travel for your residents	4	12	29	27	15	13	10	1	2	0
Competitive prices	0	11	14	26	30	8	11	8	3	2
Previous experience of the provider	5	19	28	19	14	15	6	5	2	0
Existing patient flows	64	17	9	7	5	5	2	0	3	1
Confidence in provider's management	0	7	7	12	14	28	22	15	6	2
Well developed quality assurance	2	3	3	9	21	29	28	13	5	0
Views of Community Health Council	0	0	6	3	5	10	17	31	18	23
Results of survey of local residents	0	1	2	2	1	2	10	15	32	48
Unit undertakes regular patient satisfaction surveys	0	0	0	0	2	1	6	25	42	37

Table 2: Purchasers: Contractual Partners (1991/92)

	Number	Value (£m)	% of number	% of value	Average value (£m)
NHS provider within district	488	5,610.1	17.8	78.6	11.50
NHS provider outside district	2,161	1,503.4	78.6	21.1	0.70
Private sector	13	1.5	0.5	0.0	0.12
Voluntary sector	67	9.4	2.4	0.1	0.14
Other	19	12	0.7	0.2	0.63
Total	2,748	7,136.4	100.0	100.0	2.60

Table 3: Providers: Contractual Partners 1992/93

	Number	Value (£m)	% of number	% of value	Average value:£m
Your host DHA	16	376.9	5.1	69.2	23.6
Another DHA in your Region	136	85.5	43.3	15.7	0.6
Regional Health Authority	30	40.1	9.6	7.4	1.3
GP fundholders	112	14.9	35.7	2.7	0.1
Private sector	1	0.2	0.3	0.04	0.2
Other	19	27.2	6.1	5.0	1.4
Total	314	544.7	100.0	100.0	

Table 4: Hirschman-Herfindahl Index: General Surgery; West Midlands Acute Hospitals, 1988/89 to 1990/91

Hospital	1988/89	1989/90	1990/91	1991/92
Ronkswood	7649	6155	5923	5946
Walsgrave	5254	1.0000	4819	4585
St Cross	5076	5091	3482	0701
County Hereford	5065	5057	5091	5073
Royal	4752	2181	1481	1245
George Eliot	4319	5107	4133	1655
South Warwickshire	3790	5864	7011	7275
Alexandra	3548	3696	3951	3728
Bewdley Road	3100	4423	9093	3179
Stafford	2748	2479	1566	2048
North Staffordshire R. I.	1957	1123	1985	2078
Selly Oak	1829	1927	1917	1180
The Royal	1514	1139	1704	1461
Stoke City General	1451	1179	1746	1122
Russells Hall	1403	1149	1513	1865
Sandwell	1308	2239	2318	2740
New Cross	1256	1239	1158	1309
Walsall Manor	1217	1280	4321	4515
Good Hope	1137	1225	1347	1285
East Birmingham	1116	1469	0955	1060
Walsall General	1037	1438	(**)	(**)
Dudley Road	0914	1148	1125	1004
Burton General	0811	0679	0640	0577
Warneford	0755	0834	0416	0336
Castle Street	0741	0649	0907	0908
Wordsley	0706	0894	0755	1124
Staffordshire General	0671	0674	0448	0193
Birmingham General	0659	0621	0607	0612
Queen Elizabeth	0540	0602	0560	0517
Solihull	0465	0417	0623	0635
Tenbury	0409	0436	0296	0284
Stratford	0382	(**)	(**)	(**)
Longton	0379	0174	(**)	(**)
Burton	0375	0398	0352	0358
Guest	0331	0286	0295	(**)
Tamworth	0326	0297	0256	0224
Corbett	0240	0194	0183	(**)
Biddulph	0149	(**)	(**)	(**)
Lichfield Victoria	0116	(*)	0111	0101
Evesham	(*)	0473	0283	0276
Princess Royal	(***)	1217	2478	2338
Average	1781	1985	2049	1717

(*) Hospital Patient flows too small to register a value for the index
(**) Unit closed
(***) Unit not open

3

THE PERFORMANCE OF TRUSTS

Will Bartlett and Julian Le Grand

One of the most significant elements of the internal or, as we prefer, 'quasi-market', reforms of the National Health Service has been the transformation of secondary and community health care providers from directly managed organisations into independent trusts. By April 1993, just two years after the first wave of 57 trusts started operating, there were 330 trusts in operation, comprising over half of all NHS hospital beds. By April 1994, if current expressions of interest by non-trust units are translated into action, there will be close to 500 trusts, providing 95 per cent of all hospital and community health services.

Yet trusts as such seem to have received remarkably little research attention – and certainly rather less than that given to the purchaser side of the new quasi-market, whether in the form of district health authorities or GP fundholders. Why this should be is not clear; it may reflect the heterogeneity of the organisations concerned, the difficulty of obtaining appropriate data or perhaps the biases of some of the research disciplines involved. But, whatever the reason, there seem to be very few studies that relate directly to the performance of trusts.

This chapter begins with some basic facts about trusts; what they are, and some information about their growth. The next section summarises the empirical research findings of which we are aware, distinguishing between 'direct' studies of trust performance and 'indirect' studies of progress in implementing the conditions for successful trust performance. We go on to note that a major problem with both kinds of research is that they lack an adequate theoretical model of trusts; the penultimate section offers some suggestions as to how this gap might begin to be filled. There is a brief conclusion.

Trusts: Some Basic Facts

Trusts, at least in theory, are independent non-governmental organisations providing secondary and community health care services. When a hospital or other provider unit becomes a trust, its assets are transferred from the government to the ownership of the new trustees, while a debt of equivalent value is held by the Treasury. This debt is made up of interest bearing debt and public dividend capital; for most trusts, the ratio of debt to dividend capital is 50:50.

Trusts are directly accountable to the Secretary of State for Health; special NHS Management Executive outposts have been set up to monitor trusts and hence to operationalise this accountability. Trusts have certain freedoms; they are able to set their own levels of remuneration for their workforce, and decide on the numbers and mix of staff to be employed. However they are heavily restricted with respect to capital spending. They are subject to external financing limits (EFLs) set by the Department of Health, which either limit total borrowing or, where a trust has a cash surplus, require debt to be repaid in specified amounts; and they can only dispose of their assets or acquire new ones within set limits.

The Department places three financial duties on trusts: they must earn six per cent return on assets in use; they must break even taking one year with another; and they must stay within their external financing limit. The first of these requirements is an accounting requirement. It merely means that the contracts which are drawn up with purchasers must include a six per cent charge on capital assets. In practice the actual return made on capital will vary due to unexpected changes in the value of the asset base on which the outcome rate of return is calculated at the end of the year.

The second requirement is met through two cost/price rules, *viz* that, in drawing up contracts, trusts must set their prices equal to average costs, and there must be no cross-subsidisation between services. Although surpluses can arise in practice, they can only be used to finance expenditures on the part of the trust if as a result the trust does not exceed its EFL. Should the use of surpluses for capital expenditure give rise to a total capital programme in excess of the EFL, then the EFL will be reduced to compensate.

Trusts can make new capital investment in excess of their EFL, but only if they persuade the NHS Management Executive that the costs incurred can be fully recovered through demonstrated contract income. This means that not only is the financial regime for trusts highly regulated, but also a very short term perspective on capital investment programmes is built into the system of regulation. It also means that the independence and autonomy available to trusts is highly circumscribed, and the incentives to improved performance, which might be expected to be associated with an ability to retain financial surpluses earned through improved management performance, are eliminated.

Trusts obtain most of their income from contracts from district health authorities and GP fundholders. These contracts take a number of forms: block contracts where the purchaser pays the provider an annual fee in return for access to a defined range of services (such as an accident and emergency service); cost-per-case contracts where the price of each individual treatment is specified; and cost-and-volume contracts, where a base-line level of activity is funded on a block contract basis, beyond which all funding is on a cost-per-case basis.

When the reform process was initiated, it was not envisaged that all providers would become trusts, at least in the early stages. Some were expected to remain as directly managed units (DMUs), under the authority and management of districts. DMUs would nonetheless have something close to a contractual relationship with the purchasers, with management budgets structured as contracts, but enforced through the normal management process.

However, while trusts proliferate, DMUs are a rapidly disappearing breed. The first wave of 57 trusts started operating on 1 April, 1991; it accounted for 46,000 (12 per cent) of the total number of beds in the NHS and for £1.8 bn (13.5 per cent) of total NHS revenue expenditure. The second wave of 105 trusts started in April 1992; together with the first wave, they accounted for 28 per cent of beds and 33 per cent of expenditure. The third wave, starting in April 1993, comprised 168 trusts; with the first and second waves, they accounted for 55 per cent of all beds and 67 per cent of all expenditures (Newchurch, 1993).

The timetable for the fourth wave was announced by the Secretary of State for Health in September 1992, leading to implementation by April 1994. By the end of 1992, a further 155 hospitals and other units have expressed an interest in forming part of the fourth wave. If all are approved,

95 per cent of hospital and community services in England will be provided by trusts.

The penetration of trusts has not been entirely even across the country. By April 1993, 77 per cent of the beds in the area covered by the East NHS Management Executive Outpost (East Anglia, North East Thames, North West Thames RHAs) will be in trusts, compared with, at the other extreme, 35 per cent in the Midlands (Oxford, West Midlands) and Northern Ireland outpost areas. However, other areas are catching up; most notable is the case of Scotland which in 1992 had just two trusts with 4 per cent of total beds, but by 1993 had 17, with 40 per cent of the total.

Thus, the speed of growth in the numbers of trusts is phenomenal. In the words of the Third Newchurch Guide to NHS Trusts, 'the NHS has undergone fundamental change in only three years, and reversal of this policy is now virtually impossible' (1993, p S1-23). It also creates a major challenge for researchers into the impact of trusts. Some of the initially promising areas of research, such as a comparison of the performance of trusts and non-trusts, are being rapidly closed off, and others, such as an overall evaluation of the trust mechanism of service delivery, are arguably being rendered futile (what is the point of evaluating an 'irreversible' policy change?). That perhaps is another factor affecting the number of research studies of trust performance, to which we now turn.

Trust Performance: Empirical Research

It is useful to distinguish between two kinds of approach to research on trust performance, and indeed more generally on the performance of the quasi-market reforms overall. One approach is to select a particular performance indicator, such as the rate of return on capital employed, the numbers of patients treated, or the cost per patient day, and examine the performance of trusts, and, if appropriate, non-trusts with respect to that indicator. The other is more indirect, and has two stages. The first stage involves the use of theory, chiefly micro-economic theory, to specify the conditions that must pertain in the quasi-markets in which trusts are operating, if they are to perform successfully according to specified criteria; the second stage examines the implementation process to explore the extent to which those conditions are being met. We now look at both these approaches in turn.

The Direct Approach

We are aware of four direct studies: one by Newchurch on trusts' financial performance; two by the NHS Management Executive on patient activity; and one of our own on costs. Here we summarise them briefly.

Trusts and Financial Performance: Newchurch (1993) undertook a financial appraisal of the 57 first trusts during their first year of operation. They measured performance against the performance targets imposed by the Department of Health, that trusts should earn a real rate of return on capital of at least six per cent; that trusts will break even, taking one year with another; and that trusts will operate within their external financing limits.

With respect to these three indicators, they found that:

- Only eight trusts achieved a return on capital of less than 6 per cent, with the lowest being 4.05 per cent. The average was 9.0 per cent, with the highest at 20.4 per cent. However, in part this relative success was the product of a one-off event. There was a large downward valuation of capital assets after the contract negotiations were completed, not least because of the collapse of the UK property market. In consequence, many trusts found themselves with unexpectedly generous revenues and operating returns significantly above the 6 per cent target.
- Only two trusts failed to break even. However the level of retained surpluses was low, averaging 1.9 per cent of gross income received. There were significant variations between trusts in this respect with some 'being in a position to retain up to 7 per cent of their total income.'
- Nine trusts failed to achieve their EFLs.

On the whole, the Newchurch analysts were reasonably impressed by these results, although they emphasised that they were in part due to the one-off event of capital depreciation. They also pointed out what had not happened during the year: no trust went bust, there were no large-scale involuntary redundancies and income from private patients proved to be only a marginal contribution to revenues. Overall, they commented that it is 'a remarkable if not unprecedented achievement for 57 large public sector organisations to move so rapidly and successfully to adopt such a radically different approach to their management' (1993, p. S1-3).

This judgement may be over-generous. It is important to recognise that these results were achieved within the context of a highly regulated market. For the first round of contracts negotiated in 1991/92 the Department required purchasers and providers to ensure a smooth take-off. This meant that trusts' contracts would by and large replicate previous activity and income levels. In subsequent years the requirement for a level playing field has been imposed. Trusts' pricing policy is required to incorporate a 6 per cent return on capital assets. As yet, therefore, the achieved rate of return on capital provides little information on the level of trust efficiency or, indeed, on any other aspect of their performance.

Equally, since trusts are not genuinely independent trading corporations, they cannot go bankrupt. The prices they charge in their contracts must be designed to cover their costs. If a trust should get into financial difficulties, the share-holder (the Treasury) can fund the deficit pending a reorganisation of the trust's management. Hence trusts are subject to soft budget constraints just as are DMUs. As a corollary of their status as corporatised public enterprises, trusts are unable in practice to dispose of their surpluses. These must balance out to zero over the years, and are unlikely to play a significant role as a motivator of investment, innovation, or efficiency.

If the public share in the trusts were to be sold off into private ownership the budget constraint would become hard; the rate of return would then reflect the real efficiency of their activity, and the possibility of retaining surpluses might have real economic motivating power. There is, of course, speculation that movement in this direction is part of the Government's long term agenda; if so, it would be following a path taken by some Eastern Europe countries where corporatisation of state enterprises is but a prelude to their eventual 'real' privatisation (Bartlett, 1993).

Trusts and Activity: The NHS Management Executive produced an assessment of the performance of the NHS in the half-year between April and September 1991 (NHSME, 1991), some of which relates to the performance of trusts. A further report was produced in 1992 concerned specifically with trusts and covering their performance over the whole year (NHSME, 1992b).

Both reports contain relatively little by way of actual performance data. The first considered a few indicators of activity:

- Within the acute sector, increases during the period concerned in inpatients of 1.5 per cent, in day cases of 13.6 per cent and in outpatients of 4.2 per cent. Adding together inpatients and day cases produced 'a forecast over the year of 3.7 per cent above the previous year'.
- An increase over the six months compared with the same period in 1990/91 of 5.9 per cent in heart by-pass operations, 5.5 per cent in cataract operations and 7.6 per cent in hip relacement operations.
- Reductions in the number of long wait patients (over one and over two years) in most regions.

An obvious problem with these figures from the point of view of this Chapter is that they do not differentiate between acute sector activity undertaken by trusts and non-trusts. But this is not the only difficulty with them, as has been pointed out by the Radical Statistics Health Group (1992). Although the Group makes a variety of criticisms, the principal points to which they draw attention are of two kinds. First, the figures do not distinguish between increases in hospital activity and reductions in waiting lists that are a direct consequence of the reforms, and those that are simply the result of the long term growth in such activities over time. For instance, the average annual increase in cataract operations between 1979 and 1990/91 was 8.25 per cent – well above the 5.5 per cent increase between the first six months of 1990/91 and 1991/92. Second, there have been changes in system of data collection which make year-on-year comparisons misleading – although, to be fair to the Management Executive study, most of those to which the Group draws attention took place before the implementation of the reforms, and do not apply to the specific comparison between 1990/91 and 1991/92.

The second report contained even fewer figures, simply pointing out that for trusts there was an increase in the first year inpatient admissions of 5.4 per cent, in day cases of 20.5 per cent and in total activity of 8.2 per cent, rather larger than the 1991 Report forecast. The comparable figures for DMUs were 3.8 per cent for inpatient admissions, 21.6 per cent for day cases and 6.9 per cent for total activity. However, these figures ignore the 'self-selection effect': that is, the fact that the early trusts were, according to some criteria, already more efficient than their DMU counterparts. We shall return to this point later.

Another fundamental problem with this kind of research is that it does not distinguish between changes in the performance indicator chosen that arise because of the structure of the reforms and those that arise from the fact of reform. It is well known that changes in organisational structure are often accompanied by improvements in productivity, regardless of the type of change being introduced (the so-called Hawthorne effect). In the case of the NHS the reforms were accompanied by massive Ministerial and managerial exhortation, which are likely to have had a positive impact on productivity. Indeed there is evidence – see Chapter Two – to suggest that, in the early days of the reforms, most managers felt positively about them although it is not clear whether this was due to Ministerial exhortation or a more general Hawthorne effect.

Perhaps even more importantly, the changes were accompanied by a significant increase in the resources going to the NHS. For the year 1991/92 these have been estimated as 6.1 per cent and for 1992/93 as 5.5 per cent in real terms (Department of Health, 1993, p.94). With resource changes of this magnitude, it would be very surprising indeed if there were not significant changes in activity, regardless of the impact of the reforms.

Trusts and Costs: More insight into the characteristics of both first and second wave trusts can be gained from our own project on hospital costs (Bartlett and Le Grand, 1992 and forthcoming). This work sought to make comparisons of unit operating costs between hospitals involved in applications for trust status and other hospitals. In order to do this we examined the CIPFA Health Databases for 1989/90 and 1990/91, which is the most comprehensive available source on hospital costs.

There were two samples of hospitals in England and Wales corresponding to these accounting years. The hospitals were drawn from all regions of England and Wales, and from all size groups. In most categories the first wave trust applicants were found to have lower mean unit costs than the non-applicants (see Table 1 at the end of this chapter). For example, the mean ward unit costs of the trust hospitals were £57.41 compared to £64.48 for the non-trusts. Mean unit administrative costs in the trusts were £2,958 compared to £3,681 in the non-trusts. Indeed in 25 out of 36 categories, trust applicants were found to have lower unit costs than other hospitals. These differences were statistically significant at the five per cent level for operating theatres, administration, haematology, catering, portering, at the 10 per cent level for grounds and gardens, and at the one per cent level for wards, and water and sewerage. In each of these eight categories, the trust applicants had lower unit costs than the rest. Only in the case of occupational therapy were unit costs for trust applicants significantly higher, at the five per cent level, than for others.

However, differences in average unit costs between trust applicants and other hospitals may reflect differences other than trust status. Such factors can be controlled for via a properly estimated cost function and the final part of the analysis concentrated on the econometric estimation of such a function (Bartlett and Le Grand, forthcoming). The estimated cost function was designed to explain the variation in ward unit costs between hospitals in terms of non-linear function of capacity measured by the number of available beds (bed size), and bed size squared to capture economies or dis-economies of scale; a location variable to capture the possibly higher costs associated with a London location; a crude case-mix variable which indicates whether a hospital is treating 'acute' or 'mainly acute' cases; and a dummy variable to represent trust status. This suggested that the average ward unit costs in the trust hospitals were lower than in the other hospitals, even allowing for other factors which enter into the explanation of cost variation between hospitals.

A similar exercise was undertaken covering the second wave trust applicants, this time for the period 1990/91. The sample of 155 hospitals was drawn from the CIPFA Health Database for 1991. Again there were significant differences in the costs of trust applicants and non-trusts, particularly for managerial areas (see Table 2). However, the results of the econometric estimation of the cost function showed that differences in ward unit costs in the sample hospitals were primarily determined by differences in patient days, bed size and case-mix. As before, the relationship between unit costs and trust status was negative, indicating a lower average cost level for second wave trust applicants compared to non-applicants. However, the cost difference was less than in the case of first wave applicants, and, more importantly, this time the difference was statistically insignificant.

The overall conclusion from the study was that there is persuasive evidence that the first wave trust applicants were a self-selecting group of hospitals which had lower average unit costs, especially in the non-clinical departments, but also for a range of clinical activities summarised in ward unit costs. Any research showing improved performance of the first wave trust applicants relative to DMUs, such as the NHS Management Executive study discussed above, must therefore be treated cautiously, as these are likely to have been those hospitals which were already performing better than the others under the old system.

The second set of results showed that there were still some similar, but smaller, cost differences as between second wave trust applicants and DMUs. However, these differences were substantially smaller, and statistical tests show that much of the difference was due to differences in case-mix, size, patient flow and regional location, rather than to intrinsically better managerial performance of these units. Thus, as the transition takes place, it seems that higher costs units will be pulled into trust status, and the apparent overall performance improvement of trusts, is likely to disappear. Of course this does not reflect any possible improvement resulting from the operation of units under trust status in subsequent years. The point, however, is that such performance improvement would need to be independently demonstrated: simple *post-facto* comparison of first, or even second wave, trusts with other units cannot, of itself, establish it.

The Indirect Approach

The indirect approach uses economic micro-analysis to specify the conditions necessary for the markets concerned to work, according to specified criteria, and then to examine the process of implementation of those reforms to see whether the conditions are being met. If they are being met, then it would be reasonable to assume that the reforms are being successful; if they are not, then there is a *prima facie* case for asserting that they are failing.

A full description of the application of this approach applied to the NHS and other quasi-market reforms can be found elsewhere (Le Grand and Bartlett, 1993). Here we briefly summarise the principal conclusions, particularly with respect to trusts.

The criteria chosen for evaluation were productive efficiency; the extension of user choice; responsiveness to users' wants and needs; and equity, interpreted to mean that treatment must be related to need. In order to meet the efficiency, choice and responsiveness criteria, it was argued that a quasi-market must meet the following conditions. First, the market structure must be competitive on both the purchaser and provider sides; second, both purchasers and providers must have good information concerning the costs and quality of the service being provided; third, transactions costs (the costs of specifying contracts and of monitoring contract implementation) must be low; and fourth, both purchasers and providers must be motivated to respond to market signals. To meet the equity criterion, there must be no opportunity for either purchaser of provider to cream-skim: that is, to select the cheapest (and by implication less needy) clients for whom to purchase or provide service.

Perhaps contrary to popular perception, many trusts —see Chapter Two — do appear to operate in a competitive environment. The problem here would seem to be on the purchaser side, with an increased pressure on DHAs to merge with each other and with FHSAs. Trusts seem to be steadily improving their information systems and costing procedures: again the problem for the quasi-market here appears to be on the purchaser side, with DHAs particularly badly placed to monitor quality (but not GP fundholders; see Chapter Four. Transactions costs for trusts appear to be high when dealing with fundholders, partly because of their numbers and partly because they appear to be increasingly on a cost-per-case basis; conversely they are relatively low for dealings with DHAs, partly because contracts are generally in block form. Trusts do appear to be motivated by financial considerations – probably to a sufficient extent to enable the quasi-market to work. Finally, the extensive use of block contracts by DHAs does give trusts both the incentive and the opportunity to cream-skim; how much actually goes on in practice is a matter for speculation.

In short, at least as far as trusts are concerned, the conditions for the quasi-market to promote greater efficiency, choice and responsiveness do appear to be broadly in place, or, at least, moving in the right direction. On the other hand, there is room for concern about the equity criterion.

On balance we feel that at this stage in the progress of the reforms, the indirect approach to evaluation has more potential than the direct approach. To recapitulate, the principal problems with the direct approach to evaluating the impact of trusts, and indeed more generally the NHS reforms, are as follows. First, the reforms have been introduced simultaneously throughout the system, leaving little opportunity for 'controlled' comparisons. Second, they are on such a scale that they take a long time to implement and an even longer time for their impact to be felt. Policy makers and other analysts cannot always wait the necessary ten years, or however long it takes for the reforms to work through, to obtain feedback on the extent of their success or failure. Third, so as to reduce the political, professional and managerial opposition that radical systemic reforms of any kind invariably encounter, they are often accompanied by persuasive measures of various kinds whose effects obscure the consequences of the reform themselves. Thus the politicians may engage in 'moral' propaganda, leading to an increase in work effort by the key people involved; or they may increase the resources going into the service concerned so as to buy off the opposition. In either case, there will be improvements in the service 'output' that will apparently stem from the working of the reforms themselves, but in fact have little to do with them. The indirect approach suffers from none of these problems.

However, there is a major problem with both kinds of research. This concerns their theoretical base. The direct research reported here is almost completely atheoretical. The performance indicators selected are not based on a well defined set of criteria; and there is no underlying theory of the way that trusts will or should behave towards them. The indirect research does specify evaluation criteria; and it uses theory to analyse the operations of markets. But it too lacks an underlying model of trust behaviour. In the remaining sections of this chapter we offer some suggestions as to how this gap may be rectified.

Towards a Theory of Trusts

A possible starting point for developing a theory of trusts is the literature on what are called in the United States nonprofit organisations or, more succinctly, nonprofits. The literature is large; the most useful includes Hansmann (1980, 1987), Rose-Ackerman (1986) and Weisbrod (1988). There is a much less developed literature in the UK; two recent contributions include Perri 6 (1992) in the US economics tradition, and Billis (1993) with a rather different organisational perspective. Although, as we shall see, NHS trusts do not fit perfectly into this category, they probably come closer to doing so than to either of the standard alternative forms of economic organisation: the profit-maximising firm and the government agency.

Non-profit organisations are usually defined in the literature as non-governmental service units that are barred from distributing their net earnings, if any, to individuals who exercise control over them, such as members, officers, directors, or trustees. Net earnings must be retained and devoted in their entirety to financing further production of the services that the organisation was formed to provide; that is, they must have a 'non-distribution constraint' (Hansmann, 1980). A related feature of non-profit organisations concerns their ownership structure. Typically, nonprofits will differ from for-profit firms in their property rights arrangements:

normally nonprofits are not organised as private firms under individual ownership or as joint stock companies. In the UK nonprofits are often registered under the laws governing mutual organisations (the Industrial and Provident Societies Acts), charities (the Charities Acts) or as public corporations as in the case of NHS trusts. (In fact, a special mechanism – the creation of 'special trustees' – has been introduced for NHS trusts to govern the trusts' use of assets resulting from past charitable donations.) Since nonprofits have no equity capital they face difficulties in raising finance on the private capital market. Trusts also have no automatic right to seek private finance nor to re-invest their surpluses. Although trusts can borrow from the Treasury, their ability to expand is further restricted by the requirement that they remain within their EFLs. In other words, the trusts' non-distribution constraint is extremely tight. This limits their ability to respond to market opportunities.

The non-distribution constraint is not unproblematic. In practice, non-profit organisations may evade it through inflating the salaries of managers or other employees, or through the generous provision of job-related perks etc. In such cases, the organisation might be better modelled as a labour-managed firm; this is a point to which we return.

Hansmann goes on to distinguish between four kinds of nonprofit dona-tive mutual, donative entrepeneurial, commercial mutual and commercial entrepreneurial. Donative organisations are those that receive most of their incomes from grants or donations; commercial ones receive the bulk of their income from prices charged for their services. Since NHS trusts primarily derive their income from contracts placed with them by health authorities and GP fundholders, they clearly fall into the latter category. Commercial mutual organisations are controlled by directors, directly elected or in some way selected by their clients or customers; commercial entrepreneurial nonprofits, on the other hand, are largely free of such control and are usually controlled by a self-perpetuating board of directors.

Here it is not so clear which category accurately captures trusts. A trust's board of directors is appointed by the Secretary of State, who in turn is accountable to Parliament. Since Parliament is elected, and since the electorate is likely to include most of a trust's users or customers, it could be argued that a trust is a mutual organisation. However, the chain of accountability is both long and weak and, to say the least, it is very questionable how much actual influence users can have on the board of trustees through this mechanism. Trusts are probably better thought of as closer to the entrepreneurial end of the spectrum.

Much of the US literature on nonprofits has a particular focus: *viz*, explaining why nonprofits arise in certain sectors of the economy and not others. The arguments can be used not only to explain their existence in those sectors but also to justify it: for they show that, under certain circumstances, nonprofits are likely to be more efficient than either for-profit firms or government agencies.

These arguments are of particular interest with respect to NHS trusts, not only because they might help explain why the Government introduced the relevant forms in the first place, but also why it did not go the whole hog and completely privatise health care provision. Such a move would have been perfectly feasible; the Government could have sold off hospitals and other provider units to the highest bidder, raising revenue in the process.

There are probably a number of good political reasons why the Government chose not to go down this route. Even for a Government used to risking temporary unpopularity, arguing the case for selling off the nation's hospitals would not have been easy. However, the nonprofit literature provides economic arguments as to why such an approach might be undesirable. One of the conditions for markets to be successful, in the sense of promoting greater efficiency, is that purchasers in that market have access to good information concerning the quality of the service. If they do not, then providers can lower their costs, and thereby increase their profits, by driving down quality. Nonprofits, on the other hand, are more likely to be motivated by considerations about the quality of the service, and therefore less likely to exploit their informational advantage.

With respect to the superiority of nonprofits over directly managed government agencies, the argument is less well-developed. It is usually couched in terms of a combination of the costs the public agencies face in monitoring their staff and the quality of their output, and the costs of political interference (Krashinksy, 1986).

Underlying these analyses is a more fundamental theoretical issue. The authors concerned rarely specify what they believe nonprofits are trying to achieve. Yet this is crucial to any understanding of any nonprofits, including NHS trusts; for unless we know what the aims and objectives of those in control of trusts are we will not be able to understand the behaviour of trusts, nor predict how they will respond to the incentive structures they face.

The first is that their principal objective is profit-maximisation. This may seem bizarre, given their label of nonprofit; but the rationale would be that, even with a non-distribution constraint, managers of nonprofits will personally benefit from generating large surpluses either because they directly derive utility therefrom, or because they benefit from the improvements in the quality of working conditions that may follow from the re-investment of surpluses in the business. In the context of hospitals, various authors have argued that nonprofits are interested in maximising profits (see, for example, Davis 1972), or a combination of profit and patient benefit, in terms of quality and quantity (Ellis and McGuire, 1987).

A second possible objective is that of service maximisation, subject to a break-even constraint. So, for example, studies by Newhouse (1971) and Joseph (1975) emphasised that the social purpose of a non-profit hospital could be reflected by including the quantity of services supplied as one of the factors that the hospital wishes to maximise. Newhouse also emphasised the role of the hospital management, or board of trustees, as principal decision maker. He suggested that these decision makers were interested in prestige, and that this would be most influenced by the quality of service. Newhouse therefore suggested that non-profit hospitals could be modelled as maximizing a combination of quantity and quality of services supplied.

In contrast, Pauly and Redisch (1973), argued that clinicians (physicians in the US terminology) take the prime role in decision making. They modelled the nonprofit hospital as a producer co-operative in which clinicians with fixed hours of work maximise net per capita income. This is a version of what has been termed in the literature the labour-managed firm. Labour-managed firms are firms in which the management of the firm is identified with (or acts as an agent of) those employees who are 'members' of the firm (Ward, 1958, Vanek, 1970, Bartlett and Uvalic, 1986).

In the case of UK hospitals, one could plausibly regard the senior clinical staff (the consultants) as the principal 'worker-members' of the organisation. More specifically, one could identify the clinical directorates which form a typical UK hospital management structure as a set of simultaneously competing and co-operating labour-managed partnerships. In a recent study of the evolution of management practice in NHS hospitals, Strong and Robinson (1990) describe the long tradition of 'syndicalism' – a traditional form of craft based unionism – amongst the UK medical profession. Despite the trend towards increased powers for general managers following the 1984 reorganisation, which has been strengthened with the creation of NHS trusts, the internal management of hospitals is still largely governed by the interests of the clinical directors who are now often directly responsible for managing their own budgets. Indeed, in some cases clinical directorates are permitted to retain intra organisational financial surpluses, so as to create incentives for clinical teams to stay within their budgets. This type of incentive structure is likely to generate competition for resources between clinical directorates, which nevertheless need to co-operate with one another in achieving the broader aims of the hospital general management.

Combining these two approaches, Harris (1977) argued that both administrators (trustees, managers) and clinicians share decision-making authority within a hospital, and so the overall aim of a hospital depends upon the outcome of a bargaining process between the various groups. Applying this to the UK case, it is worth noting that the hospital management may have different objectives to the clinical directorates. No doubt there would be bargaining over resources between the 'syndicates' of the clinical directors and the hospital management within an NHS trust. Indeed, part of the function of the reforms would appear to have been to give more power to management *vis-a-vis* the clinical directors. But it seems likely that the possibly divergent interests of managements and clinicians will both need to be represented in any general analysis of the objectives of an NHS trust. Clinicians may be interested in increasing personal incomes, the size of their clinical directorate (although this could be rationalised as a means of maximizing long run incomes of the trust's 'member-workers'), and in quality (*ie* patient benefit) for professional reasons; managers may be interested in reducing overall labour costs to meet financial targets, in increasing overall growth of the trust for career and status reasons, and in quality for its prestige and reputation effects. Thus any satisfactory model of an NHS trust as a non-profit provider is likely to include a combination of income, growth and quality of provision among its objectives. The weights attached to these elements will depend on the weights which various groups within the trust attach to them, and their respective influence and bargaining power.

An alternative to any of these models would be to adopt a 'satisficing' rather than a maximising approach. Here managers or clinicians would be more concerned with achieving a 'satisfying' level of income, work effort, or quality than in 'maximising' their performance with respect to any of these factors. However, again it would be necessary to ascertain which factors were the crucial elements in giving satisfaction, and how they were weighted in the trust's overall objective structure.

It is crucial to decide which of these models, if any, comes closest to describing the aims or objectives of trusts. For, until this is established, it will be impossible to predict with any accuracy how trusts will respond to the incentive structures of the NHS internal market – and hence impossible to adjust that incentive structure to achieve policy aims.

To take one example involving possible policy implications, a prediction of the theory of the labour-managed firm is that such firms, in so far as income maximization is a prime motivator, are less responsive to market signals than profit-maximizing firms. Increased prices give rise to increased incomes, rather than to increased employment and output. Further, if labour-managed firms include growth as well as income maximisation among their aims, it is likely that such growth will be different to that in a publicly managed hierarchy, or in a profit maximizing firm. Specifically, one would expect the labour-managed firm to grow in a fashion which increased the incomes (or improved the perks and working conditions) of the decision making groups as much as possible. Such growth would be likely to be relatively capital-intensive, so as to reduce the growth of the number of workers among whom any perks or residual income may be divided. There would therefore be an emphasis on substitution of capital for labour, and on substitution of non-tenured and unskilled labour for skilled tenured labour. If this were the case then trusts might develop as providers of specialised high quality services, using predominantly capital-intensive technologys. Although there may be some incentive advantages in an organisation in which teams of clinicians, in clinical directorates, have a key role in decision making in a hospital trust, this would still be medicine primarily in the interest of the doctor, rather than medicine in the interest of the patient. Much would depend upon how effectively purchasers could exercise a countervailing or competitive influence on trust management on behalf of their patients, and on the nature of the incentive effects of the contracts which they could draw up with them.

Conclusion

So what does the early research tell us about the performance of trusts? The answer has to be: not very much, at least in the case of the 'direct' research. The first wave trusts did, on the whole, succeed in meeting their financial objectives; however, this is not very surprising, given that the market in which they were operating was very heavily managed and that they were a self-selecting group of hospitals that were significantly more efficient than their non-trust equivalents. In addition, there has been growth in various forms of hospital activity since the introduction of the reforms; however, this may be due to a variety of factors unconnected with the reforms, notably the substantial increase in resources that has accompanied their introduction.

The 'indirect' research, on the other hand, is rather more promising. It suggests that many of the conditions for quasi-market efficiency are in place, at least as far as the trust side of the market is concerned. However, there may be problems for equity, particularly where the use of block contracts is concerned.

Finally, both kinds of research suffer from an absence of an appropriate model of trust behaviour. It is here that the next research efforts should be directed.

Table 1: Department Unit Costs by Trust Status, 1989/90

Department	Trust	Non-trust	t-stat	prob
Wards	57.41	64.48	1.95	.053
Out patients	17.17	17.18	0.00	.99
Daycare	21.39	23.32	0.49	.63
Audiology	15.46	13.97	0.37	.71
Chiropody	18.08	73.56	0.87	.39
Dietetics	11.52	12.89	0.86	.39
ECG	4.22	5.07	1.20	.23
EEG	32.21	30.98	0.22	.83
Accident & emergency	14.63	12.94	1.27	.21
Nuclear medicine	8.89	8.88	0.11	.92
Occupational therapy	33.97	15.25	2.14**	.038
Theatre	201.79	238.04	2.18**	.031
Chemical pathology	5.02	4.99	0.04	.97
Cytogenetics	32.17	63.60	1.35	.198
Haemetology	3.87	4.84	2.29***	.024
Histopathology	16.98	18.03	0.27	.79
Immunology	12.99	13.49	0.07	.94
Microbiology	6.28	4.64	1.01	.32
Pharmacy	323.81	367.33	1.03	.31
Radiology	592.03	528.39	1.06	.295
Speech therapy	25.81	25.17	0.18	.86
Catering	4.96	5.58	2.28**	.024
Laundry	13.02	12.74	0.28	.78
Linen	80.80	91.47	1.49	.14
Administration	2958.19	3680.61	2.26**	.024
Medical records	1803.02	2235.06	1.53	.128
Training & education	379.05	501.58	1.52	.13
Domestic/cleaning	1958.18	1788.72	1.13	.26
Portering	1512.58	2110.17	2.53**	.012
Transport	943.81	1049.90	0.36	.72
Eng maintenance	326.92	352.85	0.88	.378
Building maintenance	191.71	203.63	0.66	.51
Energy	278.55	310.48	1.58	.11
Water and sewerage	262.86	352.54	2.83***	.005
Grounds & gardens	2310.77	2984.86	1.84*	.068
General estate	188.89	206.07	0.93	.33
Beds	320.81	312.78	0.20	.84

Note: Trusts are first wave. Significance levels are indicated by asterisks as follows: * significant at 10%; ** at 5%; *** at 1%. The significance levels are calculated on the assumption of pooled or separate variance estimates on the basis of a prior F-test. The prob value indicates the observed level of statistical significance of the t-test ($\times$ 100%). Single outliers have been eliminated from the calculations.

Table 2   Departmental Unit Costs by Trust Status, 1990/91

Department	Trust	Non-trust	t-stat	prob
Wards	67.94	72.32	1.88*	.06
Outpatients	20.43	17.99	1.81*	.07
Daycare	29.37	25.11	0.56	.58
Audiology	12.82	14.76	0.62	.54
Chiropody	8.23	18.23	0.98	.36
Dietetics	12.06	12.82	0.49	.62
ECG	4.36	7.91	1.27	.21
EEG	54.45	39.16	1.60	.13
Accident & emergency	17.19	16.99	0.21	.83
Nuclear medicine	6.70	8.46	0.67	.51
Occupational therapy	28.11	24.18	0.24	.81
Theatre	262.58	251.82	0.60	.55
Chemical pathology	5.91	5.04	1.23	.22
Haematology	4.68	4.75	0.18	.86
Histopathology	15.09	14.27	0.27	.79
Immunology	12.10	9.67	0.44	.67
Microbiology	4.55	4.58	0.06	.95
Pharmacy	335.11	369.27	0.84	.40
Radiology	561.69	634.22	1.23	.22
Speech therapy	29.73	18.05	1.35	.19
Catering	5.43	6.17	2.58**	.012
Laundry	16.83	14.66	0.71	.48
Linen	119.44	114.47	0.15	.88
Administration	4396.47	4753.04	0.84	.40
Medical records	2293.64	2637.62	1.29	.20
Training & education	468.82	659.30	2.13**	.04
Domestic/cleaning	18070.10	1782.84	0.19	.85
Portering	2072.54	2364.64	1.88*	.06
Transport	1131.45	1564.86	0.93	.35
Eng maintenance	436.90	396.75	1.03	.31
Building maintenance	185.13	202.14	0.84	.40
Energy	318.86	312.25	0.31	.76
Water & sewerage	415.18	493.03	1.43	.16
Grounds & gardens	2226.93	3452.17	2.87***	.005
General estate	43.96	44.24	0.01	.99
Beds	416.47	430.75		

Note: *Trusts are second wave. Significance levels are indicated by asterisks as follows:* ***** *significant at 10%;* ****** *at 5%;* ******* *at 1%. The significance levels are calculated on the assumption of pooled or separate variance estimates on the basis of a prior F-test. The prob value indicates the observed level of statistical significance of the t-test (× 100%). Single outliers have been eliminated from the calculations.*

4

GP FUNDHOLDING: WILD CARD OR WINNING HAND?

Howard Glennerster, Manos Matsaganis, Pat Owens
and Stephanie Hancock

The fundholding element in the NHS reforms appears to have been something of a late arrival to the Prime Ministerial committee's discussions in 1988. The presentation of the scheme in *Working for Patients* made it sound rather like a side show and certainly that was the way it was viewed by regional and district officials whom we interviewed in early 1990. Yet it has become far more than that. Some observers claim that fundholding is the real cutting edge of the reforms or alternatively a major source of disruption and inequity (Ham, 1993). What lay behind this element in the reforms and what were the initiators trying to achieve?

It is important to realise that the origins of fundholding lie deep in the history of British health care and pre-date Mrs Thatcher's review of the NHS in 1989. For most of this century, and certainly since the inception of the National Health Service, general practice has lost ground to the hospital. This was, of course, partly the result of advances in medicine but it was also a matter of financial and professional power. Before 1948 the voluntary hospitals and the consultants within them depended for their livelihood on GPs referring their paying patients to them. After 1948 the hospitals were directly funded by the state and the GPs became supplicants, seeking treatment for a patient on the consultant's waiting list. There was thus a latent desire among GPs for any change that would shift the balance of power back in their direction.

The actual idea of giving budgets to GPs to buy services from hospitals can be traced back, in its earliest form, to Professor Alan Maynard who was developing the idea in York in the early 1980s and presented it to a seminar organised by the Office of Health Economics in 1984 (Maynard, 1986). A believer in markets in general, he recognised that they did not work well in health, not least because consumers lacked real knowledge and choice. However, a GP could act as the consumer's informed guide and health service purchaser. This was the nearest thing to a consumer led market that you were likely to get in health. Moreover, it would create a countervailing force to challenge the monopolistic inefficiencies of hospitals.

Quite independently work had been going on in the Department of Health on reforming primary health care. On a visit to the United States a group from the Department were struck by the flexibility and leverage health maintenance organisations (HMOs) had. With an annual premium from each of their patients covering all health needs, they could decide whether to provide treatment themselves, employ their own specialist staff or use a range of local hospitals. On their return, the team developed a version of the HMO idea and fed it into the primary health care green paper draft. It was removed as too radical! However, the idea was reintroduced into the NHS review in 1988 and was taken up by the new Secretary of State, Kenneth Clarke, who had been a junior Minister in the Department at the time of the earlier discussions. The review group did not drop its preference for the district model of purchasing but it did allow this experiment with GP purchasing to go alongside it.

The Scheme

Those in the Department of Health were well aware of the dangers in the HMO model and they constructed the fundholding variant to minimise these dangers. First, general practices were very small compared to American HMOs. One patient costing a lot to treat could bankrupt a small budget. To avoid this, the scheme was limited to non-emergency and relatively cheap treatments. There was also a provision that if the cost to the practice of hospital treatment for any patient exceeded £5,000 in any year the district would foot the bill. Finally, only large practices could join the scheme. The qualifying patient list size was originally set at 11,000, then it was dropped to 9,000 and then later reduced to 7,000 for practices joining after 1 April 1993. However practices could combine: two practices with 3,500 patients each, for example, could form a single unit for fundholding purposes and qualify.

Thus the elements of the scheme at its introduction in April 1991 were:

- Practices with more than 9,000 patients in 1991 could apply to join the scheme. Regions drew up a list of criteria to screen applicants. The aim was to ensure that they were managerially and technically capable of handling the scheme and were fully committed to it.
- Practices received a budget allocation that could only be spent on a defined set of purposes. It could not be used to increase the doctors' income or to benefit the practice generally. This budget was not paid as cash to the practices but held by the Family Health Service Authorities and used to pay hospitals when a practice told them to do so.
- The budget covered five main areas:

  Hospital inpatient care for a restricted range of operations. These covered: ophthalmology; ear nose and throat; thoracic surgery; operations on the cardiovascular system; general surgery; gynaecology; orthopaedics.
  All outpatient visits.
  Diagnostic tests done on an outpatient basis. These included blood tests, urine tests and X-rays.
  Pharmaceuticals prescribed by the practice. The drug budget would be calculated in exactly the same way as the indicative budget within which non-fundholding practices would be expected to keep. However, if fundholders made savings they could use these on other parts of the fund or they could use the fund to pay for any drug overspend.
  Practice staff. Again fundholders would not be paid any more than other GPs for their practice staff but instead of having to get approval for each staff member, and new approval each time a receptionist left, for example, fundholders would simply be given a sum of money and told to pay their staff salaries from that sum.

- Although they were calculated separately, the sums in individual budgets were pooled. A saving on one could be used to spend more under another heading.
- From April 1993 the scope of the fund was extended to include community health services; district nursing; health visiting; chiropody; dietetics; all community and outpatient mental health services; mental health counselling; health services for people with learning disabilities. Terminal care and midwifery were excluded.

In the first year, practices' scope for shopping around or for employing their own staff in connection with these new services were severely restricted. They had to contract for all the community services from an existing health service community unit.

Efficiency Catalysts

The scheme was targeted on those parts of the NHS, especially the hospital sector, that were most inefficient. These included:

Non-emergency cases: This is where long waiting lists exist. While life-threatening conditions are relatively well catered for in the NHS, the non-emergency areas of medicine are not. Hospital doctors get relatively little satisfaction from undertaking the marginal hip joint operation. The more the team and the nurses take on, the harder they need to work. Indeed, if a consultant has a private clinic, there is an incentive to keep a long waiting list, in the knowledge that this may encourage patients to go to the private clinic instead. It was clear from our interviews that GPs were convinced this was a major reason why many of their consultants' waiting lists remained persistently high. A major motivation for some in the third wave was, as one GP put it, 'to dish these crooks'.

Outpatients: These are low on a hospital doctor's agenda. Appointments schemes are poorly run, many patients fail to turn up or are seen by junior doctors. The easiest thing for a junior doctor to do is to carry out a routine check-up and then request the patient to come back in six months when he or she will be off in another job.

Pharmaceuticals: Indicative drug budgets have had little effect on drug spending. Fundholding was an attempt to introduce a positive incentive for doctors to think more carefully about their prescribing, since they would be able to spend money saved on other aspects of care.

Community services: Though district nurses and health visitors are meant to work closely with GPs, as part of the primary health care team, they are actually employed by a separate community services unit. This can make co-ordination difficult even though individual doctors often enjoy very good working relationships with their community colleagues. A nurse employed by a GP, for example, cannot go into a patient's home to perform duties she could in the surgery. In the long run, the argument went, these functions could be more rationally managed from a single budget.

These, then, were the efficiency arguments for the scheme. However, there were also some matching fears expressed in our interviews with officials and GPs.

Budget volatility: The experience of HMOs in America suggested that, despite the efforts of those designing the scheme, the budget variability would be too great for the small practices to handle. It was feared that many would over spend and find themselves unable to treat patients at the end of the financial year (Weiner and Ferris, 1990).

No management skills: Practices were unused to handling such large budgets and simply would not be able to recruit people with the skills needed.

Cream skimming: Again evidence from America suggested that with a fixed income per patient, practices would have an incentive to avoid accepting patients with a high risk of being expensive (Luft and Miller, 1988).

Under treatment or under referral: Some argued that if the practice had to pay for treatment itself, there would be an incentive for doctors to put off treatment or not treat at all. Similarly, there would be a temptation to treat too many patients themselves, for example, to set up private companies and refer to them for minor operations.

Equity considerations: two standards: In addition to these efficiency arguments against the scheme, there were also equity objections. Probably the most widespread fear was that consultants would be tempted to give preferential treatment to patients from fundholders because it would boost their incomes or the revenue their unit gained. It was also feared that fundholders would get bigger budgets and be favoured in other ways compared to patients of non-fundholding GPs. This was to prove the most controversial part of an already controversial set of changes.

The Research

The research was designed to test these hopes and fears. It was, essentially, a study of administrative process and not of health outcomes. The latter would have required a far larger budget and a different disciplinary starting point. Our approach was grounded in economics and social administration. Would the market work in the way its advocates predicted? Would fundholders prove better contractors than districts? Would they manage to keep within budget? Would their prescribing patterns change? How would fundholding affect their internal practice organisation and approach to care? Was there any evidence of cream skimming?

The study concentrated on three regions, two in London and the home counties and one predominantly rural. One region had within it the highest concentration of fundholding GPs in one FHSA anywhere in the country. We interviewed those administering the scheme in other regions but most closely followed events in these three.

Region A had 13 first wave fundholders, 10 second wavers and 29 third wavers. Region B had 23 first wavers, 21 second wavers and 45 third wavers. Region C the rural region had 9 first wavers, 4 second wavers and 41 third wavers.

We chose a sample of 17 practices which had expressed interest in joining the scheme early in 1990 and which reflected the range of different kinds of practice and geographical spread. Our research officer accompanied the regional officers on initial visits to intending practices. Two felt, in the end they did not want to collaborate with the research because of the time they thought it would take. We continued to interview another five but they decided they did not want to enter fundholding in the first wave. This left us with ten practices which became first wave fundholders and which have continued in the scheme to the time when this report was written in March 1993. With the help of an additional grant from the King's Fund, we were able to compare the experience of third wave practices, the next big cohort, with the first wave group. In 1992 we chose another sample of 16 practices in the same way from those expressing an intention to join the third wave in April 1993. All did become third wavers. Table 1 gives a brief outline of the sample practices' characteristics.

We interviewed those in the Department of Health responsible for the scheme, regional officers in the three regions, FHSA officials, one or more partners and the practice manager in the sample practices. These interviews were carried out every three months for the first eighteen months and then, less frequently, later in the project. We used a semi-structured 90 minute interview. We were able to attend all the planning meetings in one region which determined the detailed implementation of the scheme.

Table 1: Sample Practices' Characteristics: First Wave

Practice	Partners	Locations	Patients
1	3	Inner London (not poor)	9,500
2	6	Small town	16,000
3	5	Large town (deprived)	12,800
4	6	Large town	12,500
5	5	Village/rural	9,100
6	6	Small town	13,500
7	6	Village/rural (remote)	13,500
8	6	Village/rural	11,000
9	6	Outer London (mixed)	15,200
10	4	Outer London	10,500

Sample Practices' Characteristics: Third Wave

Practice	Partners	Locations	Patients
1	5	Inner London	10,000
2	2	Outer London (suburbs)	3,200
3	4	Inner London (not poor)	9,000
4	6	Small town	11,000
5	3	Small town	7,000
6	3	Large town	7,800
7	6	Village/rural	11,000
8	6	Outer London (poor)	12,500
9	4	Outer London	7,400
10	4	Outer London (poor)	7,500
11	7	Large town (poor)	12,230
12	4	Village/rural	6,500
13	6	City	13,000
14	6	Small town (semi-rural)	11,500
15	8	Town	13,500
16	6	Town	7,500

We attended seminars and workshops and conferences to make sure our emerging ideas were not inconsistent with views expressed by GPs in the country more widely. From this it became clear that some of the enthusiasm we found was a south of England phenomenon, especially in the first wave.

We collected all the summary financial and prescribing data from our practices on a monthly basis and a range of documentary and statistical material about them. Regions and FHSAs were also helpful with aggregate data. Finally, in order to throw more light on the expense of particular patients, we enlisted the support of one of our practices. We drew a one in ten sample of their practice population, randomly drawn from the alphabetical list. The practice summarised all the medical history and screening information they had about their patients, together with the patient's postal code and assigned a social deprivation score on the basis of the Jarman index of deprivation. We then matched this anonymised material with the expenditure on that patient from the fund. This enabled us to see whether the practice could predict the kinds of patient that would be expensive, and enabled us to see how far the Department of Health's formula would compensate the practice for the extra cost of predictably expensive patients.

Implementing the Scheme

Typical of reforms in the Thatcher era, this scheme was, at its inception, no more than an outline idea. None of the detail was in place at that stage. The rules of the game had to be invented as it went along. For some time it was unclear just what treatments would be covered by the scheme or how tertiary referrals from consultants on to another specialty would be treated. The financial software for the practices had to be invented from scratch in a few months.

This phase of the scheme has been discussed by the authors in their preliminary report (Glennerster, Matsaganis and Owens, 1992) and will not be described in detail here. However, it should be said that given the lack of a blueprint and the timescale involved the administrative feat was considerable. The scheme was fortunate in the lead people at the Department of Health. The medical adviser was the key initiator who had evolved the idea in the mid-1980s. The administrator, an outsider from another department, was an enthusiastic convert. This was important, since the scheme did not have many friends in the Department. He was also an administrative entrepreneur who delighted in the freedom of action this unusual role gave him.

Each region had a nominated and publicly named individual responsible for fundholding and these met at the Department roughly once a month to discuss issues that had arisen and to hear what new or developing rules the Department were suggesting. Telephone contact was frequent and problems sorted out in one region were then communicated as case law to other regions. These officials visited practices a lot and, since they talked at numerous conferences, they became known and contactable by individual first wave practices. Unusually, for civil servants, they knew what was happening in the front line. When Ministers changed or came under pressure they were whisked off to see some of the enthusiastic practices and their faith restored. Whatever the merits of the scheme, its early implementation is a lesson in how to achieve change in an otherwise bureaucratic environment.

The regional officers were much more cautious or even downright sceptical. They would be held responsible if particular practices proved incapable of handling the budget. Not surprisingly they set fairly demanding standards for practices wanting to join the first wave. They had to have good computer systems up and running, a good managerial capacity, a united view amongst the partners about fundholding and be good practices in the view of their FHSAs.

All the regions were surprised by the response. They expected perhaps half a dozen interested practices. In fact, Region A had 58; Region B, 78 and Region C, 36. However, many did not qualify or were persuaded to come back next year so that a much smaller number actually entered the first wave. The first wavers were both unusually good and committed. Hardly any were to be found in the inner city core. They had good premises and staff and were predominantly in the suburban ring round London. If there were to be advantages in the scheme, they would go to those who already enjoyed good primary health care.

As the number of practices in the scheme grew in the second and third waves, it became impossible for regions to cope with the detail involved in choosing the practices and monitoring their progress. This was devolved to FHSAs. Regions remained as backstops and above all kept responsibility for setting the budgets.

Why did GPs Join?

We spent much of our earliest interviews with the practices discussing why they had chosen to become fundholders. We asked the third wavers the same thing.

The first wavers gave a number of reasons for joining:

Improving quality of service: All the first wave practices used this phrase, or something like it to describe their primary motivation. When pressed, most described some aspect of their local hospital service they were unhappy with, frequently waiting times or particularly unhelpful consultants. None wanted to move all their patients, but most had at least one or two specialties or service they wished to change, or threaten, in order to improve matters. Some of the most passionate advocates of the new scheme were also passionately pro National Health Service. They saw the scheme as a way of shaking up a highly ineffective hospital system. As one put it: 'This is the NHS's last chance. If it does not come off I shall leave the profession.'

Referral freedom: About three-quarters of the practices were very concerned that the districts would not permit them to send patients to hospitals outside the district. They wanted to retain the freedom they had always had to refer where they wished. The capacity to pay the receiving hospital would ensure this freedom, they felt.

Service development: Slightly fewer, but still a majority, were keen to provide more on-site services, mostly counselling and physiotherapy, for example, but a few had the idea that consultants might come and do outpatient clinics. Some wanted to do minor operations. In general, though, their ambitions were modest at this point.

Budgetary freedom: All looked forward to having a staff budget and not to have to ask the FHSA's permission to employ staff.

Money and computing: Some said frankly that the computers would be worth it even if the scheme failed.

The next mountain: For many of the first wave, this was the leading edge thing to do. They were teaching practices which had made all the improvements they could. Some of the younger doctors in their late thirties or mid career had got a little bored with general practice and this was the next mountain to climb.

We asked why the practices in our third wave sample had not joined the first wave? About a third had not been eligible before the size limit had been dropped. The sheer amount of organisational change and management involved had put off most of the others, in particular many felt their computer systems were not up to the change. The fundholding option had come just about the time they were getting used to the new contract and they had felt that was quite enough change for the time being.

Some had been very cautious about how fundholding would turn out and decided to let others blaze the trail. 'We wanted to see how it shook down before we committed ourselves.' A few practices had been discouraged because they lacked peer support, indeed some had faced outright hostility from colleagues in the locality.

Some had had political doubts. They had felt the scheme would bring a two-tier service. There had also been the fear that it would introduce money into the relationship between doctor and patient. Even if not shared by all the partners, these fears had been felt by some members of the team. In most cases these views had tempered with time.

The problems had gradually come to seem less important. Local fundholders seemed to be coping without any great difficulty. The positive reasons they gave were drawn from watching the experience of the first two waves.

Service improvements: Third wavers all said they had seen how the first wavers had made the hospitals respond and take notice. They were perceived to be getting a more responsive service. Most thought their patients would be disadvantaged in the long run if they did not join. One doctor said that rather than being a 'vigorous advocate' on behalf of some of his patients, especially the most articulate, he would rather be 'a purchasing advocate' for all his patients. About a quarter of our sample had been purchasing advisers to their district health authority. They felt frustrated that the GP's voice was not adequately heard. The process was slow and there was little feedback. The district health authority was too heavily influenced by the providers to have a truly independent purchasing strategy. Fundholding would give them the chance to define their own requirements. They wanted to 'fine tune' the contracts to their own practices' needs. What was different about the third wave was that they had had a chance to compare the first wavers' contracts with the districts'. They thought they could do better than the districts.

Referral freedom: This was less important than before but a half of those interviewed felt strongly that their district had limited the scope of the hospitals they could use. One had been outraged by the fact that the district had run out of extra contractual referral funds half way through the year. He had always referred a few special cases to the regional teaching hospital and a letter telling him he could not do so had so infuriated him, he applied to be a fundholder the next day.

Changing hospitals for the patients' good: Most of the practices we interviewed claimed that they had seen an improvement in communication with hospitals in the past two years and most put this down to the influence of fundholding. Many felt that most hospitals still took a take it or leave it attitude to patients and would continue to do so unless GPs obtained some sanction over them.

Future of general practice: Most felt that fundholding was now the future for primary health care, extending its scope. As one partner put it, 'We have been the lead practice in this area for may years. All the partners opposed fundholding when it first came in. We had our usual retreat to discuss the future of the practice as we do every year or so. Fundholding was not on the agenda when we went but by the end of the weekend we had all concluded it had to be the way forward because it fitted into the way general practice had to go.'

Optimum time to apply: Most thought that this was the best time to join the scheme. They would not have to face the problems the first wave pioneers had faced. Fundholding was still relatively new, but there would still be financial inducements like computing.

Budgetary freedom: Several practices said that being free of petty staffing controls and simply having a cash limited budget was worth joining on its own. Several were in areas where the local hospital had run out of cash for non-emergency cases three months before the end of the year. They knew their fundholding colleagues had managed things better.

The next mountain: The number of sheer mountain climbers was less than in the first wave. There were fewer idealists, more hard headed pragmatists learning from the gains and problems of the first and second wavers. There was little evidence of a general decline in the competence of the practices in managerial terms, indeed most were *better* prepared than the first wavers at the same stage. A few were not, however.

The Spread of Fundholding

Our third wave interviews give some clue to the unexpected growth of fundholding. In the first year seven per cent of the population comprised fundholder patients. By the second wave the figure was 14 per cent and the third wave will cover more than a quarter of the population. The number of practices falling within the 7,000 limit will only cover. By 1993/94 25 per cent of the population of England were in fundholding practices.

The geographical spread, however, remains uneven. In one of our FHSAs, half the population were in a fundholding practice in 1992/93. Table 2 shows the regional breakdown in early 1993.

The third wave will enter areas that the first did not reach, but there are still very few poor and inner city practices in the scheme. Many are too small or their premises too cramped and the partners do not have the spare energy to take up the scheme.

Despite the growth in the numbers of the population covered, it should be stressed that the share of the total hospital and community budget involved is still quite small. In 1992/93, the share of the total taken by fundholders was only two per cent. Even in the region with the largest number of fundholders, the share of the hospital budget taken by them was still only four per cent. If everyone were registered with a fundholder, only about 15 per cent of the hospital budget would have passed through their hands in 1992/93.

Setting the Budget

One of the most difficult and as yet unsolved problems officials have faced is a very basic one – how do you calculate the budget each practice should be given?

Table 2: The Population in GP Fundholding Practices, by Region, 1993

	% Total
Mersey	35
Oxford	33
Wessex	33
Yorkshire	33
Trent	31
North West Thames	27
West Midlands	26
East Anglian	25
Northern	25
South West Thames	25
South East Thames	22
South Western	19
North Western	17
North East Thames	14

The original white paper was quite clear about this. Fundholders' budgets should be set in the same way as districts – on a formula basis (Secretaries of State, 1989). Just as an ordinary GP is paid a sum per head for each patient who signs on with the practice, so a sum would be added to cover the cost of hospital treatment.

How to set the formula? There was the rub. Existing research on GPs' referral patterns indicated that there were very considerable differences that could not be readily explained (Coulter *et al*, 1991; Roland and Coulter, 1992). Added to that, the prices for hospital treatment faced by practices would differ widely, especially in the initial phase of a market. To set some national average capitation figure would mean some practices getting much above what they needed to buy their normal supply of treatment, while other practices would get too little to sustain their usual level of referrals. The Treasury would not accept the first and the practices concerned would not have accepted the latter. The scheme would never have been launched. No answer could be found before the first budgets had to be set.

In the event, the Department decided to base the budgets on an historic cost basis. Practices would be given enough money to enable them to buy the same level of hospital care that they had obtained for their patients in the previous year. It was hoped that regional data and hospital records would enable the regions to find out how many patients each practice had referred to hospitals in the previous year. This proved very unreliable. Each practice was therefore asked to supply its own records of the number of patients it had referred to which hospital for what purpose. The period covered was sometimes as short as three months. From this the regional officers had to estimate a yearly rate of hospitalisation by specialty. They then worked out how much it should cost to treat those patients in those hospitals. The same was done with the practices' use of laboratory tests. The hospital element in the budget was then calculated so that it would enable practices to buy the same amount of services as they had used in the previous year. The drug element was calculated by the FHSA – on the same basis as that used to set the indicative budget, often last year's spend plus an 'uplift' factor. The FHSA also fixed the staff budget by taking the existing approved staff complement and an estimated salary bill.

These elements were then added to form the total budget that could be spent on patient services. These budgets varied between regions and between practices. For example, in the second year of the scheme, our lowest region gave just over £100 per patient. Thus, a practice with 10,000 patients gained a budget of just over £1 million. Budgets were set somewhat higher in the other two regions at £123 and £132 per patient. The composition of the budgets varied too. In the region with the largest number of practices the drug budget was on average £44 per patient and the hospital budget £69, (comprising inpatients' costs of £33, outpatients £29, and tests £6). In the other two regions the drugs budgets were, on average, £40 and £54 per patient and the hospital budgets £51 and £65 per patient. The variations from practice to practice were considerable. This was partly unreal, insofar as the prices charged may have been calculated in different ways, but for the most part the figures reflected the different referral patterns, and the widely different cost structures in local hospitals. Some practices spent more on drugs and less on hospital care. These figures revealed, they did not create, the inequality in resources available to patients attending different GPs in the NHS.

In the second year the regions only increased the hospital budget by about £0.80 per patient responding to criticism that they had been too generous in

Table 3: Fundholding Budgets in the Three Regions, 1991/92 and 1992/93

| | Patients | Funds | Budget Allocations (£) Per Capita | | | |
			Hospital	Drugs	Staff	Total
1991/92						
44 practices	543,143	58.7	60.68	38.61	8.73	108.09
1992/93						
44 first wave	540,830	62.5	61.51	43.80	10.48	115.65
35 second wave	386,642	47.6	65.50	46.80	10.64	123.15
All 79 practices	927,472	100.2	63.18	45.05	10.31	118.78

the first round: see Table 3. This was an uplift less than districts received that year.

In addition to these ring-fenced budgets for patient care, the practices received a management allowance to enable them to employ a part-time manager to handle the fund and assistance for computing. This management allowance amounted to £34,500 per practice and half that for the preparatory year. The costs of computer upgrading needed to operate the fund were also added.

This way of setting the budgets got the show on the road but the methodology built in a perverse incentive. It was in the interests of practices to bid up their referrals and their drug spending in the year before they became fundholders and to sustain or increase it thereafter. As one practice put it, 'we did not stint ourselves' in the run up to fundholding. Moreover, on a practical level, it was clear that the whole process of individually negotiating each budget would become intolerable when very large numbers joined the scheme.

The Department of Health returned to the task of calculating a capitation formula. A group of civil servants and regional officers began work in August 1991. A year later in July 1992 it had produced a draft proposal that was discussed with the regions, revised and made available for regions to use in the autumn to assist in setting the 1993 budgets. The drugs element was hived off and given to academics at Leeds to work on. No change was recommended in the way the staff budget was set. FHSAs were to adopt the same criteria across fundholding and non-fundholding practices. The group ran into considerable difficulties with the nationally available data linking patient characteristics with the probability of attending different hospital specialties. Outpatients proved completely intractable. In the end it was possible to show a relationship between inpatient activity rates and age and sex. No relationship could be found from the national data with the deprivation of the population. This led the Department to conclude that it should merely aim to produce a 'capitation benchmark' from which regions should begin their negotiations.

This benchmark would have three components. The first would be a predicted activity level in the fundholding procedures and specialties based on the age and sex balance of the practice population. For example, how many orthopaedic procedures would be generated from a given population if it conformed to the national average? The second element would be to produce the average cost of each procedure group. If local provider prices were very different, actual local prices would be used but the national or regional benchmark would be a useful check. Finally, a list of local factors would have to be added to adjust the formula to the practice's situation; for example, the proportion of patients with private insurance. The region would set a capitation benchmark for each practice and use that as a basis for negotiation. The research team on prescribing produced a weighting scheme by age and sex to set a benchmark for drug budgets.

In the event different regions did different things with this guidance in their 1993 negotiations. Some regions felt they had very good historical trend data about their practices' referrals and this was a surer basis for questioning their budgets than national or even regional averages. The North Western Region were in this position and so were Wessex, for example. The Northern Region did not use the capitation formula at all. Most regions and FHSAs used the national methodology modified by using regional not national activity rates and specialty costs. Having produced a guidelines budget, they would then see if there were any real outliers a long way from the figure produced by the formula. If so, a discussion with the practice would take place to identify any special factors. The result might be a tougher budget or a warning that next year's might be tough, but in very few cases was a major change made.

One region tried to push ahead with a modified formula that took account of social deprivation. This was based on the patterns of referrals indicated in a commissioned study. Because its fundholders were largely in less deprived areas this finding enabled it to justify 'benchmarks' well below previous years' budgets. Initial reductions of 15 to 20 per cent were common. This proved politically impossible to sustain. Nor was the logic in equity sustainable. If non-fundholding practices in suburban areas also had their access to hospital reduced it might have been fair. As it was the effect would have been to penalise suburban fundholders alone. The region had to back down in successive stages but the result was to exert some downward pressure on the budgets in 1993.

Contracting

Contracting was slow to get under way for the first wave practices. This was not because they were unready or uncertain but because the providers simply did not take them seriously. Most of the practices had to make repeated attempts to find anyone in the hospitals prepared to talk to them in 1990/91. Only in the two months before the scheme was to begin was there any significant response. Even then suggestions from the practices that they wanted changes or improvements were treated with incredulity. Our interview notes from three years ago make fascinating reading. Neither hospital clinicians nor managers had any idea what was about to hit them. It was clear that most simply did not understand what GP fundholding was, or thought it would have no impact on them if they ignored it. Two of our practices could not conclude contracts until the June after the scheme began in April. When the provider units did get round to responding, they assumed that the GPs would merely want to adopt the standard district block contract and arrange to buy in full from the same providers as they always had done. Many practices were reluctant to do this. They had often entered the scheme, as we saw, because of dissatisfaction with a local provider and were keen to shift, or threaten to shift custom to make the whole thing worthwhile. This infuriated not just the local hospital managers and consultants but the district health authority managers too. One district hospital official said 'It's our money you have taken. You have no right to take it elsewhere'.

Then, in the two months before vesting day things began to change, slowly at first and then very significantly. The first chink appeared with the laboratory services. There was more concern about this service than any other. Most of our practices had to wait a week to get urine or blood tests done. Documentation was poor. Yet, here there was, in every case, an alternative, either a different NHS hospital lab or a private one.

The practices used the threat of exit – withdrawing their custom – for the first time. They threatened to take their custom elsewhere. One case was fairly typical. The practice asked for improvement in the turn around time for test results. The hospital took no notice. The practice had an offer from another hospital to put on a daily collection service and placed the contract with them. A week later the first hospital phoned to say they could after all put on a daily van and do it for all the GPs in the area. 'For years we have been told this was impossible. Now with fundholding it has happened in a week', one of our practices said. In every case but one, our first wave sample achieved an improvement in their lab service by threatening to change supplier. In our first report we quoted numerous other examples. This story has now become so familiar, and is replicated by our third wave sample, that it is difficult to remember the feeling of liberation this produced in the practices. The word quickly spread to other specialties. Consultants, only a few at first, asked to come to the practices and discuss what the GPs might want. One of our practices put in their contract that they wished to have a regular meeting with the consultants in the local hospital. The partner commented to us after the first meeting, 'As I sat down and I realised what we were about to do, I thought, this is a revolution happening here. No consultant has ever talked to me about what I might think of his service or any general problems we might have in twenty years of professional life'. Now, interviewing our third wave practices, such accounts are common.

Nevertheless, in the early months of 1991, many fierce and acrimonious battles were fought by GPs and their practice managers to get hospital managers, and more importantly consultants, to accept quality targets. None of these had to do with professional medical issues, in the narrow sense, but they did relate things that mattered to the GP and the patient – the content and speed of discharge letters, the length of wait before being seen by the hospital for an initial consultation, the consultant seeing the patient on at least a certain proportion of visits. In the end, most of the practices got such quality specifications, at least as goals that they would review with the hospitals on a regular basis.

Most importantly the practices built flexibility into their contracts. Most would not contract all their business to one provider for the whole year. This gave them some leverage over the hospital if it did not perform or, if towards the end of the year, there was a backlog of cases not seen. Most *did* change their use of those key specialties that had been giving particularly bad service – a very slow and unhelpful orthopaedic consultant, a rude gynaecologist women patients had been complaining about for years. In the past alternative hospitals could not afford to take on more work. Now with a large practice bringing patients *and* money another post could be created and work accepted. While most districts were negotiating block contracts with the same providers for the same services, 'the steady state', many fundholders began with more diverse and innovative contracts. By the third year, 1993/94, many more were diversifying their providers, making more flexible contracts and specifying their own quality standards. The third wave practices were being more innovative than their first wave counterparts. Table 4 shows how the first wavers have developed their contracting strategies.

In the second and third years they became more adventurous. In year two the idea of persuading a consultant to come to the practice to do outpatient

Table 4: Contracts of First Wave Practices, 1991–93

April 1991	April 1993
1 Single block contract with district general hospitals, except tests. DHA contract specifications.	Main provider; cost per case inpatients cost and volume outpatients, mental health block. Community fixed price; several cost per case contracts with a range of specialties. Private lab, contract, cost per case.
2 Cost and volume with two main providers. Some specialist cost per case contracts.	Cost and volume with one provider; a range of cost per case contracts; community services fixed price.
3 Seven different contracts with district general hospitals, cost and volume, and block. Cost per case with two other local hospitals. Cost per case with two private hospitals.	The same plus cost and volume for community.
4 One provider cost and volume. Practice's own quality specifications.	Two main providers, cost and volume and cost per case adjusted with activity levels; path and radiology cost and volume, physio cost per case; mental health cost and volume. Two community providers.
5 Two main providers cost and volume; third similar, two others cost per case.	One main provider mostly cost and volume, but cost per case in some specialties, other providers cost per case, more detailed quality specifications. Fixed price community.
6 Two main providers cost per case; outpatient physio and radiology cost and volume.	Same plus other providers cost per case; mental health cost per case. Community fixed price.
7 Main provider cost and volume, path lab block.	Main provider block contracts by specialty; range of other providers cost per case. Two community units fixed price.
8 Block contracts with district general hospitals and community services	Acute: one main provider, cost per case; for other providers, cost per case; other specialties and services a min of cost per case and block. Quality as DHA with practice variation.
9 Main provider block contract cost per case second hospital.	Main provider mostly cost and volume; cost per case after 80 per cent activity; some specialties cost per case; other providers cost per case. Community fixed price.
10 One main provider, cost and volume. Separate path lab contract	As for 8

sessions began to catch on. Only one of our sample had made a big thing of this in the first year. By year two all were talking about it and half had some form of consultant attendance in their second year contracts. Lack of premises was the main obstacle. 'There has been a sea change on this', one GP said to us. Most of the movement seems to have come about from a combination of the fact that consultants felt they had to sell something to GPs to keep their custom and because they began to realise there were mutual gains from such an arrangement. Patients turned up and kept appointments with a practice they knew. They felt more at ease and the notes and the GP were at hand. The GP learned about new developments and diagnostic clues to look for – it kept him or her up-to-date.

Holding their own budgets also stimulated practices to think more innovatively about services they could provide on site. In most places patients' back problems were a major source of difficulty. Referral to hospital or community physiotherapy could take so long as to be pointless. Prescribing anti-inflammatories was the norm. Now fundholding provided them with a way of saving money on their drug bill or outpatient budget and using the money to employ a physiotherapist in the practice.

Psychiatric problems of a non-acute kind also took a disproportionate amount of time and referral to a psychiatric outpatients was worse than useless, they argued. After several months the individual might be seen by a junior doctor who was no help. A trained counsellor who could see the person immediately on the premises and then give a short series of sessions was much more effective. Fundholders used their outpatient budget to employ, often only a part time counsellor, for the price of relatively few outpatients referrals. In the second year more contracts of this kind began.

Fundholding does seem to have been a catalyst in challenging the boundary line between hospital outpatients and primary health care. The fact that the budget can be vired between the two previously water tight systems is the key.

Another boundary line that becomes susceptible to revision after April 1993 is that between community health services such as health visiting and community nursing, and general practice. GPs had good working relations with most of these staff with whom they have to work closely. Nevertheless, the fact that they were employed and run by another agency over whom the GPs had no influence was a cause of considerable irritation. Relations with the managers of the front line staff were often poor. The nurses employed by the practices could attend to the patient in the surgery but were not allowed to attend the patient in their own home. GPs were not able to find out which of their patients were being seen by district nurses. So the catalogue of frustrations went on, mirrored by comments by community service managers sometimes. All this was a classic example of bureaucracies at war with no incentive to collaborate and every incentive to defend boundaries.

Though a small minority — four out of our sample of 26 — would rather have had nothing to do with the community service contract, the rest were mildly or very keen to achieve more flexibility in the relationship between the two services. Most were frustrated that the regulations said they must contract all their services to an NHS community unit and not employ staff themselves, at least initially. They looked on the first year as a time when they would not attempt to change anything but find out some facts about the service and begin discussions about what they would like for the year after.

Budget Control

When the scheme was first proposed many critics, one of these authors included, argued that the practices were dangerously small (Weiner and Ferris, 1990). Evidence from the United States on health maintenance organisations suggested that any group of patients of less than 50,000 would be too small to average out the big swings in costs that might happen from one year to the next. Moreover, budget control was very difficult and practices had no experience and would not be able to track spending or control it effectively.

In the event these fears have proved completely unfounded. Only one practice in the country has had its capacity to fundhold withdrawn for overspending up to April 1993. On reflection the fears expressed in 1989/90 were founded on a simple misunderstanding and too great a reliance on the American research. The scope of the original budget was skilfully chosen. The fact that it included mainly elective procedures and outpatients on the hospital side meant that when a practice found it was overspending early in the year it could slow down the numbers it was adding to the waiting list. Conversely, and more frequently, when hospitals were falling behind they could go elsewhere and push more of their waiting list through. In short, by manipulating the queue they could come in on target at the end of the year. A fairly typical example of this can be seen from the

Figure 1   Monthly Cumulative Expenditure, of Fund-Holding Practice 7

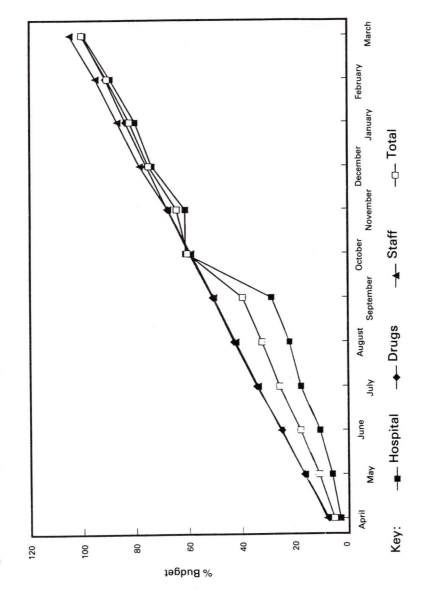

Key: — ■ — Hospital   — ◆ — Drugs   — ▲ — Staff   — □ — Total

monthly budgets – see Figure 1 – of one of our first wave practices.

Practices mostly cautiously underspent. Average underspend in our practices was 2.76 per cent: see Table 5. This average hides two significant underspends. One of these was largely caused by a miscalculation of the producer prices charged, only partly recovered by a mid-year adjustment, and, like the other case, slow throughput by the provider.

The mid-year adjustments and initial errors resulted from regions' understandable mistakes not fundholders' incapacity to budget. Indeed, the events at the beginning of 1993 showed the advantages of practice based budgeting. A number of hospitals found they had completed all the procedures they were permitted to do within their district contracts by January. That meant non-emergency patients had to be turned away. It was not that districts had received less money overall than fundholders but that the incentives in the system meant that there was no reason why hospitals should phase their work to keep to district set targets. It is in the interests of hospitals to get to their targets early and raise a political rumpus in the hope of attracting more cash.

Hospital finance directors interviewed in 1992 predicted this kind of outcome. One said:

> *It is all very well for districts to tell us that we can only treat so many patients of this or that kind. Districts do not send us patients. GPs do. They drive our business. Districts do not. They are trying to second-guess demand and impose their own arbitrary limits . . . the sooner the people who take the decision to refer patients also have the cash to back their decision, the better it will be for us.*

A Balance Sheet

Having described developments over the past three years and shown how the scheme has moved faster than even most of its advocates expected at the outset, we must now try to draw up a balance sheet. The scheme remains the most controversial element in the NHS reforms. That is because there are genuine worries and problems and not just because there are vested interests being challenged. The balance sheet has two kinds of entry. The first contains efficiency gains and losses: the second equity gains and losses.

Table 5: Budgeted and Actual Spending in the Ten Practices of the Study

Practice	Original budget	Mid-year adjustment	Final budget	Spending	Under(over) spend	Per cent budget
	£	£	£	£	£	£
1	£999,971	-111,420	885,551	771,680	113,871	12.86
2	1,807,918	–	1,807,918	1,846,255	-38,337	-2.12
3	1,791,425	38,301	1,829,726	1,809,395	20,331	1.11
4	1,572,348	-23,000	1,549,348	1,528,337	21,011	1.36
5	984,000	-51,710	1,035,710	967,027	68,683	6.63
6	1,320,000	6,079	1,326,079	1,386,151	-60,072	-4.53
7	1,416,000	–	1,416,000	1,421,604	-5,604	-0.40
8	1,172,000	–	1,172,000	988,627	183,373	15.65
9	1,800,000	4,290	1,804,290	1,786,388	17,902	0.99
10	1,644,000	–	1,644,000	1,566,247	77,753	4.73

Total 10 practices

Original budget	£14,507,662
Mid-year adjustment	-£140,460
Final budget	£14,470,622
Spending	£14,071,711
Total underspend	398,911

Per cent budget   2.76

We look first at the efficiency side of the balance sheet.

Better contractors? Districts, in our experience, tended to concentrate their efforts on strategic issues – where to spend more to obtain maximum health gains, the broad health needs of the area – not on micro-efficiency or quality issues. They were simply not in a position to be able to conduct that kind of discussion. They lacked the detailed clinical and personal experience of the day-to-day quality problems that GPs had. GPs were, in the same way, not in a position to do the strategic thinking. Their contracting was thus complementary to that done by districts. They were best at attacking the micro-level inefficiencies and the insensitivity of the monopolistic hospital mentality – the aspects of the NHS which most encourage patients to use the private sector. Where GPs had been involved in advising district health authorities, they felt the direct form of negotiation with a hospital and the thread of 'exit' was more effective.

In short, on the micro-efficiency issues, GPs were better contractors because:

- they had better information;
- they had the motivation to improve service standards because they suffered from delay and patien⁺ dissatisfaction;
- they could make marginal decisions and not be faced with big public confrontations that districts faced if they changed provider.

It would be wrong to suggest that the changes to hospital services that resulted were revolutionary. In most cases, the gains affected services from no more than two specialties or consultants, and sometimes were quite small. But they were growing and the change in the balance of power towards the GP had certainly communicated itself to the third wavers who all felt that it was something from which they could not afford their practice to be excluded.

Drug spending: The knowledge that they could use their drug spending savings for other services to patients was taken very seriously by all our practices. Most hoped to do this by switching more to generic prescribing or more rigorous thinking about partners' prescribing. Some began to hold regular monthly meetings at which a partner would give a paper reviewing the effectiveness of drugs for a particular condition and their relative cost.

The partners would then take an in-principle decision about what they would normally prescribe. In fact, the drug budgets were fixed very tightly and few actually made savings. Indeed most had to use their hospital budget to help keep within their drugs budget. Non-fundholders in difficulties must have been permitted to overshoot. It is evident from the national figures that the incentives worked on fundholders. In 1991/92 all GPs prescribed 15 per cent more in cash terms than the year before. Fundholders' increase was only 12 per cent. In 1992/93 the gap was wider. The national average increase was 12 per cent but the fundholders' increase was only 8 per cent.

In 1992/93 the projected drug overspend by non-fundholding GPs nationally on their drug budgets was 9 per cent. For fundholders the figure was 1.4 per cent (Communication from the Department of Health).

Boundaries questioned: We have seen that being able to use the budget flexibly between the outpatient referrals and GP services, and between community services and practice services, enables those concerned to ask where and how services are best located and organised. This has considerable potential for increasing efficiency.

Costs: Set against these benefits, there are plainly costs. These include fundholder management allowances, and the time of regional and FHSA staff. One of our regions, with the largest number of fundholders, calculated that the total administrative costs came to 5 per cent of the fundholding allocation. In fact, this sum included the preparatory year allowances for fundholders who were not yet receiving a fund so the figure was overstated. Perhaps 4 per cent would be a fairer figure. On the other hand, it left out the extra costs incurred by provider units in dealing with multiple fundholders rather than a single district. In comparison, district commissioning and contracting was said to take 3 per cent of the budget.

Thus GP fundholding has rather higher administrative costs than district-wide purchasing. This is inevitable. However, the crucial question is: do the efficiency gains discussed above outweigh this cost? Our belief is that they do, but this remains a judgement.

It is also wrong to simply count the administration and computing costs as dead-weight losses. This ignores the fact that there is a benefit from an individualised information system that tells the doctor where a patient is in the system, how long they have been waiting and whether they have been seen.

If the efficiency arguments appear favourable, are they outweighed by equity considerations?

Failure to treat: Angela Coulter has shown, on the basis of a matched sample, that the level of referrals to outpatients was no different for fundholders compared with non-fundholders (Coulter and Bradlow, 1993). Hence it does not seem that fundholders have failed to refer patients in order to save costs, as some people feared.

A two tier service?: The complaint levelled against fundholding from the start was that it would bring two standards to the service. Three years of interviewing in GP practices, that vary from dingy cramped premises with harassed receptionists in a poor inner city area, to quiet and efficient modern premises with rose gardens, branch clinics and computers linking the surgeries in a rural area, would disabuse anyone that there ever was a single tier service in Britain. The claim needs clarifying.

Some claimed that consultants would be forced to give preferential treatment to fundholding patients on their list regardless of need. One highly publicised case that suggested that this might be the case just before vesting day in 1991 led to such an uproar that the Department of Health issued guidance to hospital managers to prevent such an occurrence.

However, on a more general level, some increase in inequality was bound to follow if, indeed, the scheme was a success. The more effective the leverage and the gains outlined above the more the resultant inequality. This follows directly from a scheme that applies to only, at most, 40 per cent of the population. The policy conclusion to draw is less clear. To pursue equity by withdrawing the evident gains and make many people losers would be one solution but not one that would appeal to the authors. Our belief is that the benefits of bottom-up funding and negotiation have to be extended to those who are not fundholders. We discuss this more at the end of the chapter. The scheme has been most successful in suburban and rural areas, as we saw. That follows from the fact that this is where the best practices already were. The solution again lies, in our view, in bringing up the quality of the poorer practices.

Another complaint is that money has been spent on computers for one group of GPs and not others. This is, again, a consequence of there being two separate systems of funding and contracting and is not an intrinsic unfairness of the scheme. The computers and contract managers are in district offices in one version of contracting and in the practices in the other. If there are side benefits of this enhanced computer capacity to the practice that is a case for the scheme not against it.

A final complaint has been that the practices were allocated more money to buy services than the money available to non-fundholders via district allocations. It turns out that the reverse is true. In developing the national formula the Department of Health were able to produce a figure for what they would expect fundholders should have gained on the first wave allocations. It was 15 per cent above what they actually got. One of our regions repeated the exercise using regional price data and found fundholders had gained about the same. Another region did a similar exercise and found fundholders underfunded by about 12 per cent. In another county GPs received more than a region-wide formula would have allocated. All in all it is difficult to make a case that fundholders have been systematically over-funded. Some recent instances of trusts charging fundholders *higher* prices are, however, disturbing.

Cream skimming: So far then we are unconvinced by the equity case against fundholding. There is, however, one important respect in which the case remains important. An early fear was that fundholding GPs would turn away expensive patients. In fact, they have had no incentive to do so under the old rules of setting budgets. An expensive set of patients would have meant a high base line budget. If the budget setting moves to a formula basis then the situation will change. The formula drawn up by the Department of Health includes age and sex as factors that will lead to differential spending, but that is all.

We asked our practices to tell us what conditions they would look for to predict high spending. With the co-operation of one practice with good screening information on all its patients, we took a sample of one in ten of their patients, about 1,500 in the sample. We asked them to extract a summary of the medical histories screening data and the post code to which a deprivation score could be attached. We then matched the data on medical history with the actual spending from the fund on that patient.

A number of fascinating things emerged. First, the whole fund was expended on only 27 per cent of the patients. The most expensive five per cent of patients took 68 per cent of the expenditure. If you could lose a part of that five per cent, just one in five of them, you would be doing very well as a practice. Could you choose who to lose or put off from joining the practice on the basis of the information you had on the patients' medical history? Our research suggested that the answer was yes. Table 6 shows the cost to the fund of those with various histories or chronic conditions. In a two stage model we replicated the kind of formula the Department of Health are proposing to use which takes age and sex into account weighting older age groups more heavily. We then modeled the impact of known clinical histories. The first column of predicted costs simply takes account of the age and sex factors in the Department of Health formula. Assuming the formula were accurate for this practice it would get enough

Table 6: Two Alternative Models

Patient group	No. of patients	Average Cost Per Patient (£)		
		Actual	Predicted by:	
			Age & sex	Clinical history
Smoker	159	89.55	52.55	56.12
'Clean' record	703	29.49	31.15	45.17
Cancer	28	121.92	88.94	168.79
Heart/stroke	205	112.22	76.31	104.70
Stomach/liver	94	76.19	66.86	81.16
Kidney	48	133.92	68.38	111.30
Lungs	173	72.61	55.40	73.05
Spine	326	70.18	71.92	81.17
Minor surgery	238	112.80	70.99	94.41
Disability	19	82.97	62.80	99.58
Mental disorder	164	117.75	59.51	88.18
Diabetes	37	153.63	73.98	163.10
Total		56.71	55.42	55.50

Note: *The column headed 'clinical history' includes diagnostic information from the practice's medical records as well as the patient's age and sex* extra to cover the costs of the elderly. The practice would gain nothing by excluding old people. However, a comparison between the two predicted cost columns shows that a history of cancer or stroke, or a diabetic condition, would increase the probability of cost to the budget substantially over and above what the simple age and sex based formula predicted (Matsaganis and Glennerster, forthcoming).

Does this matter? How would practices respond in this situation? Evidence from the United States suggests that it matters a lot. Health maintenance organisations that are financed in an analogous way to fundholders have responded by finding all kinds of subtle and not so subtle ways of excluding patients from membership whom they predict will be expensive.

GP fundholders are, however, in a different position to some extent. They do not stand to lose personally if a patient is very costly. Other patients in the fund will get less good treatment. The damage is in any case limited to the £5,000 stop loss provision in the fundholding scheme.

It remains the case that even if there were no cream skimming it would be important for equity reasons to design a formula that rewarded practices for potentially costly patients. This could be done by adding a weight for patients on a practice list who had chronic conditions, or previous histories of the kind we identified in our research, as well as a social deprivation factor. Clearly our study would need to be replicated and extended to a wider sample, but it does suggest that the addition of a weighting for patients with a history of cancer, stroke, gall bladder, ulcer, kidney, lung problems and physical disability or mental disorder would catch most of the potentially high cost patients. It would not be too difficult to ask practices to include such numbers in a statistical return. It would be in their financial interest to do so. They could also be audited reasonably easily.

Action of an administrative kind could also be taken – giving patients of fundholders the right of access to the list, for example. Given that the financial incentives are not strictly equivalent to those facing HMOs in the United States, such a belt and braces approach should meet the danger of cream skimming.

The Future

We have argued that fundholding is probably one of the few parts of the reforms that is having the competitive efficiency effects on the hospital system that the reformers hoped for. On the other hand it only applies to a minority of patients and is therefore open to criticism for its equity effects. There are also long term worries about cream skimming or risk selection.

More to the point, the scheme is a threat to the established centres of power in the NHS – hospital consultants, especially those with private clinics, and the officers employed in district health authorities, regions and indeed the NHS Management Executive itself that is the top of this hierarchy. Fundholders have few friends in the system. As fundholders take more of the budget, districts' role is more questionable. We have an unstable administrative equilibrium.

Many fundholders fear that 'the empire will strike back'. Regions will make life very difficult for fundholders by restricting their budgets. FHSAs, whom GPs see as on their side, will be merged with districts. Districts will develop locality purchasing giving non-fundholders greater say in districts' contracting. The latter competition between the two systems of purchasing could be healthy. Bureaucrats tend to want neat and tidy universal systems, however.

One possible scenario is therefore that the empire will win. Fundholding will be seen as a temporary excursion and abandoned, possibly by a future Labour government with nothing to replace it. That would probably lead to a substantial exodus from the NHS of fundholders setting up private insurance based HMOs. The Labour Party would have finally broken up the NHS, which would be par for the course in stupidity!

Another scenario is that the empire will partly win. Districts and FHSAs will merge to form a health care purchasing authority but some elements of fundholding might remain (Stacey, Bosanquet, Griffiths, 1993). Under this model an elected committee of GPs would negotiate contracts for secondary care with hospitals for a population similar to a present district. Tertiary care contracts for really expensive units would be negotiated directly by the authority. This would give more power to GPs on a representative basis but not in the direct form fundholding gives.

At the other extreme, fundholding could become the basis for a revived and extended concept of primary care. Bottom-up funding would replace top-down funding as the basis for NHS finance. Fundholders and non-fundholders grouped under the FHSA's wing, would receive capitation funding that covered the present scope of the fund plus maternity, parts of general medicine and possibly community care too. Rarer and expensive procedures and long term care contracts would have to be jointly purchased at FHSA level where unmet health needs assessment and consumer surveys would be located. Regions or districts combined into much larger units could be responsible for capital planning – responding to revealed preferences and demand coming from the primary care contractors and the capital plans put forward by the trusts.

The 1991 reforms look like the beginning, not the end, of a process of change.

5

CHOICE OF HOSPITAL FOR ELECTIVE SURGERY REFERRAL: GPs' AND PATIENTS' VIEWS

Ann Mahon, David Wilkin and Carl Whitehouse

The creation of the National Health Service in 1948 represented the rejection of market principles in favour of a collectivist approach to health care provision. Klein (1983) argues that two implicit assumptions were made in the adoption of this approach. First, that there is a collective interest in the provision of health care over and above individual self-interest, and second, that health care is different from other consumer goods in that it is the producer – not the consumer – who knows best. Traditionally, then, the responsibility for ensuring the quality of health services lay with those who also defined the need for these services – managers and health professionals. The notion of consumer choice was irrelevant in the context of the philosophy that the NHS would provide the best possible care for everyone (Mooney *et al*, 1986) and that health priorities would be self-selecting (Teeling-Smith, 1984). In this sense, the justification of the NHS was the claim that it would meet the needs of all patients by providing the highest quality of care without the necessity for consumers to exercise choice.

In recent years the notion of the patient as a consumer of health care has developed. Stacey (1976) identifies two distinct sources from which this notion has arisen. The first is the application of an economic industrial model to the health service and the second is from the consumer movement. The 1960s saw the growth of a movement towards establishing the rights and interests of users of public services.

In the NHS the growth of self-help groups, community pressure groups, patient participation groups and the creation of Community Health Councils in 1974 were, in part, a response to increasing concerns over public accountability in a bureaucratic and paternalistic health service (Klein and Lewis, 1976; Bates, 1983; Winkler, 1989). Consumerism in this era took the form of public participation, a collectivist approach designed to influence and change the health service from the outside rather than the inside (National Consumer Council, 1992). This form of consumerism can be viewed as an attempt to democratise the health service by urging professionals and managers to take users' views into account, rather than a direct attempt to empower individual consumers of health care.

One widespread criticism of consumer groups and Community Health Councils has been the extent to which they truly represent health services users (Bates, 1983; Richardson and Bray, 1987; Pollack, 1992). The consumerism of the 1990s, however, goes further than questioning the representativeness of collective bodies by questioning the belief that consumers can exert an influence through such bodies at all. The collectivist approach to consumerism, traditionally associated with the NHS, has been replaced by an individualistic approach that attempts to achieve responsiveness to users through the introduction of a market ethos into the management and structure of the NHS.

This approach was first developed by Griffiths (1983) in the NHS Management Review, was further developed in the primary health care review *Promoting Better Health* (Department of Health and Social Security, 1987b) and most recently and most forcefully in *Working for Patients*. The adoption of this approach to consumerism requires that 'the interests of the consumer have to be central to every decision taken by the authorities and its management – it is not a "bolt on" option to be used occasionally' (Griffiths, 1988, p. 202). If the creation of the NHS in 1948 represented the rejection of market principles, the 1990 reforms represented their adoption, without changing traditional funding arrangements through general taxation. Thus the consumer movement approach to consumerism is distinct from the economic industrial model in that the latter adopts an individualistic approach whilst the former adopts a collectivist approach.

Working for Patients

The changes introduced by the reforms were intended to secure two objectives relating directly to the patient as a consumer:

> to give patients, wherever they live in the UK, better health care and greater choice of the services available; and,
> greater satisfaction and rewards for those working in the NHS who successfully respond to local needs and preferences. (Secretaries of State, 1989, p. 3)

The emphasis in the white paper was on services where patients and GPs have time to choose when and where to seek hospital treatment. The focus was therefore on services providing treatment for non-urgent or elective procedures such as hernia or varicose veins and other services not available at all district hospitals, such as ear, nose and throat services.

The various policy initiatives embraced by the reforms – the distinction between the purchasers and providers of care, the introduction of trust status hospitals and community services, the introduction of a contract culture for hospital services and GP fundholding – were all described in terms of their ability to promote the quality of health care services in response to the needs and preferences of consumers.

The mechanism for achieving the aims outlined in the white paper is the internal market in which providers – directly managed units, NHS trusts and private hospitals – compete with each other to secure contracts with NHS purchasers – health authorities and GP fundholders. It argues that through the channels of the internal market 'money will follow patients'; purchasers will place contracts with hospitals that meet the needs and preferences of consumers. Less responsive services will be spurred into action and standards of health services will be raised. Providers will have an incentive to attract patients and the revenue that comes with them and so will make sure that the services they offer correspond to what patients want. Health authorities and providers were urged to incorporate the views of users at all levels in their management structures. The district and regional health authorities, traditionally regarded as public representatives, have been slimmed down to reflect their new managerial and business role in the NHS.

To speak of a patient as a consumer of health care and to equate the introduction of a market ethos into the management and organisational structure of the NHS with increased choice has prompted considerable debate. The term consumer is an economic term and, for some, it is inappropriate to speak of the patient as a consumer because consumers are essentially those who consume the goods produced by industry (Stacey, 1976). The economic model overlooks the fact that health services do things to people rather than for people, that the consumer is the object of work. For others, to speak of the patient as a consumer in the NHS is inappropriate because general taxation funding arrangements mean that patients are not in a position to exert direct influence over the providers of care. They have no power of exit. From this viewpoint patient choice will become a reality only if patients can pay directly for their health care (Green and Neuberger, 1990).

Despite these reservations concerning the use of the term consumer in the public sector and its application to health care, it has now become fashionable to speak of the patient as a consumer of health care. Pollitt (1989) has identified five dimensions of consumerism which are necessary to empower users and potential users; access, choice, information, redress of grievances, and representation.

The approach to consumerism adopted in the white paper equates the promotion of quality and efficiency with responsiveness to users' needs and preferences. This assumes that patients will act in a rational way and, given the choice, will opt to use services that will result in better health care. The impact of health promotion initiatives suggest this is not always the case (Blaxter, 1990) and a recent survey found considerable discrepancies between the priorities of patients, managers and doctors with anti-smoking education being a higher priority for doctors and managers than for the public (Groves, 1993). Furthermore in order to make informed choices, information on a range of different aspects of care, for example treatment options and outcome, would need to be available in a form that enables meaningful comparison between a range of services. Currently, however, it is problematic even to make meaningful comparisons for outpatient waiting times between individual consultants, specialties and hospitals; a recent review suggests that one of the unintended consequences of the devolution of management is an increasing fragmentation of the data network (Wilkin and Roland, 1993).

There appears to be a general consensus that making more information available will result in a more rational approach to decision-making. Little is known, however, about how this information is used by patients and GPs. Some studies suggest that while patients do want to be well informed they do not want to use the information to make decisions about their own health care, preferring to leave it to the professionals (Beisecker, 1988). One American study found the production of hospital 'death lists' had no impact on hospital choice and suggested that the basic assumptions behind information strategies are wrong, with physicians' preferences and convenience being more influential than objective information about hospitals (Vladeck *et al*, 1988).

Despite the rhetoric of increased choice for patients, the proposals outlined in the white paper serve to enhance the powers of managers and GP fundholders. References to quality standards included reducing waiting times, offering individual appointments, providing quiet and pleasant waiting areas and clear information about hospital facilities. The Patient's Charter, launched in October 1991, defined the standards of care that patients can expect to receive and set out seven existing rights and three new ones; information on local services, guaranteed admission times to hospital and investigation of all complaints. Essentially these aspects of quality are concerned with customer relations and whilst elements of these proposals touch on the dimensions of consumerism identified by Pollitt they are not elaborated. Public representation is treated as a peripheral concern – there is no reference to direct contact with patients, and Community Health Councils are mentioned only once in a chapter entitled 'Other issues'. Reference to audit is made exclusively to medical peer review with no reference to consumer audit.

In promoting consumerism, the white paper advocates delegating managerial control nearer to consumers but not directly to them. Thus trusts and GP fundholders are seen as vehicles for promoting consumerism and, indeed, are viewed as synonymous with the consumer so that, as *Working for Patients* puts it:

Offering choice to patients means involving general practitioners far more in key decisions (p. 36)
and
The relationship which general practitioners have with both patients and hospitals make them uniquely placed to improve patients' choice of good quality services. (p. 48).

Essentially, then, the white paper adopts a normative approach to consumerism: it assumes that GPs and managers will act in the best interests of patients and in a way that reflects their needs and preferences. Patients' views do not, however, necessarily correspond with official views of quality. One study reported considerable discrepancies between official criteria of quality and the views of patients in general practice (Haigh Smith and Armstrong, 1989).

In the past GPs were, in theory, free to refer patients to any NHS consultant in the UK. The introduction of contracts has removed this freedom and effectively reduced the choices available to those GPs who are not fundholders. Concern that referrals outside of these contract arrangements would be subject to the scrutiny of purchasers working in a cash limited budget, was expressed vigorously by GPs (British Medical Association, 1989; Jebb, 1991). Although the white paper promised that money will follow patients, the extent to which money follows patients' preferences depends on the contracts set on their behalf by districts and GP fundholders.

In the case of GP fundholders, decision-making and negotiating power is brought closer to patients and consequently may result in a higher standard of care for patients. However the concept of fundholding has been the subject of much debate. One view is that operating within a cash limited budget will increase the potential for selection bias and may delay referrals, thus restricting choice and access to health care for some patients, and endangering the trust relationship between patients and GPs (Scheffler, 1989). Many of these concerns are speculative and based on anecdotal evidence: initial research in Oxford found no evidence that the outpatient referral patterns of fundholders were influenced by budgetary pressures (Coulter and Bradlow, 1993). Others have expressed concerns that fundholding GPs will secure better care and treatment for their patients at the expense of patients in non-fundholding practices (Little, 1991).

Choice of hospital will depend on the contracts set on patients' behalf by purchasing authorities, be they GP fundholders or district health authorities. Patients must be willing and able to travel to services that offer better, faster and more cost-effective treatment if the internal market is to function effectively. There is some evidence to suggest this may be the case. A Marplan opinion poll conducted in 1988, reported considerable willingness to travel for treatment amongst a sample of the general population, with 38 per cent of adults saying they would be prepared to travel anywhere in the UK, and 60 per cent saying they were prepared to travel more than 25 miles (Davies, 1988). Other studies have reported considerable willingness to travel amongst the patient population; one study in the northern region reported that 74 per cent of patients waiting for routine surgery accepted the offer to travel for earlier treatment elsewhere (Stewart and Donaldson, 1991).

These studies suggest a considerable willingness by the public and patients to travel to services offering quicker treatment. A study of public opinion in Bath found somewhat less enthusiasm, reporting that just over half of respondents would definitely travel to a hospital outside of the district to reduce their wait for surgery (Richardson et al, 1992). A study in the Midlands found that amongst a group of 60 patients who had been waiting some time to be seen 42 per cent were not prepared to travel in order to be seen more quickly (French et al, 1990). Some doctors, too, are sceptical about referring patients some distance from home because of the problems of complications and follow-up (Curley et al, 1993).

The reforms have prompted much speculation about the impact they will have on choice of hospital. However, whilst there is a diverse literature on GPs' referrals to hospital, most studies have been concerned with referral rates and patterns of referral (Roland and Coulter, 1992; Coulter et al, 1991). Few studies have looked at which hospitals GPs refer to and why, or at GPs' perceptions of the factors that influence such choice (French et al, 1991; Odell, 1983). Similarly lay decision-making in hospital choice is a relatively neglected area of study although there have been many patient satisfaction surveys, typically reporting high levels of satisfaction and support for the NHS (Locker and Dunt, 1978; Carr-Hill, 1992). There has been little patient focused research, although Cartwright's studies of patients' attitudes to the care given by general practitioner services have demonstrated the importance of the patients' perspective (Cartwright, 1967; Cartwright and Anderson, 1981).

The Research Project

The purpose of the research reported in this chapter was to evaluate the NHS reforms in terms of their effects on patients' choices of hospital and choices exercised on their behalf by GPs. The research focused on referrals for elective surgery in the specialties of general surgery, ophthalmology and orthopaedics, since it is in these areas where there is considerable potential for increased choice. Indeed elective surgery was the focus for many of the initial changes and it was examples of elective surgical procedures, such as hip replacement, which were commonly used to illustrate the potential advantages of the internal market. The objectives of the study were:

- To examine the nature and extent of the choices offered to patients by their GPs, patients' perceptions of choice and the factors involved in choice, and the desire for more information in the period immediately preceding the reforms.
- To describe GPs' experiences and perceptions of choice and the factors involved in their decision-making in the period immediately preceding the reforms.
- Following the introduction of the reforms, to assess the impact of the changes on the choices available to patients and GPs.

Study Design and Methods: This was a before and after study employing primarily postal survey methods with some face-to-face interviews in the pilot stages of fieldwork. A number of methods of identifying a population of patients referred to hospital for elective surgery were considered. Focusing on new outpatient attenders was rejected on the grounds that, for many patients, it would have been some time since the referral consultation with their GP took place. It was decided therefore that newly referred patients would be identified through contact with hospitals.

Five NHS hospitals were selected: two district general hospitals, two specialist hospitals (ophthalmology and orthopaedic) and one teaching hospital. The hospitals reflected a range of NHS hospitals and were situated in urban, suburban, and rural locations in the North Western Regional Health Authority.

We were concerned to maintain a link between the patients' and GPs' surveys and this was done via the study hospitals, with each providing us with a list of referring GPs.

Patient Surveys: The patient population was defined as all patients newly referred to one of the three surgical specialties during a six week period. Preliminary interviews conducted during 1990 with 47 patients attending outpatients clinics at three of the study hospitals formed the basis for the design of the first postal questionnaire sent out in 1991. Five main areas were covered in the questionnaire; the referral decision, patient involvement in choice of hospital and consultant, desire for more information, factors perceived to be influential in choice, attitudes to travel for earlier consultation and waiting times. Patients were also asked about the reason for referral, age, gender, educational status and postcode.

A total of 3,821 questionnaires were distributed with appointment letters to patients at the five NHS hospitals between January and March 1991. Assistance with translation was offered in areas having a high proportion of patients from ethnic minorities; 1,655 completed questionnaires were returned making a response rate of 43 per cent. The same methods of distribution were employed in the second survey conducted between May and June 1992 when 3,397 questionnaires were distributed to newly referred patients. This second questionnaire was modified somewhat with the inclusion of additional questions relating to the NHS reforms and the Patient's Charter: 1,459 completed questionnaires were returned making a response rate also of 43 per cent.

GP Surveys: The GP population was identified as all GPs known to have referred at least one patient to at least one of the three surgical specialties at the study hospitals during the preceding year. Lists of GPs were obtained from the five NHS hospitals and one private hospital. A list of 502 GPs was compiled during winter 1991. Twenty-one of these GPs were approached for interview and 19 agreed.

These pilot interviews formed the basis on which the 1991 questionnaire was designed. It included a range of questions about the factors that influence choice of hospital, attitudes to patient involvement in choice and GPs' perceptions of the effects of the NHS reforms. This questionnaire was distributed to the remaining 481 GPs in January 1991. Thirty-two GPs were subsequently found to have moved, retired or died leaving a total of 449 eligible for inclusion in the study. 260 completed questionnaires were returned making a response rate of 58 per cent. Four additional questionnaires, photocopied by a group practice, were also returned and are included in the analyses.

A second survey was conducted during May and June 1992. The second questionnaire included an additional question about GPs' attitudes to referring patients further afield. Postal questionnaires were distributed to the original sample of GPs plus an additional sample of 261 GPs obtained using the same methods as in the 1991 survey. This gave a total of 710 GPs. Thirteen GPs from the earlier sample were known to have left their practice and were not sent a questionnaire. In addition two GPs who refused to be interviewed in the pilot study were sent a questionnaire. In total 699 questionnaires were distributed during spring 1992. Twenty-seven were subsequently found to be no longer in practice for a number of reasons leaving 672 GPs eligible for inclusion in the study. Sixty-seven (10 per cent) of the sample were fundholders. 382 completed questionnaires were returned making a response rate of 57 per cent. Thirty-seven (10 per cent) of the respondents were fundholders. 174 GPs responded to both surveys representing 67 per cent of the original respondents and 75 per cent of those who remained eligible for inclusion in the study. Six of these respondents were subsequently found to have moved practice and have been excluded from the analyses. Of those GPs responding to both the 1991 and 1992 surveys, 13 (8 per cent) had become fundholders during the study period. The results presented are based on the 168 GPs responding to both surveys and the 382 GPs responding to the follow-up survey.

Methodological Considerations

The low response rate achieved in the two patient surveys is of some concern because of the bias it may have introduced. The main reason for the low response must be the fact that no follow-up of non-respondents was possible and the response rates are therefore based on a single mailing of the questionnaire. Another reason might be that the availability of choice is not a salient issue for many patients. The pilot interviews conducted with outpatients and the findings from our surveys suggest this may be the case. In addition it may be that patients did not see the research as important or interesting. Response rates are also likely to be lower amongst the sick and elderly and patients may have been suffering from conditions that affected their ability to respond (French, 1981). In addition self-completion questionnaires are generally less appealing than face-to-face interviews (Oppenheim, 1966).

There were, however, considerable advantages in the methods that we chose to employ in this research. Identification of newly referred outpatients at the study hospitals enabled us to target patients at the time they received their outpatients appointment and therefore the time that elapsed between the initial referral consultation with their GP was short and problems of memory recall were minimised. Furthermore it enabled us to maintain the link with the GP surveys.

The response rate achieved in the GP surveys was similar across both surveys – 58 per cent in 1991, 57 per cent in 1992 – and somewhat better than that achieved for the patient surveys. These rates are, nevertheless, somewhat disappointing. There is some anecdotal evidence that suggests the response rates from postal surveys of GPs has been reducing in recent years, perhaps because of the increasing administrative burden placed on them as a result of the GP contract and more recently the NHS reforms.

Despite these reservations, we believe that the results add significantly to our knowledge about the nature and extent of patients' and GPs' involvement in choice of hospital and this is of particular importance in an area where there has been little previous research.

Key Findings: NHS Patients

Involvement in Choice of Hospital and Consultant: The level of patient involvement in choice of hospital and consultant was low and there was little change in the reported levels of involvement in the first year of the reforms. Only one in ten patients reported they had been offered a choice of hospital by their GP (1991 9.9%; 1992 10.9%) and one in twenty said they had asked their GP about other hospitals they could go to (1991 4.7%; 1992 5.4%). The level of involvement in choice of consultant was somewhat lower with only one in twenty patients reporting they had been offered a choice of consultant by their GP (1991 4.9%; 1992 5.5%). It is of note that a considerable proportion of patients did not know to which hospital (1991 24.6%; 1991 28.7%) or to which consultant (1991 67.7%; 1992 66.6%) they had been referred before receiving their appointment letter from the hospital.

Patients referred to general surgery, older patients and patients with no experience of further education reported the lowest levels of involvement, and this finding was consistent across both surveys, whilst patients referred to the specialist orthopaedic hospital reported the highest level of involvement.

Most patients reported that the choice of hospital was made by their GP (1991 70.8%; 1992 75.7%) and less than one in ten patients said that they had chosen the hospital themselves (1991 9.4%; 1992 8.3%). Despite the low level of patient involvement in choice, the vast majority were satisfied, with nine out of ten saying they were happy with the way the choice of hospital was made (1991 89.9%; 1992 90.7%). Older patients and those with no further education reported higher levels of satisfaction – findings which are consistent with many patient satisfaction surveys (Locker and Dunt, 1978).

Despite the high levels of satisfaction, many patients would have liked to have had more choice of hospital and more information about other hospitals and consultants they could have gone to, and the proportion expressing this desire for more information was similar in both surveys. Four in ten patients wanted more information about other hospitals (1991 43.7%; 1992 43.7%) and about other consultants (1991 40.3%; 1992 43.5%) and a half of patients wanted more information about waiting times for hospitals (1991 49.6%; 1992 50.8%) and for consultants (1991 50.7%; 1992 49.3%). This desire for more information was most strongly expressed by patients referred to local district general hospitals: older patients and patients with no further education were less likely to want more information.

Impact of the Reforms on Choice: In the 1992 survey patients were asked what effect the reforms had on the choices available to them. Eight out of ten patients perceived the reforms to have had no effect or were unable to say what the effect on the choices available to them had been. 4.3 per cent felt they had a lot more choice and 11.4 per cent a little more choice while one in twenty (5.4 per cent) felt they had less choice. Whilst this finding suggests that the impact of the NHS reforms has been minimal, it also raises questions about patients' awareness of the changes that have taken place. This interpretation is reinforced by respondents' ignorance of the Patient's Charter. Despite the publicity that accompanied the launch of the Charter in October 1991, over 40 per cent of our respondents had not heard of it. Over half of those with no further education had not heard of the Patient's Charter compared with a third of those with further education.

Attitudes to Travel: Over a third of all respondents said they would not be prepared to travel any further to be seen more quickly (1991 39.6%; 1992 35.5%) and less than a quarter of all respondents were prepared to travel up to or more than 30 miles (1991 24.7%; 1992 23.2%). Patients referred to specialist hospitals were more prepared to travel longer distances than those referred to other hospitals (Table 1). Unsurprisingly, there were few changes in attitudes to travel between the two surveys. It is of note however that the proportion of eye hospital patients who reported they would travel 'no further' actually increased over the study period.

Patients referred to an orthopaedic specialist were generally more willing to travel and to travel longer distances than patients referred to general surgery or ophthalmology, so that nearly a third of orthopaedic patients were prepared to travel more than ten miles (1991 32.9%; 1992 29%)

Table 1: Patients' Attitudes to Travel for Earlier Appointment by Hospital of Referral and by Year

	Specialist Orthopaedic		Specialist Ophthalmology		District General Hospital: 1		Teaching Hospital		District General Hospital: 2	
	1991	1992	1991	1992	1991	1992	1991	1992	1991	1992
No. of Respondents	152	130	461	170	207	419	473	336	216	331
Prepared to travel %										
No further	42.1	40.8	47.7	54.7	34.3	32.9	36.2	32.4	33.3	29.9
Up to 10 miles	18.4	20.8	26.9	22.3	46.8	42.5	41.0	49.4	44.5	49.5
Up to 30 miles	13.8	17.7	7.4	10.0	10.6	16.2	10.1	8.9	10.6	8.5
More than 30 miles	25.7	20.8	18.0	12.9	8.2	8.3	12.7	9.3	11.6	12.1

compared with a fifth of patients referred to general survey (1991 20.9%; 1992 19.5%) and ophthalmology (1991 23.8%; 1992 18.9%). Older patients in particular were unwilling to travel or prepared to travel only short distances, so that nine out of ten of respondents over 65 years were unwilling to travel more than 10 miles (1991 87%; 1992 89.9%).

It might be expected that willingness to travel is related to the length of time patients were having to wait before being seen, the distance that patients were already travelling or the nature of the condition for which they had been referred. Although patients who were being seen relatively quickly were slightly less inclined to travel further, the differences were small; in the first survey, 77.2 per cent of those patients being seen within one month were not prepared to travel more than 10 miles compared with 75 per cent of those waiting a year or more; in the follow-up surveys these figures were 80.1 per cent and 63.9 per cent respectively.

Willingness to travel was, however, clearly related to district of residence. Patients referred to a hospital in their own health district were less willing to travel further distances, whilst those already travelling some distance to a hospital out of their own district or region reported a greater willingness to travel further and these differences persisted across both surveys.

Whilst willingness to travel was clearly related to specialty of referral, it did not appear to be closely related to diagnostic groups. For example, in the first survey 43 per cent of patients referred for hernia reported they were prepared to travel no further and 15.9 per cent were prepared to travel more than 30 miles whilst for patients with cataracts these figures were 43 per cent and 14 per cent. Similarly, the follow-up survey found no relation between diagnostic groups and attitudes to travel.

Our findings with respect to patients' willingness to travel appear to be at variance with some existing evidence. However it should be noted that the Marplan study (Davies, 1988) asked 'well' people, not patients, about willingness to travel in very general terms, which may have led to the adoption of a 'worst case scenario'. For example these respondents may have thought in terms of emergency or life threatening illnesses and consequently would consider travelling very long distances for treatment. In our surveys, respondents were patients older than the general population and suffering from conditions that may well have affected their ability to travel. Furthermore, many of our respondents were suffering from conditions that they had lived with for some time and many had had previous experience of the hospital services to which they had been referred. In these circumstances it is perhaps not surprising that most are unwilling to travel long distances. Our findings do conflict with those reporting considerable willingness to travel within a population of patients. (Stewart and Donaldson, 1991). However a selection process appears to precede the offer of earlier treatment elsewhere and such findings must be interpreted with caution. Thus some older patients and patients suffering from conditions deemed unsuitable for travel may be denied the opportunity for earlier treatment.

These findings suggest that patients cannot be seen as a homogeneous group and that willingness to travel depends on the type of services that patients are seeking, so that those seeking more specialist care which may not be available locally reported a greater willingness to travel, whilst patients referred for treatment that is or should be available locally are less willing to travel, supporting the view that the relative availability of services influences the awareness, attractiveness and utilisation of facilities (Morrill and Erickson, 1968). Our findings suggest that this may remain the case even when patients themselves perceive waiting times to be an important factor in hospital choice and when alternatives offering shorter waiting times are available.

Key Findings: GPs

It is evident from the patient surveys that the GP plays a central role in the choice of hospital and that most patients appear to be happy to leave this decision to their GP. Little is known, however, about why doctors choose one hospital rather than another. Our surveys of GPs attempted to identify what factors were influential in the choice of hospital and what impact the introduction of the reforms has had on their perceptions of choice.

Factors Influencing the Choice of Hospital: GPs were asked to select from a list of factors which they considered commonly influenced their choice of hospital. In the follow-up survey two additional factors, not relevant in the earlier survey, were added to the list; 'only hospital I have a contract with' and 'low treatment costs'. Table 2 compares the frequency with which the various factors were selected by the group of 168 GPs who responded to both surveys. Across both surveys, fewer factors were selected for ophthalmology

Table 2: Factors Influencing General Practitioners' Choice of Hospital

Choice factors	General surgery 1991	1992	Ophthalmology 1991	1992	Orthopaedics 1991	1992
% GPs (Rank Order)						
Only hospital available	14.5(15)	18.2(14)	31.9(10)	36.2(7)	15.2(15)	13.3(14)
Only hospital with contract	N/A	4.2(16)	N/A	4.3(16)	N/A	4.2(16)
Local and convenient	95.2(1)	92.1(1)	69.9(1)	69.3(1)	85.5(1)	83(1)
Familiar with hospital	69.1(5)	64.2(6)	47.9(5)	45.4(6)	53.9(6)	52.7(6)
Good overall service	52.1(10)	55.2(8)	34.4(8)	35.6(8)	40.6(8)	43(8)
Sub specialty available	35.2(13)	29.7(13)	14.7(14)	10.4(14)	30.3(13)	21.2(13)*
Good clinical care	78.2(3)	69.7(4)*	56.4(3)	52.1(4)	64.2(4)	61.2(4)
Patients' clinical needs	39.4(12)	35.2(12)	31.3(11)	29.4(11)	34.5(11)	35.8(12)
Waiting time for appointment	57.0(8)	54.5(7)	39.3(7)	33.1(9)	46.1(7)	46.7(7)
Waiting time for surgery	52.7(9)	49.7(10)	30.1(12)	27.6(3)	40(9)	37(11)
Low costs	N/A	1.8(17)	N/A	1.2(17)	N/A	1.2(17)
Good communications	51.5(11)	49.1(11)	27(13)	29.4(11)	31.5(12)	37.6(10)
Patients' preference	70.9(4)	73.3(3)	57.1(2)	62(2)	64.8(3)	69.1(2)
Patients' previous attendance	68.5(6)	67.3(5)	56.4(3)	54.6(3)	62.4(5)	61.2(4)
Patients' personality	15.2(14)	11.5(15)	9.8(15)	6.7(15)	13.9(14)	9.7(15)
Consultants manner	64.2(7)	55.2(8)	33.7(9)	30.1(10)	38.8(10)	42.4(9)
Know consultant	84.8(2)	80(2)	45.4(6)	46.6(5)	66.1(2)	67.3(3)

N/A = Not asked

than for general surgery or orthopaedics, suggesting that choice is more limited for ophthalmology referral. Several factors emerged as being of particular influence for all specialties. Proximity and convenience were a major determinant of hospital choice for all specialties – a finding consistent with other studies (French *et al*, 1990). Other factors that ranked highly for all specialties include knowledge of consultant, good clinical care, patients' previous attendance and patients' preference. The two additional factors added in the follow-up survey appear to have had little influence on hospital choice.

GPs clearly perceive patient preference to be a common influence on their choice of hospital, with this factor ranking no less than fourth place across the three specialties and across both surveys. However, when asked to select what they perceived to be the single most important factor, patient preference was selected by less than one in twenty GPs for any specialty, whilst the general standard of clinical care and proximity and convenience were the most frequently mentioned as the single most important factor. This suggests that, whilst GPs clearly appear to recognise the importance of patients' views, they ultimately take second place to professional judgement. Nevertheless, the majority of GPs mentioned patients' preference as being a factor that frequently influenced their choice of hospital.

Approximately a half of the GPs reported that they 'always' or 'quite often' considered it appropriate to offer their patients a choice of hospital, one in five thought it 'never' or 'rarely' appropriate to offer such choice and nearly a quarter said that patients 'often' or 'always' asked for a specific hospital. There were no changes in GPs' attitudes towards patients' involvement in choice over the study period. Such perceptions appear to be at variance with patients' perceptions of their involvement in choice reported earlier in this chapter.

There were however differences between fundholding and non-fundholding GPs with respect to the frequency with which the various choice factors were mentioned. Across all specialties GP fundholders were less likely to perceive there to be only one hospital available so that for general surgery five per cent of fundholders hold this perception compared with 18 per cent of non-fundholders and for ophthalmology these figures were 22 per cent and 31 per cent respectively, while for orthopaedics one fundholder perceived there to be only one hospital compared with 15 per cent of non-fundholders. Locality and convenience was mentioned by similar proportions of fundholders and non-fundholders for general surgery and for both groups this was the most frequently mentioned factor. For ophthalmology and orthopaedics distance was less frequently mentioned by fundholders. Several factors were more frequently mentioned by fundholding GPs, in particular waiting times for first appointment and waiting times for surgery, and this was the case for all three specialties so that for general surgery 70 per cent of fundholders mentioned waiting time for first appointment as a factor that frequently influenced the choice of hospital compared with 50 per cent of non-fundholders. Similar differences were reported for ophthalmology while for orthopaedics waiting time for first appointment was the more frequently mentioned by fundholders than any other single factor so that 78 per cent mentioned this compared to 45 per cent of non-fundholders. There were, however no differences between fundholders and non-fundholders in reported attitudes towards patients' involvement in choice.

The reasons for such differences are not clear. However the results of the 1991 survey conducted prior to the introduction of the contract system suggest that the GPs who subsequently became fundholders were more likely to consider such factors as being more influential in the period preceding the reforms. The number – 13 – on which this interpretation is based is small and, furthermore, the GPs would have been in the preparatory phase of fundholding at the time the study was conducted.

Impact of the Reforms on Choice: Overall the findings with respect to GPs' perceptions of the factors that influence choice and their attitudes to patients' involvement in choice give the overall impression of little change during the first year of the reforms, although there are clear differences between fundholders and non-fundholders.

This impression of little change is reflected by GPs' own perceptions of the effects of the reforms on the choices available to them. In the first survey nearly half of the GPs envisaged the effects of the reforms would be to reduce the choices available to them, only one in twenty thought that choice would be increased and a quarter felt they would make no difference. 22 per cent did not know what effects the reforms would have. The concern that choice would be reduced under the new system does not appear to have materialised. In the follow-up survey, over three-quarters of GPs reported that the reforms had made no difference to the choices available to them. 17 per cent felt that choice had been reduced and only one in twenty perceived choice to have increased. Fundholders were more likely to perceive the reforms to have increased the choices available to them although it is of note that six out of ten fundholders perceived the reforms to have made no difference to choice. None of the fundholders reported a reduction in choice.

Attitudes to Referring Patients Further Afield: In the follow-up survey, GPs were asked how far they would consider sending their patients for routine elective surgery referral. This question was not asked in the first survey. Overall most GPs were reluctant to refer their patients very far afield. 64 per cent were not prepared to refer more than 10 miles for general surgery, 56 per cent for ophthalmology and 53 per cent for orthopaedics. Indeed, one in six of all GPs reported that they would only consider their local hospital for general surgery referral, whilst one in ten held this view for ophthalmology and orthopaedics. Fundholding GPs differed from other GPs in that they appeared to be considerably more willing to refer their patients some distance from home for routine elective surgery: see Table 3. One-third of fundholders said that they would be prepared to refer their patients more than 50 miles for routine elective surgery for all three specialties, compared with less than one in ten of non-fundholders. Generally GPs, both fundholders and non-fundholders, were less willing to consider referring further afield for general surgery than for ophthalmology and orthopaedics, a finding consistent with patients' attitudes to travel reported earlier.

The results of our study are not indicative of a major change in patients' and GPs' experiences of hospital choice. However, comparison of fund-holding and non-fundholding GPs shows clear and consistent differences between the two groups of doctors. The follow-up surveys were conducted in the early stages of the internal market and the longer term effects of the reforms remain largely unknown. The impression of little change during the study period must be viewed in the context of the 'steady state' or 'smooth take off' approach to contracting adopted by most districts and regions in response to the NHS Management Executive directive (Ham, 1991). The vast majority of patients and GPs responding to our survey were located in the North West Region, which adopted a particularly cautious approach to contracting by setting block contracts for all hospital services region-wide (North West Regional Health Authority, 1990).

Nevertheless the findings do provide us with important information and

Table 3: Distance GPs are Prepared to Refer Patients for Routine Elective Surgery by Fundholding Status and Specialty: 1992

Distance prepared to send patients	General Surgery		Ophthalmology		Orthopaedics	
	Fund-holders Nos (%)	Non-Fundholders Nos (%)	Fund-holders Nos (%)	Non-Fundholders Nos (%)	Fund holders Nos (%)	Non-Fundholders Nos (%)
Local hospital only	1 (2.8)	61 (18.7)	0 (0)	41 (12.6)	0 (0)	41 (12.1)
Up to 10 miles	13 (36.2)	158 (48.3)	9 (25)	152 (46.6)	8 (22.2)	144 (44.5)
Up to 30 miles	7 (19.4)	63 (19.3)	10 (27.8)	76 (23.3)	11 (30.6)	78 (24.3)
Up to or more than 50 miles	15 (41.7)	45 (13.8)	17 (47.3)	57 (17.5)	17 (47.3)	62 (19.1)

allow us to speculate on the implications of the white paper for the promotion of a consumer orientated health service.

Conclusion

Consumerism in the health service has become widely accepted, although the usefulness of the term is questionable given the different meanings and values that are associated with it. If the aims of the reforms were to increase the level of patient involvement in choice, the scope to do this remains huge. However, if choice is expected to increase because of the introduction of a market ethos into the health service then disappointment is inevitable. The changes introduced conform to what Winkler (1987) has identified as the supermarket model of consumerism. This model emphasises customer relations but fails to address the wider issues of representation and the associated concepts of participation and empowerment.

But the consumerism outlined in the white paper is not just concerned with customer relations, it is also about control of costs, outcomes and efficiency. The extent to which the multiple objectives pursued by the NHS reforms can be achieved remains to be seen. Our results suggest that efficiency and normative definitions of quality may be achieved at the expense of patients' preferences. The issue of patient travel illustrates the potential for conflict between the principles of patient choice, efficiency and quality and ultimately some trade-off between these competing principles will occur. Rewarding services that offer better, faster and cheaper treatment is a basic premise of the health service reforms. Basic data on which to make informed decisions do not exist. Furthermore, as the results of our surveys have shown, costs, speed and quality of care are not the only factors considered when making the choice of hospital. Distance is a major influence for GPs and many patients prefer not to travel or to travel short distances only for earlier treatment. Whilst waiting times clearly are influential in hospital choice they do not appear to be a major determinant. It is of note, however, that fundholders' perceptions were more akin to market principles than those of non-fundholders in that they more frequently considered waiting times and were more willing to consider referring their patients further afield. The extent to which the choices of fundholders reflect those of their patients warrants further investigation.

The collectivist approach to consumerism has been replaced by an individualistic model and as Winkler notes 'those who believe in the market don't see the need for an agency to represent users' interests' (1989, p. 2). Although the delegation of management brings decision making closer to the consumer, it remains the case that managers are responsible for the planning and delivery of services. As such the needs for external representation remains crucial. The challenge must be to shift from the narrow definition of consumerism adopted by the white paper to a model or models that adopt broader definitions of consumerism and move away from normative definitions of quality and efficiency to ones that give credence to patients' views. There is no consensus on how this might be done but a number of models are currently in existence including, for example, Community Health Councils, patient participation groups and consumer audit. Unless there is the commitment and investment to develop these, and other initiatives, the rhetoric of patient choice in the health service will remain divorced from the reality of the experiences of most NHS patients.

6

MONITORING CHANGES IN HEALTH SERVICES FOR OLDER PEOPLE

Dee Jones, Carolyn Lester, Robert West

A principal objective of the NHS reforms is to put patients' interests first. The Government intends that this objective should be achieved by providing better health care and greater choice within a 'client-centred' and 'needs led' health service. The project described in this chapter sets out to monitor and evaluate the changes designed to achieve these aims in relation to the services provided for older people.

The decision to concentrate on services for older people was made for a number of reasons. The lion's share of health care both in the hospital and the community sector is consumed by older people (Griffiths, 1988) and the proportion of older people in the population, particularly those aged 80 years and over, will continue to increase in the foreseeable future. Studies of random samples of older people were therefore considered appropriate for assessing the impact of change on hospital and community services; and, because a high proportion of health service activity is with older people, this method offered the advantage of increased research efficiency. Furthermore older people as a more vulnerable group within the population – both possibly more frail and with less political clout – may be particularly susceptible to organisational change in the health service.

Two studies were included within this project; one to assess the impact of change within the community services and the other to assess change within the hospital services. The issue of transfer between the two sectors, which is of considerable concern to researchers, service providers and government, (Department of Health, 1989), is also addressed within each of these studies. Both studies sought to assess change and the effect of change from a patient/client/user perspective rather than from a provider perspective; that is, they examined changes as they affected users rather than the structure, organisation or management of the health services, or other providing agencies.

Health status and quality of life were measured in both studies, although it was not anticipated that changes that would take place within two years were likely to produce measurable health changes. Nonetheless their measurement allows standardisation of the important, independent variables and also provides baseline information on large representative samples against which future findings could be compared.

The Community Study

For the provision of health and community care services the principal issues of *Working for Patients* concerned access, availability and choice. The studies sought principally to address these issues by seeking views from users or potential users as to what services were available to them, how available they were, how well availability matched their perceived needs and whether or not they had any recommendations for improvements. The philosophy underlying the proposed changes was that of the implied 'efficiency of the market': *ie* where choice exists, within reasonable distance, competition leads to improved service which is rewarded for some providers by increased use, increased 'sales': the providers of a poor or inadequate service perish. In major metropolitan areas where alternatives co-exist this could lead to rationalisation in some specialties, for example one hospital aiming for the regional cardiology/cardiac surgery spot while a neighbouring hospital aims for the neurology/neurosurgery spot.

It appears that application of the philosophy was expected to extend to less-populated areas, where one district general hospital was an effective monopoly provider, and possibly even to alternative services, for example clinical psychology and occupational therapy. In the hurry to implement the new Act and to create a 'market' for health care, it was not clear how some of these aims would be achieved and even whether establishing contracts for care might act against the concept of extending choice. For the purposes of the studies described in this chapter, however, availability of alternatives and choice between alternatives were assumed and users or potential users were asked whether or not they perceived alternatives and exercised choice.

To investigate availability and accessibility of health services thoroughly, this study first measured the health status of each respondent, using standard scales, then assessed need for assistance in each service and finally the extent to which these needs were met by statutory services, including hospital, primary health care team and community health services. Quality of care issues were also examined for each service by asking each respondent about choice, provision of information and communication between services and users.

Since the new GP contract was being introduced at much the same time as *Working for Patients* and the Patient's Charter, certain aspects of primary care, including health assessment of those aged over 75 years, and their medication were investigated more fully.

The Hospital Study

This study sought to investigate the impact of the health reforms on hospital care, with particular emphasis on the quality issues outlined in the reforms: choice, information, participation in decision-making, communication between staff and patients, appropriateness of care and degree to which services are client-centred and meet individual's needs, both on admission and on transfer back to the community. This focuses the discussion outlined above towards, for example, choice between hospitals, where it exists. It was perceived as important to mount a separate study concentrating on hospital care, since hospital care accounts for a large proportion of NHS activity and since hospitalisation can be a traumatic experience for the patient. An important aim of the NHS reforms was to improve the quality of the hospital service, with emphasis on short waiting lists and short waiting times for outpatients, congenial surroundings, a welcome by a member of staff on admission and clear information. These were all designed to make the patient feel more at ease in strange surroundings at a time of stress. The study therefore examined aspects of admission, hospital stay, discharge planning and transfer back into the community, either to residential nursing homes or their own homes. The transition between hospital and community has been the subject of many studies and guidelines (Department of Health, 1989b; Skeet, 1970; Waters, 1987). These aim to reduce the barriers and gaps between sectors so producing seamless care, whereby users can move smoothly from one sector to another or benefit from the interlocking services provided by different sectors or agencies.

Research Methods

The two studies followed the same principles for identifying change in the early years of the introduction of the reforms. Representative samples of the general population were asked about their experience of health services in 1990 when the reforms were being proposed and discussed but before they had been introduced. New representative samples were asked the same set of questions in the same format in 1992 after the changes had been introduced. The same before and after principles were employed in both the community study and the patient discharge study.

Since the time frame for the introduction of the NHS reforms was short, and since the proposed reforms were being given quite widespread publicity, it was desirable to move quite quickly with the first stage of the studies in order to obtain baseline data from typical populations as far as possible before any changes in practice or in attitudes and expectations had occurred. The semi-structured interviews and questionnaires employed in the study, therefore, were based on interviews and questionnaires that had been used in previous studies in comparable situations. The repeat study in 1992 was based on new samples of the population drawn in the same way as in the previous samples. Thus both the 'before' subjects, in the 1990 samples, and the 'after' subjects, in the 1992 samples, were approached *de novo*.

Both studies were undertaken in three district health authorities in South Wales. These cover some 50 miles east to west and some 30 miles north to south. Their population numbers some 1.6 million and includes a wide range of occupations – agriculture, heavy industry now somewhat in 'retirement', modern light manufacture and assembly industries, services, education and provincial government. Previous comparisons suggest that these districts are representative of the social and occupational mix of England and Wales generally (Webber and Craig, 1978). Similarly, their health service and community service provisions were typical of health and community service provision generally. There was no particular reason to think that the reforms were likely to have any more or any less effect on these districts than on any other three districts in the country.

The Community Study: The community study used Family Health Services Authorities' registers as sampling frames. Three random samples of 500 in each of the three authorities were drawn in 1990 and again independently in 1992. These samples constitute a little below one per cent of elderly persons in the three counties. Each person was interviewed in his/her home by a trained, experienced fieldworker using a semi-structured interview schedule. The interviewer introduced herself with a cover letter and identification, outlined the nature of the study, and requested an interview of about 45 minutes.

The interview schedule asked about health and quality of life generally, including several standard previously validated measures, including disability, dependency, mobility, perceived health status, anxiety and depression. Having summarised the person's general state of health, specific areas of temporary limitation or incapacity and need for assistance, the structured interview moved on to ask about the person's need for, use of, opinions of and satisfaction with community health and social services including district nurse, health visitor, bath attendant, day hospital, social worker, home help, meals-on-wheels, lunch club, chiropodist and dental services. A substantial portion of the interview investigated the person's contact with, and opinion of, primary health care. Rather more varied and detailed questions were asked about the general practitioner services, since these address a wider range of needs for the sick. Moreover, these services were the first to show signs of reorganisation under the NHS and Community Care Act, with the introduction of charter standards for access and availability, screening policies for the elderly and fundholding. The questions focused on aspects of primary care, which the NHS changes were intended to reform, and included enquiries into provision of information, assessment of health and change of GP or practice. Respondents were asked about consultation with GPs and practice nurses and they were asked if aspects of their health, *eg* sight, hearing, feet, continence, blood pressure and urine, had been assessed in the previous year. A complete list of prescribed medications was compiled and brief details of referral to hospital, hospital waiting list and inpatient care were sought. The whole interview took approximately 30 minutes to an hour to administer, depending on the person's state of health, their use of community health services and ability to communicate.

The interview schedule closed with the interviewer's assessment of the person's understanding of questions and reliability of their answers, within the context of the respondent's apparent health or disability. The whole interview schedule was repeated by another interviewer for a small selected sub-sample to assess test reliability; for quality control, selected questions were asked again of selected persons by telephone by the study's research officer or principal investigator. Overall, there were 1,500 in the 'before' sample and 1,500 in the 'after' sample, making 3,000 in all.

The Hospital Study: The hospital study was based on three random samples of elderly patients discharged home from hospitals in the three district health authorities, which were co-terminous with the three counties of the community study. Although the majority of hospital admissions were concentrated in relatively few district general hospitals (three or four per district), all, except long-stay (chronic geriatric and mental illness) hospitals which discharged 100 or more elderly patients per quarter were included in the study. In the largest district the sample included discharges from as many as 10 hospitals. Samples of 400 recently discharged patients aged 65 and over excluding hospital transfers and day cases were drawn in 1990; equivalent to approximately two per cent of the discharges per annum of elderly patients from these districts. These samples were obtained using Hospital Activity Analysis or in some hospitals, where computer linkage with the Welsh Health Services Information Unit was slow, directly from hospital medical records. Discharges were drawn from one month and identified some four to six weeks after discharge.

For cost reasons the discharge study was based entirely on a postal questionnaire rather than interviews. After checking local county death registers for deaths since discharge from hospital, questionnaires were posted to patients three months after discharge, with an explanatory letter. Non-responders were sent a second letter and a duplicate questionnaire and second time non-responders were telephoned or visited and asked if they wished to have help in completing the questionnaire, since an appreciable proportion of elderly patients have some visual handicap or may find difficulty with self completion (McIver, 1992).

The 12 page questionnaire first asked about choice of hospital and notice of admission, information about hospital and the advice about hospital facilities, optional extras, what to bring, visiting hours, complaints procedure, etc, received prior to admission and on admission. The next section asked about patients' opinions of basic hospital facilities *eg* cleanliness, privacy, meals, visiting hours, and (optional) extra facilities *eg* own room, own television, own phone, own food, and about ease of communication with doctors, nurses and other hospital staff. The third section asked specifically about discharge planning, who discussed discharge arrangements with the patient, whether there were home visits or liaison with community services prior to discharge, how much notice was given of discharge, how well that suited relatives or friends in making necessary arrangements and about advice given with respect to seeing a general practitioner and about medication. The fourth section, for those patients who went into residential or nursing care, asked about choice of homes and decision of where to go when discharged. The final section investigated the assistance provided by health and social services during the first week at home and at three months after discharge. Patients' perceived health status, mobility and functional impairment were also assessed.

These topics were investigated by both closed questions, in order to record standard responses, and open questions – which were later coded – to collect more detailed information. For example, closed questions including satisfaction ratings were used for specific aspects of care *eg* cleanliness, quality and choice of food and communication with staff, for comparability purposes, and to elicit positive and negative opinions, patients were invited to comment in an open-ended section asking what they liked and/or disliked about their hospital stay and what improvements, if any, they would suggest.

A shorter four page questionnaire was enclosed in the same envelope for the discharged patient's principal carer. The carer's questionnaire asked their opinions of the patient's hospital stay, their involvement in discharge planning, notice of discharge and their views of help provided by the statutory community and social services.

As with the community study, repeatability was checked in a small sub-sample of patients by asking again selected questions by telephone. Three new samples were drawn in a similar manner in 1992 from the same three districts. Thus in the before and after studies a total of 2,400 discharged patients in three districts were included.

Results: Community Study

Of the 1,500 people in the community-based study, 1,413 were interviewed in 1990 and 1,405 in 1992, giving a 94 per cent response rate for each sample. Just over 60 per cent of those interviewed were female and 42 per cent were aged 75 or over in both years.

At the time of the first interview there were no fundholding general practices but when patients were interviewed in 1992, there were five, one in district A and four in district B. Far more practices became fundholders after this study: in Spring 1993 there were 18 in district A, 7 in district B and 13 in district C.

Only eight per cent of patients described their GPs as single-handed. There was an increase in practice nurses or in patients' awareness of practice nurses: in 1990 1,057 (75 per cent) of patients reported the presence of a practice nurse compared with 1,192 (85 per cent) in 1992. Interestingly more of those aged 65–74 reported that there was a practice nurse than did those of 75 and over. Virtually all practices (98 per cent) had receptionists and most practices operated an appointment system (85 per cent in 1990 and 89 per cent in 1992). Nearly half the patients preferred an appointment system for all attendances while about 15 per cent preferred a system allowing both appointments and casual attendance and about 20 per cent preferred an 'open' first come, first served system. Accompanying a very slight shift towards appointments systems between 1990 and 1992, there was a modest improvement in time-keeping, with slightly more (32 compared with 27 per cent) being seen within 10 minutes of appointment time and fewer (91 compared with

Table 1: Written Information Received by Respondent

| | 1990 | | | | 1992 | | | |
| | <75 | | ≥75 | | <75 | | ≥75 | |
	No.	%	No.	%	No.	%	No.	%
None	632	77	484	82	509	63	381	64
Hours only	32	4	28	5	12	2	4	1
Services only	3	<1	5	1	3	<1	10	2
Hours and services	84	10	31	5	257	32	165	28
Don't know	68	8	46	8	23	3	39	7
Total	819	100	594	101	806	100	599	101

110) reporting waiting more than half an hour after appointment time.

Under the terms of their new contract, GPs are required to provide practice information leaflets for their patients including surgery hours, information on practice staff and services provided, for example a well-person clinic. In 1990 only eight per cent of patients could recall having received information on both hours and services but in 1992 this had increased, although only to about one third: see Table 1. This rather low proportion may reflect recall, since in both years patients aged 65–74 were more likely to report receiving written information than those aged 75 or over.

Few patients reported changing practices with which they were registered within the preceding two years and there was no difference in the proportion who did: 86 (6 per cent) in 1990 and 78 (6 per cent) in 1992. The main reasons for changing in both years were practical considerations like moving house or doctor retiring, or dying, distance from surgery or partnership split. Ten patients in 1990 and 17 in 1992 changed because they were dissatisfied with their GPs and very few (three in 1992) because of personal disagreement or because their doctor had asked them to (four in total). About three per cent in both years said that they wished to change their GP but had not done so as yet, the main reasons being lack of choice within a reasonable distance and not knowing how to change. Some were perhaps not serious about changing as they 'could not be bothered to do anything about it' and others did not wish to offend their present GP (one in 1990 and five in 1992) but a few (seven in total) appear to have tried and failed, in that their chosen GP had declined to accept them.

As expected, most elderly people are in contact with their GP: of those interviewed in 1990, 1,176 (83 per cent) had consulted within the previous year and 479 (34 per cent) within the previous 4 weeks. Similar frequencies were reported in 1992, when those aged 75 and over were rather more likely to have consulted within the previous year than those aged 65–74.

In 1990, 53 per cent of patients who had requested an out-of-hours home visit said that a GP from their own practice (as opposed to a rota of local practices or deputising service) had attended; the proportion increased in 1992 to 59 per cent. Similarly when patients telephoned the surgery for advice, 63 per cent spoke to the GP in 1990, and 77 per cent in 1992. These responses for out-of-hours visits and telephone advice indicate an overall increase in GPs' availability to their patients.

About ten per cent in both years were visited by their GP, with a higher frequency among those aged 75 and over. Difficulty in obtaining a home visit was reported by about four per cent in both years. Half of these claimed that this was because the GP was reluctant to make home visits, while a quarter attributed the difficulty to the receptionist's attitude and the final quarter gave practical reasons like no home telephone, or difficulty getting a reply when telephoning the surgery.

In 1990, 386 patients reported consultation with a practice nurse within the past year. In 1992, this number had increased to 546 (39 per cent overall and 46 per cent of those who knew there was a nurse). More patients reported seeing a practice nurse five or more times in a year (12 per cent in 1990 and 18 per cent in 1992) and more patients reported that they could consult the nurse directly without first consulting the doctor (546 compared with 436). The main reasons for consulting the practice nurse in 1990 were to have blood pressure taken (132), a blood test (69), 'flu injection (61) and to have ears syringed (53). The main changes in 1992 were increases in the number of 'flu injections (157) and in the number of health checks (49). Blood tests were slightly more common among women and 'flu injections and ear syringing among men. Only 13 women reported consultations with the practice nurse for gynaecological reasons.

The new contract requires GPs to offer annual health checks to all patients aged 75 and over. Respondents were asked if a check or enquiry had been made by a member of the primary care team on sight, hearing, feet, continence and blood pressure. They were also asked which member of the practice team had tested or enquired about each item. In 1990 few patients reported being assessed for sight, hearing, foot problems or for continence, rather more reported a urine test, but more than half reported that they had had their blood pressure taken: the numbers were similar below or above age 75: see Table 2. By 1992 more patients aged 75 and over reported being assessed. For example assessment of those of 75 and over nearly doubled between 1990 and 1992 for foot problems (four to nine per cent) and urine testing (13 to 22 per cent). For both asssessments, rates for under 75s were lower than for those aged 75 and over in 1992.

Very few (one per cent) reported tests or enquiries by a health visitor: see Table 3. The main change between 1990 and 1992 was the number of reported tests by the practice nurse, and the main change by the practice

Table 2: Assessment in Primary Care

| | 1990 | | | | 1992 | | | |
| | <75 (n=819) | | ≥75 (n=594) | | <75 (n=806) | | ≥75 n=599) | |
	No.	%	No.	%	No.	%	No.	%
Sight	38	5	36	6	44	5	53	9
Hearing	41	5	44	7	45	6	66	11
Feet	33	4	23	4	33	4	51	9
Continence	32	4	26	4	26	3	57	10
Blood pressure	481	59	317	53	463	57	385	64
Urine	13	17	79	13	161	20	134	22

nurse was an increase in testing of blood pressure (16 to 31 per cent) and urine tests (33 to 38 per cent).

Almost all (95 per cent) who had called upon primary health care services in the past two years were very or fairly satisfied with their GP. There was a small movement between 1990 and 1992 from fairly satisfied to very satisfied for specific aspects of GP care; for example the numbers who were very satisfied in respect of information increased by 83, explanations by 69 and time spent on consultations by 32. More than 99 per cent of respondents were very or fairly satisfied with the practice nurse in both years, and there was a similar small movement from fairly to very satisfied (83 to 87 per cent). Almost all were satisfied with the receptionist (96 per cent) and with organisational aspects like the comfort of the waiting area and convenience of surgery times. Patients were rather less well satisfied with waiting time for appointments – ie how close to their appointment times they were seen – (92 per cent). In general patients seemed to be even more satisfied with primary care at the time of the second survey.

Nearly three-quarters of elderly respondents in these studies reported taking prescribed medication within the previous 24 hours (72 per cent in 1990 and 73 per cent in 1992) with very slightly higher proportions among those aged 75 and over. The mean number of prescribed drugs taken

Table 3: Assessment by Member of Primary Care Team

	Sight				Hearing				Feet				Continence				Blood Pressure				Urine			
	1990 (n=1412)		1992 (n=1402)		1990 (n=1412)		1992 (n=1402)		1990 (n=1412)		1992 (n=1409)		1990 (n=1412)		1992 (n=1400)		1990 (n=1412)		1992 (n=1403)		1990 (n=1412)		1992 (n=139)	
	No.	%	No.	%	No.	%	No.	%	No.	%	No.	%	No.	%	No.	%	No.	%	No.	%	No.	%	No.	%
GP	64	5	77	5	72	4	79	6	48	3	64	4	52	4	56	4	669	47	571	41	148	10	176	13
Health visitor	0	0	1	<1	0	0	1	<1	2	<1	4	<1	2	<1	4	<1	2	<1	10	1	0	0	6	<1
Practice nurse	10	1	18	1	13	1	30	2	6	<1	22	2	4	<1	22	2	127	9	266	19	74	5	113	8
Total	1,412		1,402		1,412		1,402		1,412		1,409		1,412		1,400		1,412		1,403		1,412		1,397	

within the preceding 24 hours increased slightly from 1.93 in 1990 to 2.03 in 1992. These figures include those taking no medication: including only those taking some medication, the means were 2.69 in 1990 and 2.78 in 1992.

The proportion of patients receiving the services of a health visitor (5 per cent) or day hospital (2 per cent) remained similar in 1990 and 1992 – see Table 4 – but there was a slight fall in numbers receiving district nursing (13 to 10 per cent) and chiropody (29 to 26 per cent). Few of those who used the district nursing service (25 in 1990 and 15 in 1992) considered that the service was too infrequent. Rather more of those visited by health visitors considered that they needed visiting more often. Users of chiropody reported more difficulty with the frequency of visits: more than a quarter considered that they did not receive it as often as needed, the main problem being toe-nails growing too long between visits. Two diabetics in 1990 and six in 1992 thought that their medical condition necessitated more frequent treatment.

Numbers waiting for hospital outpatient appointments were similar in both years at seven per cent, but the mean waiting time increased from 3.9 to 4.9 months. Numbers waiting for day or inpatient treatment increased from 35 (2 per cent) in 1990 to 51 (4 per cent) in 1992 and most of this increase from 9 (2 per cent) to 22 (4 per cent) was among those aged 75 and over. The mean waiting time for day or inpatient treatment also increased from 6.8 months to 7.5 months, and even more for those aged 75 and over (8.8 to 10.1 months).

Summary: Though the high response rate makes this study highly representative, it should be borne in mind that information was derived solely from the recollections and perceptions of elderly people and was not verified with practice records. The proportion of patients who changed their GP within the previous two years, and the very small number who had been asked to change by their doctor, does not appear to have been affected by the reforms. Fears had been expressed that health service reforms would encourage GPs to rid themselves of patients who were heavy users of health care, but results of this study give no credence to these fears.

Even allowing for some failure of recall, the numbers of people receiving information from the GP remained low. It is possible that practices did not post leaflets systematically, but handed them to patients opportunistically, but if this were so, those patients who had seen the doctor within the

Table 4: Community Health Services Received as Often as Needed (received within previous two years only)

	1990				1992			
	Services received (all respondents)		Often as needed (recipients)		Services received (all respondents)		Often as needed (recipients)	
	No.	%	No.	%	No.	%	No.	%
District nurse	190	13	172	91	146	10	138	95
Health visitor	66	5	55	83	76	5	63	83
Chiropodist	403	29	285	71	370	26	277	75
Day hospital	30	2	28	93	25	2	25	100

preceding year (84 per cent) should have received a leaflet. It is difficult to explain why two-thirds did not recall receipt of information, given that all practices are now required to produce an information leaflet (Department of Health, 1989b). However, our examination of the practice leaflets showed wide variation in the amount, type and quality of information. It is possible that some people who received a leaflet failed to assimilate its contents; a previous study reported that practice leaflets varied greatly in their readability (Albert and Chadwick, 1992).

Practice structure does not appear to have changed a great deal, apart from most now employing a practice nurse. The addition of the practice nurse to the primary care team may be partially due to the requirement for health checks for the over 75s as this aspect of primary care is often undertaken by the nurse (Pathy *et al*, 1992).

There may have been a true increase in practices operating an appointment system, or merely an increase in patient awareness following receipt of a practice leaflet, as information on appointment or non-appointment surgeries is included in practice leaflets. Better adherence to appointment times suggests that practices are improving that aspect of their service. A slight increase in attendance 'out-of-hours' by a patient's own GP may be due to contractual terms specifying the number of hours that GPs should be available, and higher fees for those undertaking their own night visits (Department of Health, 1989b). The apparent increase in the number of patients who succeed in speaking to their own doctor by telephone is perhaps also due to greater availability of practice leaflets with advice on the best time to telephone.

The increased numbers of patients aged 75 and over who had seen their GP within the previous year may be due to offers of a health check, or to other reasons like more publicity about the availability of 'flu injections. Explanation for the increase in consultation with the practice nurse may be due to the introduction of assessments of the over 75s, awareness of a new member of the practice team or awareness of what can be dealt with appropriately by a practice nurse.

Explanation for increasing numbers of assessments of older people lies with the GP contract. That the numbers who recalled enquiry or testing for sight, hearing, feet and continence remained low could be that they are generally unobtrusive, for example, hearing may be assessed by whether or not a patient is able to participate in normal conversation during the consultation. Patients' recall may therefore be an underestimation of some assessments, except when assessment involves a formal procedure, for example taking blood pressure. However there was still a substantial number who thought that they had not had their blood pressure checked, despite the proven effectiveness of anti-hypertensive drugs in this age group (Coope and Warrender, 1986). Previous accounts of assessing elderly people have not described in detail how assessments were carried out (Pathy *et al*, 1992; Barber and Wallis, 1978; Vetter *et al*, 1984 and 1986).

The increase of prescribed drugs in those aged 75 and over is likely to be largely attributable to new prescribing following the initiation of annual health checks. While in the short term this may appear to increase prescribing costs, the long term effect may be economically beneficial to the NHS as need for more costly hospital care may decrease (Coope and Warrender, 1986).

Though one of the main aims of health service reforms was to reduce waiting lists, numbers of patients waiting for outpatient, day patient and inpatient hospital care increased in those aged 75 and over, and again this may be due to increased referrals following GP assessments. Here also it might be argued that the increased cost in the short term of more current referrals may avoid future costs of emergency admissions and more disabled elderly people in the community.

Results: Hospital Study

Questionnaires were sent to 1,084 patients in 1990 with 960 completed, and 1,237 in 1992 with 1,025 completed, giving response rates of 89 and 83 per cent. Fifty-four per cent of the respondents were women in 1990: 51 per cent in 1992. At the time of the studies there were no trust hospitals in any of the three health authorities but at the time of writing, Spring 1993, one in district A and two in district B have taken on trust status.

Half of all patients in both years were categorised as urgent or emergency admissions. The main specialties to which people were admitted were geriatric medicine (21 per cent), general medicine (22 per cent), general surgery (18 per cent), ophthalmology (8 per cent), trauma and orthopaedic surgery (7 per cent) and urology (7 per cent); the remaining specialties each comprised two per cent or less of the total.

Rather over one-third of non-emergency patients (38 per cent in 1990 and 37 per cent in 1992) were admitted to hospital within a month of being told that they would need inpatient treatment. Thirty-four people in 1990 and

43 in 1992 reported waiting more than a year to be admitted to hospital. Overall average waiting times increased slightly; the mean reported waiting time changed from 5 months to 5.3 months.

The amount of notice of admission given to patients varied from one day or less (16 per cent) to more than a week (32 per cent in 1990 and 38 per cent in 1992). Most patients were very satisfied (75 per cent) or fairly satisfied (13 per cent) with the amount of notice in both years but 20 in 1990 and 41 in 1992 were very unsatisfied.

In terms of hospital communication, fewer patients remembered being given written information before or after admission on a range of topics in 1992 than in 1990. The information that patients could recall were 'what patients should bring to hospital' (64 per cent in 1990 and 59 per cent in 1992), facilities provided for patients within the hospital (49 per cent and 39 per cent), availability of optional extras which could be paid for (20 per cent and 17 per cent), visiting times (75 per cent and 55 per cent), complaints procedure (30 per cent and 21 per cent), and suggestions procedure (27 per cent and 18 per cent). Booklets or leaflets providing information for patients were sought from study hospitals. In district A one of the six hospitals, in district B four of ten and in district C one of five had not produced such a booklet.

Few patients reported difficulty in communicating with health professionals in either year, only one per cent in 1990 and three per cent in 1992 said that communication with nurses was difficult or very difficult. There was an increase in the number of patients who thought nurses were busy and hospitals understaffed. Communication with doctors was found to be difficult by five per cent in 1990 and three per cent in 1992. Very few patients in either year reported problems in communication with therapists.

A few patients, 14 in 1990 and 9 in 1992, reported that they had been given no medical information at all during their hospital stay. In 1992 there was a small increase in the number of patients who thought that the amount of information they had been given was right for their needs (73 to 79 per cent). There was also a significant improvement in patients' ability to understand the medical information they were given (79 to 83 per cent).

For patients whose admissions were booked or planned, there was a small reported decrease in the number who felt that they had a choice of hospital to which they were admitted (13 to 10 per cent). The main reasons given for choosing a particular hospital were that it was the best hospital for the planned treatment (31 and 17), proximity to home (15 and 19), proximity to a relative's home (5 and 2), and shortness of the waiting list (3 and 6).

Although the vast majority of patients (97 and 95 per cent) had not been offered any optional extras which they could pay for at the time of their admission, there did seem to be an increase in offers of private rooms (9 and 20) and individual televisions (4 and 9). While three-quarters of all patients did not wish to be offered optional extras, if they had to pay for them, some patients would have liked a private room (6 per cent), own television (6 per cent), own telephone (3 per cent) and a wider choice of food (10 per cent).

Patients' opinions of hospital cleanliness did not indicate any improvement: see Table 5. Some people (8 per cent) thought that the cleanliness of lavatories was poor or very poor and when patients were given the opportunity to make critical comments on their hospital stay, 16 (1990) and 21 (1992) complained of dirty or inadequate toilet and/or bathroom facilities.

The quality of hospital food was rated as poor or very poor by 14 per cent of patients in both years: see Table 6. In the open question 35 (1990) and 40 people (1992) mentioned the unpleasantness of food and six diabetic patients in each year reported that their condition was adversely affected by incorrect diet whilst in hospital. Younger patients tended to be more critical of both cleanliness of lavatories and quality of food.

Patients' satisfaction with the amount of privacy provided in hospital was similar in both years, with 60 per cent in 1990 and 57 per cent in 1992 very satisfied. While 30 per cent in 1990 and 32 per cent in 1992 were fairly satisfied, some of these qualified their reply by saying that they were only satisfied within what they saw as the constraints of the NHS. Eight per cent in 1990 and six per cent in 1992 were fairly unsatisfied and one per cent in 1990 and three per cent very unsatisfied with privacy. There was, therefore, a small decrease in satisfaction overall, with movement from very to fairly satisfied and from fairly to very unsatisfied. The main reasons given for dissatisfaction with privacy were crowded wards (28 and 25), other patients' mental condition (18 and 19), other patients' physical condition (12 and 25), insensitivity of staff (13 and 15), and building work in progress (12 and 6).

There seems to have been very little change in how patients considered their discharge from hospital was arranged, with 38 per cent of patients

Table 5: Patient Opinion of Hospital Cleanliness

	Ward				Lavatory				Bathroom				Public Areas			
	1990		1992		1990		1992		1990		1992		1990		1992	
	No.	%	No.	%	No.	%	No.	%	No.	%	No.	%	No.	%	No.	%
Very good	715	75	738	74	604	64	595	61	587	65	583	61	557	61	540	57
Good	215	23	232	23	260	28	310	32	274	30	308	32	292	32	321	34
Poor	18	2	18	2	62	7	54	6	34	4	49	5	46	5	64	7
Very poor	3	<1	9	1	13	1	20	2	8	1	18	2	16	2	21	2
Total	951	100	997	100	939	100	979	100	903	100	958	100	911	100	946	100

Table 6: Patient Opinion of Hospital Food

| | Quality | | | | Choice | | | | Suitability | | | |
| | 1990 | | 1992 | | 1990 | | 1992 | | 1990 | | 1992 | |
	No.	%	No.	%	No.	%	No.	%	No.	%	No.	%
Very good	376	40	397	40	357	39	346	36	352	39	354	36
Good	422	45	453	46	386	43	446	46	388	42	421	43
Poor	96	10	101	10	121	13	129	13	117	13	131	14
Very poor	37	4	39	4	43	5	44	5	55	6	64	7
Total	931	99	990	100	907	100	965	100	912	100	970	100

in 1990 and 39 per cent in 1992 reporting that there was no discussion of discharge with hospital staff. Fewer patients discussed discharge with a doctor (21 per cent and 17 per cent) but more did talk with a nurse (36 per cent and 39 per cent) or an occupational therapist (4 per cent and 6 per cent), providing some indication that hospital policy may have undergone some changes. On leaving hospital 41 patients in each year were transferred to residential care, 25 as new admissions in 1990 and 18 in 1992.

Summary: Most aspects of hospital care showed no marked improvement from 1990 to 1992. The implementation of change in large organisations is inevitably a slow process and it is possible that in most hospitals the full effect of the reforms is yet to be established. This study has not been able to demonstrate any increase in patient choice. In most cases the belief that a patient can make an informed choice of hospital is fallacious. Most patients are treated within their own health authority where there is usually little choice of hospital and, when patients are offered alternatives, most have insufficient understanding of which hospital is able to provide the 'best' treatment and many are constrained by the cost and difficulty of travel to hospitals in other health authorities. Patients may wish to choose to pay for optional extras or have a better choice of food but these are opportunities not widely available.

The health service reforms aimed to cut waiting lists but patients had waited longer for their hospital treatment in 1992 than in 1990. Results in the primary care study also showed that patients who were waiting to be admitted had waited longer in 1992 than in 1990. This confirms that although the number of people waiting for more than two years may have been reduced, it is at the expense of people waiting for shorter times. The reason is probably that the total number of beds available has not increased.

There has been an increase in the numbers of patients given seven or more days' notice of admission, which suggests that hospitals are becoming more aware of the patient's perspective and are attempting to give more notice where it is possible to book non-urgent admissions in advance. Despite this trend more patients were very dissatisfied with the amount of notice they were given, which perhaps indicates that the public may be expecting hospitals to set higher standards, as a result of the publicity surrounding the reforms.

Despite emphasis on better information for patients, it appears that fewer patients are receiving information about their hospitals before admission.

This may be a temporary deficit, as some hospitals were in the process of producing new booklets with more detailed information. Though formal information provision by administration may not yet have improved, staff at ward level seem to be increasing their efforts to communicate effectively with patients.

Conclusions

The studies described in this chapter complement those described in other chapters in several different ways. While others have focussed on change or the mechanism of change and have examined health care practice or interviewed health care practitioners about aspects of the NHS reforms, these studies have been concerned more with the end effects on patients of management or organisational change. The final judgement on the NHS reforms lies logically with patients. While patients' judgement in the long term may be derived from accumulated experience of 'hard' criteria on health status and quality of life, useful insights of how the NHS reforms are affecting patients show up in patients' views.

It is important also for health planners, health policy makers and politicians to have feedback as to how the reforms are changing health care, for reassurance if satisfactory, or for early warning if reforms are failing to achieve the desired objective. An example, perhaps, might be the effect of issuing directives on two year waiting lists without increasing resources. This has tended to increase numbers waiting and to increase average waiting times of those with waits under two years. Early feedback of the effect on outcome measures can prove useful also to managers in fine-tuning or in revising policy before it is 'set in concrete'. An example here might be the details of community care planning.

While it is our view that in the final analysis the answer to the question of effectiveness of the NHS reforms lies with the health status and quality of life of the population, it is not to be expected that significant improvements in these can be observed in the short term. Even with the well-recognized and powerful effect of smoking on longevity, it takes many years of changing smoking habits before significant improvements in life expectancy are observed. Our studies have measured health status at baseline on a number of standard scales and it may well be worth repeating these measures after a full five or even ten years to see if health status and quality of life improve.

The justification for interviewing or questioning large numbers of users or potential users lies in the range of services covered and the representative nature of the sample achieved. It complements the detailed 'anthropological' type of study of a few selected major users of particular services, because detailed study can tell as much about the server or the served as about the service, while the larger representative study can describe the variety that makes up a typical NHS service. Readers should need no reminding that, in a labour intensive service like health care, the effectiveness and quality of individual services depends greatly on contributions of individual practitioners. There are acknowledged difficulties in obtaining useful criticisms of the health services through consumer views. Patients are all too grateful, too relieved to be alive and often reluctant to criticise a service that may very probably have the opportunity to serve a critic less well next time (Carr-Hill 1992). These reservations are particularly true of elderly people, many of whom still perceive the service as 'charity' rather than a nationally owned service for which they have paid since 1947.

Closed questions can be artificially restrictive and virtually impossible to answer if they fail to distinguish different aspects of a service perceived relevant by the patient; for example food may look good, appetising and nutritious but be completely inappropriate for a patient after tonsillectomy. The open questions eliciting suggestions, together with the closed question scaling the quality of the service, allows and, particularly in interviews, encourages modest criticism as well as suggestions. An example here is how nurses are almost invariably described as 'angels', but at interview a patient may suggest more attention be paid to privacy, noise and respect for patients' autonomy, all of which could be gentle criticism of insensitive and thoughtless behaviour by those self-same 'angels'.

The case for selecting elderly people for these studies was explained earlier. Ideally, the impact of the NHS reforms should be assessed on all ages. Greater value for money in this research was obtained by targeting major users. There would be considerable dilution if the study included younger people, since most would not have direct personal experience of any of the individual services in recent recall. Nevertheless, the methodology is generally applicable to studying the impact of the reforms on the middle-aged and the young, although the detail of the questionnaires and interviewing schedules might need modification in places.

Our studies have given some answers on four broad issues emanating from NHS reforms: accessibility, choice, communication and quality. With regard to accessibility, the numbers looking for new GPs, the numbers describing difficulty getting to a surgery or obtaining a home visit and the numbers on the hospital waiting lists could be regarded as relevant statistics. None of these appear to have moved appreciably in the right direction; this study and others suggest that the numbers waiting for hospital treatment may have increased. Choice was potentially available at both the service level, between practices or between hospitals and in detail, for example between open ward and private room, for particular foods or for optional extras while in hospital. With regard to choice of hospital, there is little change because in many parts of the country there are few real alternatives and also other NHS reforms concerning contracting and fundholding may have actually acted against freedom of choice, in that the health authorities or general practices may have contracted to send all hernias or hips to one hospital, whether or not it is perceived by the patient as the convenient or pleasant or good hospital. There are signs that some aspects of communication, such as information on services provided by health centres, have been addressed more quickly than some of the other issues. Many aspects of quality, as perceived by patients, have shown little change. Uncomfortable examples here are the criticism of food quality and cleanliness of toilets and public areas in hospitals. While contracting-out catering and cleaning services may in the long term lead to better food and cleaner hospitals, the short term indications are that efficiency has taken precedence over effectiveness. With regard to clinical care, most doctors appreciate the importance of keeping effectiveness before efficiency. It would behove management of many of the services within the totality of health care to ensure that the job is done and done effectively before being too concerned about how to cut the cost of doing it.

The study has shown up some significant changes, such as the increase in health assessments, both among those aged over 75, for whom it was intended, and among those aged 65 to 74. Although possibly under-reported because doctors may practice assessments subtly, or under-promoted because doctors think it is a waste of time, this is clearly a direct consequence of a recent change in the GP's contract. For many other changes causality may not be so easily inferred. *Working for Patients* was fairly general and non-specific, as were several of the subsequent Patient Charter standards, and many changes have been introduced one on top of the other. In some areas, two reforms or two aspects of the same reform may be acting against each other. Even changes outside the realm of health care, like public transport, can powerfully influence how convenient or inconvenient a recent hospitalisation is perceived.

Ideally, the researcher would like to experiment with one reform at a time in a controlled way, in other words to change one district or region to GP fundholding while keeping another unaltered, and then experiment with another reform. The recent reforms in the NHS are far from ideal from the researcher's point of view because so many changes are occurring together and in an uncontrolled and unpiloted way. The studies reported in different chapters of this book identified that changes consequent upon *Working for Patients* and the accompanying reforms developed differently in different parts of the country. It might well be that studies based in more widely separated regions, ranging from the South East to the North West, would have allowed us to report more significant change over the early years of the reforms.

As to the future, the current wave of change in the NHS is so widespread that the ripples will take years to settle. Many changes are bound to be seen with the passage of time. Managers, both strategic long term purchasers and local providers, will require studies of this sort to monitor change, to fine-tune developments or to correct errors as early as possible and to see if the final objectives of patient care are achieved.

7

MONITORING MEDICAL AUDIT

Susan Kerrison, Tim Packwood and Martin Buxton

Audit is a technique with a long history. Many articles within the medical literature have argued that audit skilfully executed could both improve patient care and benefit the organisation of medical work. Therefore it was no surprise that the decision announced in *Working for Patients* requiring all doctors to undertake audit proved one of the least controversial aspects of the reforms. Yet despite this auspicious start, audit has proved problematic. Prior to the reforms, few had experience of routinely undertaking audit. Although robust in its analysis of the audit technique, the medical literature provided little advice or description on how the method should be applied across the range of different organisational contexts in which doctors work in the NHS (Packwood, Kerrison, Buxton, 1992). If audit was to be successful then doctors needed to become skilled at organising the structure and process of audit. Who should be included at the various stages of the process? Who should undertake which work? What should happen to the products of the audit? Moreover, as doctors have begun to gain experience of audit and to consider how best it might be organised, a more fundamental question has emerged: what is the purpose of audit? Unless the answer to this question is clear, it is inevitably difficult to organise the process effectively.

Ostensibly, the Government gave a clear definition of audit in Working Paper 6 (Department of Health, 1989c):

> *Audit is the systematic, critical analysis of the quality of medical care, including the procedures used for diagnosis and treatment, the use of resources, and the resulting outcome and quality of life for the patient.*

But organising a process to fulfil this purpose is far from straightforward, as the central aim of this definition, 'quality of medical care', can be a vexed and slippery concept. Both Donabedian (1988) and Maxwell (1984) have set out definitions of quality but their work pre-dates widespread attempts to use the term as a basis for policy. Consequently, as quality of care has become more discussed and used as a basis for action, the meaning of the term has changed and is now contested. Quality may refer to an attribute of a product or it may refer to a system of management, as in Total Quality Management (Pfeffer and Coote, 1991).

Clearly, the organisational framework in which the term is used and the views of those who participate in applying it will have considerable influence over its operational meaning. Working Paper 6, the Standing Medical Advisory Committee (Department of Health, 1990) and the subsequent circular (Department of Health, 1991a) elaborated a framework which characterised audit as a confidential peer review process, owned and led by the medical profession. The monies allocated to audit in 1991/92 and in subsequent years, a total of some £150 million to date, were ring-fenced and distributed through regional and local audit committees composed solely of clinicians. This ring-fencing – coupled with the confidential nature of the process – afforded the medical profession the opportunity to control who should take part in the process and who was to have access to the results. These factors tended to set audit apart from other related policies. Although there were to be links with other quality initiatives and postgraduate medical education, audit and these policies were not to be organisationally integrated. Furthermore, the structured analysis of medical work was promoted in a non-threatening manner as an educational experience for doctors. It was hoped that change would be stimulated by increased knowledge about organisation and outcomes of medical practice gained from the application of the audit technique.

Nevertheless, despite this emphasis on medical ownership, local non-medical managers were given some oversight of the process. The circular indicated that the audit programme should be discussed and agreed with local managers and that the aggregate results were to be made available to them. More controversially, managers were also given the power to initiate audit. In practice, these powers of oversight proved weak. The confidential nature of the process, its separateness from other policies and the mechanism for allocating monies, all gave audit the characteristic of being enclosed within the medical profession. Encased in such a framework, it was unlikely that the operational definition of quality of care would be based on anything other than medical values. With these characteristics, it was not surprising that audit was seen as an extension of the profession's current self-management arrangements.

Others, however, had different expectations of this process. Audit was introduced at a time when the extent of the profession's self-management arrangements were being called into question and demands being made for doctors to be more accountable for resource use. A key mechanism for exercising managerial accountability in modern organisations is measuring the extent to which departments, groups, products or processes conform to predetermined standards (Day and Klein, 1987, Harrison, 1992). As conformance to standards is also the central mechanism of audit, it is not surprising that audit may be seen as a tool for increasing the accountability of doctors.

In an article on the relationship between the state and the profession, Klein (1990) notes that since the inception of the NHS a contract has existed between the two where the former sets an overall budget for the NHS and 'the NHS provides a setting where doctors can exercise their skills with almost complete autonomy.' The imperative to contain the costs of health care has led to policies which attempt to re-negotiate this contract to include wider societal or institutional interests in decisions about the way resources are allocated between different groups of patients. For example, the Griffiths management reforms of the early 1980s sought to change the balance of power between doctors and managers by proposing that medicine should be part of the managerial sphere of influence. When this proved unsuccessful in delivering the desired leverage over medical decision-making, the reverse technique of involving doctors in management was attempted through the Resource Management Initiative (Packwood, Keen, Buxton, 1991). In this latter approach, doctors were encouraged to assimilate management ideas by taking a greater interest in, and responsibility for, the resource implications of their clinical activities, often by appointing clinical directors who would take responsibility for the husbandry of clinical resources. This policy trend culminated in the 1991 reforms where the central feature – the internal market – may be seen as providing a powerful tool for re-directing the way clinical resources are used. Potentially, audit has an important role within this market as it could provide information about effectiveness and efficiency of medical care for commissioners to use to monitor and influence medical decision making (Kerrison, 1993).

But there is a further aspect of current changes to the NHS which muddies the waters for audit. Like many other contemporary institutions, the NHS is beginning to adopt the concept of 'quality management'. The similarities between 'quality management' – and more particularly 'total quality management' – and the audit process seen in terms of the 'quality of medical care' – lead people to believe they are part of the same activity. But the philosophy of quality management presents a number of challenges to medical audit. First, the drive of quality management to embrace all sections of the organisation is in conflict with the insularity of medical audit as currently implemented. Second, in practice, quality management appears to be a top-down activity initiated and cascaded by senior management (Centre for the Evaluation of Public Policy and Practice, 1991). This conflicts with the self-management ethos of medical audit. Third, medical audit, as defined in Working Paper 6, focuses attention on the patient. In contrast the main focus of quality management is less clear. Its intended focus is on the customer, a term which can refer not only to the patient but also to others who may have an interest in the services doctors provide. These may include other departments or professions in organisations in which doctors work and commissioners of services (Centre for the Evaluation of Public Policy and Practice, 1991). The plurality of customers for the products of quality management differentiates it from audit which is essentially an activity focused either inwardly on the concerns of the medical profession or entirely on the patient.

Thus audit occupies a somewhat contradictory position in relation to the reforms and other changes in NHS management practice. On the one hand, the reforms can be seen as the latest in a series of policies aimed at exerting more control over medical decision making, while on the other hand Working Paper 6 portrays audit in terms of a continuation of the medical profession's existing self-management arrangements. Moreover, although it might appear that the philosophy of audit is congruent with the new management initiatives, the framework implemented for audit sets it apart from them.

In practical terms, these different perspectives result in audit seeking to fulfil three quite distinct purposes which give rise to three quite different lines of accountability. The first purpose is to provide a local peer review activity which would be educational in nature. In this case it is suggested that accountability would be through a doctors' peer group. The second purpose is to provide an information source for commissioners. This would enable commissioners to have increased oversight of medical decision making. The third purpose is that audit should be part of the total management process of institutions. In this case doctors would arguably become more accountable to the institutions in which they work. Clearly, audit is more complex and controversial than was first apparent.

The Study and its Methods

Although the expectations of audit have varied, it has generally been implemented in terms of the framework laid out in Working Paper 6 and the subsequent circular. In this chapter we describe how the implementation has been accomplished to date and, bearing in mind that audit is characterised as an educational activity, provide an assessment of the extent to which it has been successful in increasing the peer accountability of doctors. Clearly this criterion of success will not satisfy those who wish to see an increase in the external accountability of doctors. Hence, as further attention is likely to be directed to this issue by the current debate about the status of the medical profession (Elston 1991), we have speculated on three other future scenarios for audit which meet these external demands.

The evidence on which our description and analysis is based came from two sources. The principal source is a case study of the implementation of audit in general medicine at four hospital sites. These sites were selected to offer contrasts in terms of the level of involvement of doctors in management, size, availability of information technology and level of engagement in quality assurance programmes. Thus one hospital in our sample had a well embedded clinical directorate structure with heavy investment in information technology, while another was organised around the traditional medical structure based on specialties and had underdeveloped information systems. In choosing the sites, the opinions of regional audit co-ordinators were sought about the level of audit development in these hospitals because we were keen to choose hospitals which were neither at the forefront nor backward in their development of the system. Data were collected at these sites between 1991 and 1992. The method consisted of observation of speciality audit meetings and local audit committee meetings, and interviews with key participants: namely, clinicians, audit co-ordinators, clinical tutors and with those on the periphery of audit, nurses – both managers and ward sisters – and local hospital managers. We also undertook surveys of the views of junior doctors.

Supporting evidence is provided by data from a national survey of medical audit support staff carried out in the autumn of 1991 in conjunction with the King's Fund Medical Audit Information Service. The aim of this survey was to provide basic descriptive details of the background and work of a new occupational group within the NHS, *ie* audit support staff, and to ascertain their perception of the process, its problems and successes. In all, 557 questionnaires were sent out to medical unit support staff known to the King's Fund Medical Audit Information Service and 382 were returned, representing a response rate of 69 per cent. A full account of the methods used and the findings can be found in Kerrison, Packwood and Buxton (1993).

Audit in Practice

Given the framework laid out in Working Paper 6, it was not surprising that we found that audit at our sites was planned, organised and executed as an attempt at local medical self-management. The choices made by local clinicians about who was to be involved in its planning and execution, choices about the subjects to be audited, and the problems sites had in applying the audit technique – such as the lack of guidelines and information technology – guided audit further along this path.

Organising Audit: The audit process was, in the main, planned by those who had been appointed as lead clinicians of the various specialties. Initially they chose the topics and organised the meetings. It might have been expected from Working Paper 6 that the local audit committee or local managers might have had an input into the audit programme, but this was not the case. Indeed at most of our sites this would have been difficult, as the programmes tended to be formulated on an *ad hoc* basis, in some cases from meeting to meeting. Similarly purchasers or commissioners of services appeared to have little role in shaping the process at the sites studied. In this respect the sites appeared typical of hospitals in general. Only eight per cent who responded to our survey reported being involved in formulating criteria or standards for use in contracts and 17 per cent reported being involved in providing audit information for monitoring contracts. However, there were two groups who as time went on became more involved in the planning process. At two sites, junior doctors were increasingly encouraged to choose topics and undertake audit. It also became quite apparent that audit support staff, encouraged by the training they received and informed by their contacts with other hospitals, would encourage clinicians to pursue particular audit topics.

Although the sites studied varied considerably both in terms of size and organisational factors – and this might have been expected to impinge on the audit process – in practice, these factors appeared to have very little effect on the shape of audit. For example, the size of the hospital had little impact on the number of participants attending specialty audit meetings. In fact, paradoxically, at the largest hospital with 900 beds, audit meetings had the smallest number of participants. This hospital had a directorate structure but audit in general medicine was carried out at a sub-directorate level with only two consultants and six junior doctors participating in the particular sub-specialty group that we observed. In contrast, at the smallest hospital, meetings consisted of some 15–20 people with between three and six consultants attending.

Overall attendance at meetings averaged two-thirds to three-quarters of all those who were designated as part of the general medicine audit group. Not surprisingly, the size of the meeting had an influence on its ambience. The smallest audit group, with less than ten people, had the air of a team meeting with the consultants encouraging everyone to participate in a lively debate. The largest group, which met at 8.30 am with usually more than ten consultants and 20 junior doctors present, was quite formal. Productive and lively debate took place among consultants but it often appeared difficult for junior doctors to participate. The style at the other two audit groups was of an informal lunchtime meeting with junior doctors fully participating in the debate.

The numbers at meetings were often swelled by the presence of other occupational groups: pathologists, nurses, pharmacists, radiologists, information technologists all attended meetings at the sites in our study at one time or another, but the dominant group was always consultant physicians and their juniors. With the exception of members from some service departments, such as haematologists and pharmacists who attended meetings with the purpose of developing joint policies with physicians, other occupational groups appeared to have a status similar to that of guests. They often appeared as guest presenters, or guest experts invited to comment on the proceedings or as part of the audience, but they were not full participants.

These observations apply in particular to nurses. Like all guests they were made welcome but appeared to find it difficult to criticise the host. In other words, the presence of other professional groups does not necessarily mean that clinical audit, in the sense of joint audit with other professions, is being undertaken. At no site was joint formulation of guidelines initiated, no joint collection of data occurred nor were joint policies formulated with other professions or occupational groups. The sites where formalised quality assurance initiatives were in operation, such as the King's Fund Hospital Accreditation Scheme or Total Quality Management, were no different in this respect. At these sites these initiatives did not appear to facilitate the integration of medical audit and quality assurance.

Thus audit emerges from the choices made during the process of organisation as almost the exclusive territory of the medical profession. Indeed it may not have been possible for the lead clinicians who organised the audit programme to develop it otherwise given that some of their colleagues, albeit a minority, were hostile to the introduction of audit, suspicious of the Government's motives, fearful of the time costs that might be involved and unconvinced about its benefits. But even as a process encapsulated within medicine, sites had difficulty in making the audit technique work for them, either educationally or in terms of changing policies. There were difficulties in applying the method, utilising the outcome of the meetings, using the process as an educational experience and generally in making peer accountability work.

Using the audit method: The majority of audits (37 out of 55) were criteria based *ie* an attempt was made to set standards and measure conformance to these standards. In the majority of cases the whole audit was presented at one meeting. The criteria used were announced, the data presented, conclusions drawn and action discussed all in the space of a lunchtime. The meetings often had the air of being a particular form of case presentation, a format familiar to all doctors, with 'the case' being the audit. The doctors attending played the role of audience to a performance rather than participants in a decision making process. The consequence of this was that debate over variation in practice was limited and the educational value of having a broad discussion on the best criteria was diminished.

Choosing criteria on which to base the judgement about the quality of care, one of the key steps in this form of audit, also proved problematic.

The process of formulating criteria or guidelines is now taking place at the national level under the auspices of professional bodies such as the Royal College of Physicians. But a usable body of guidelines has yet to emerge. Survey results presented to one conference on this subject (Collier, 1991) suggested that very few hospitals were using any guidelines, whether formulated internally or externally. The sites we observed were no exception and, in consequence, explicit criteria based on the literature, on national guidelines, or on a formal local consensus were used in only a minority of audits (10 out of 37). Although two sites explicitly stated that formulating criteria was part of the aim of audit, only rarely was the required time and energy put into this activity. Interviews suggested that many doctors were resistant to the use of standards, particularly those which were felt overly to restrict their clinical freedom. Consultants would argue that they wanted 'guidelines' not 'tramlines'.

In the absence of ready-made guidelines or criteria, presenters were faced with a problem. On a number of occasions they solved this by formulating the criteria themselves and making these explicit to the audience, but in 12 out of the 37 audits the nature of the criteria appeared not to be stated and were left as implicit.

Another problem associated with the execution of audit at these sites was the small sample sizes on which it was based. With the exception of one site, which on three occasions used a sample of more than 50 cases, sample sizes for the 37 criteria audits were almost always small. In 24 of these audits the sample size was less than 20 cases.

Small sample sizes may be a consequence of reliance on case notes instead of computerised records as the data source. Case notes were used for all criteria audits at our sites and although advocated by many experts as the cornerstone of audit, it makes the process very labour intensive. Although audit co-ordinators have been appointed to undertake some of this data collection, they were only routinely used for this purpose at one of our sites. Even at this site, however, audit still seemed to require considerable investment of time by clinicians. The senior registrar who undertook the audit with the largest sample, some 100 cases, estimated that it took her one week to collect the data from the notes. Using those whose time is limited to review case notes is a disincentive to basing audit on a larger sample.

Even those sites with some form of computerised record systems experienced problems utilising them for audit. Only one of our study sites had an integrated case-mix data system but, during the study period, this system was largely inaccessible to clinicians, due to distributional problems. Only one attempt was made to use a large case-mix database for audit and this proved unrewarding. Other sites had purchased stand-alone computers to facilitate audit but these systems were still in an early stage of development. Our survey suggested that the low use of hospital-wide databases of the sites studied is typical of audit in general with only 10 per cent of respondents reporting using a case-mix management system for audit purposes and only 20 per cent using an order communicating system.

In general the use of large databases for audit exposed a number of problems. First, the database may not contain information in the form required for audit. For example, on a number of occasions computerised systems seemed unable to identify the sample to audit. One presenter had attempted to identify gastro-intestinal haemorrhages through a variety of computer systems. But as the databases were based on diagnoses they appeared to be of little use for this purpose. Another site had difficulty in using their radiology computer to identify a sample of patients who had had a CT scan by consultant. A second problem is that clinicians may have difficulty in gaining access to, or retrieving data from, the system. Third, clinicians may lack the skills necessary to analyse large data sets. The epidemiological and statistical skills required are not well developed within the medical curriculum.

Finally, the criteria audit we observed tended to concentrate on the technical aspects of care. Donabedian (1988) argues that medical care has many components – structure, technical care, interpersonal relationships and use of resources. All of these should be audited. Indeed audit is being introduced at a time when great emphasis is being placed on both customer satisfaction and efficiency in the use of resources. Our survey suggested that there was interest in including customer satisfaction in audit, as 37 per cent of audit support staff reported using data on patients' views. In contrast, there was little evidence of any assessment of the use of resources, with only three per cent of audit support staff reporting using cost data.

Undoubtedly, increasing the scope of audit to include customer satisfaction is problematic as it requires a separate data collection process, often using methodologies which have been devised by other professions and concepts which are unfamiliar to clinicians. But the same problems do not apply to cost data. Although costing may be conceptually difficult, the data could be made available to the audit process. Yet such data were seldom used. It appeared that clinicians at our sites did not place great emphasis on resource use as the proper focus of audit. It may be that their views of the purposes of audit were rather more traditional than those outlined in the white paper. But this is unlikely to be the only reason for placing little emphasis on these subjects. The audit method itself may constrain its scope. The fact that audit has become synonymous with the one methodological approach of measuring conformance to standards may limit clinicians' capacity for assessing other important components of health care, such as the relationship between doctor and patient, which do not fit easily within this methodological framework.

The characteristics of audit in practice outlined above clearly place constraints on its effective use. First, concentration on the technical aspects of inpatient care means that the work of consultants may disappear from view given that it is junior doctors who, in medicine, provide most of the care for these patients. Second, reliance on implicit criteria or individual expert opinion can weaken the process both in terms of education and quality assurance. When implicit criteria are used it is difficult to know the basis on which criticisms are being made, and expectations about how things should be done are not made clear. Third, the use of small samples also has certain disadvantages. Undoubtedly much can be learnt from the management of an individual case but with such small samples it is difficult to identify patterns of care. This can then lead to a tendency to see all the difficulties identified as anomalies rather than as generalised problems. These factors together mean that audit must remain unquantifiable, no comparisons with other groups can be made and attempts to judge improvements by repeating the process are difficult. This loose application of the audit technique limits it as a tool for oversight by commissioners, or even its use by hospitals who wish to judge the performance of their consultants by the standards of a wider community, and constrains it to function as a tool for localised medical self-management.

The methodological problems outlined above suggest that the sites found it difficult to apply a structured audit technique systematically to their work. Indeed clinicians seemed to have doubts about the validity of standardising their practice to include every case as required by the audit method. An example illustrates this point. A consultant cardiologist auditing the management of cardiac failure remarked that there was good evidence that a particular drug was of no use in this sort of cardiac failure but, 'they all knew of cases like this one', he taps the case notes he is reviewing, 'where the drug has been administered and the patient appears to have recovered well because of it'. Such examples bring out the tension between standardisation based on knowledge gained from clinical trials and the value placed on the everyday experience of practice. They do not bode well for attempts to increase the use of standardised rules in the assessment of everyday medical practice.

The outcomes of audit: Despite limiting the audit technique's usefulness to purchasers and managers, the difficulties we observed might have proved inconsequential had the process brought about clearly discernible changes to the way doctors managed their work. But there was often uncertainty about what should happen as a result of the audit. It appeared to be the accepted convention that the chair of the meeting had some responsibility for drawing attention to the results of the audit, either in summary at the end or as they emerged during, or were discussed, after the presentation. This was not always easy since there were quite likely to be conflicting opinions as to just what had emerged. There was also the related issue of who was going to take any action on the basis of the results and how anyone would know whether or not any such action had been successful. It was our experience that, by the end of the meeting, the audience was liable to have drifted away, leaving the chair, presenter and the audit support staff to pick up the pieces. These views appeared to be shared by junior doctors. Over half of the respondents to our survey of junior doctors felt that they had no clear idea of what action should be taken as a result of the audit meeting. Two-thirds felt that they had no clear idea of who would be responsible for taking further action. Moreover, it was rare for proposals for action to be followed-up from meeting to meeting. There was no space allotted to 'matters arising from the minutes' on the agenda for these meetings.

Nevertheless, despite these problems some changes in practice or policies did emerge. For example, at two sites, guidelines on the treatment of asthma and investigating anaemia were formulated, and policies on blood transfusions were implemented. It also appears from our survey of medical audit support staff that in their view a number of successful audits were being undertaken. One hundred and ninety two of the 382 medical audit support who responded gave examples of audits they considered successful. These revealed that audits of considerable depth and breadth were being undertaken. Examples we observed included both criteria audits about the technical aspects of care and audits of wider scope: interdisciplinary audits, those using cost data and those which involved obtaining patients' views about their care. According to our respondents, factors which contributed towards the success of audit included choosing a subject which was perceived as a 'problem by many'; an audit design which was straightforward and easy to analyse; enthusiastic and well motivated clinicians; involvement of audit support staff at all stages; and audits which brought people together to develop a common perspective.

From an analysis of these audits, it looks as if the main products of audit are policies or protocols developed by, and for, clinicians without any reference to external agencies. This reinforces the view that currently one of the main uses of audit is for the self-management of the medical profession.

Audit and Accountability

No matter whether audit is seen as part of medical self-management or as a tool to aid others in the management of doctors, the exercise of accountability is central to any management activity. Exercising accountability through the mechanism of conformance to standards requires agreement between those who are being held to account and those who have oversight about the standards or yardsticks to be used to assess performance, as well as access to the data used to measure conformance (Day and Klein, 1987). Stone (1980) in a comparative investigation of the governance of the medical profession in Germany and USA notes that to be effective groups charged with oversight need to be able to observe what is happening, criticise and act. Within the current framework for audit there are three groups that are charged with this role; peer groups of doctors, local audit committees consisting of mainly clinicians with a small number of managers, and local hospital managers. The context in which audit has been introduced suggests that there may also be other contenders for this role waiting in the wings but at present their influence appears weak.

The current philosophy of audit suggests that the strongest degree of oversight is to come from a doctor's peers. But this leaves unresolved the fundamental problem of who will be legitimately accepted as a particular doctor's peer. The word is usually taken to mean a colleague of equal status and standing, but many audit groups are not made up of peers. For example, at all the sites we studied, specialty audit meetings were made up of consultants and junior doctors who were subordinate to the consultants and managerially and professionally accountable to them. Given this hierarchy, junior doctors' willingness to openly criticise consultants will be very limited. Moreover, even consultants may not accept each other as peers. The restricted scope of the audit process combined with the increased specialisation of medicine can call into question the validity of the peer relationship. For example, in the same audit group, there may be consultants who have a specialist interest in diabetes and those who have a specialist interest in respiratory medicine. A respiratory physician may be very reluctant to criticise a colleague's handling of diabetic cases, particularly when audit concentrates heavily on the technical aspects of care. When this situation is coupled with a lack of widely agreed standards, with scepticism about their usefulness, and unsophisticated methods with small samples, then the basis on which one consultant may criticise another or insist on action is insecure.

Unfortunately the local audit committee was no more successful in providing oversight for audit. As noted earlier, local audit committees had little input into the planning of specialty audits, little say in the standards used and were unlikely to see the results of audit. Some local audit committees did find a role for themselves in representing the interests of audit to a wider community in the hospital. They organised training days in audit, distributed newsletters and liaised with management. But for others, audit was a professionally determined activity and they saw no reason to negotiate the purposes or expectations of audit with other groups. Unfortunately, one of the consequences of this philosophy was that it tended to constrain the role of audit committees and gave them a very narrow remit for action. All committees did however try to develop a formalised reporting structure with proformas on which specialties were supposed to report the audit they had undertaken together with their findings. But these seldom appeared to be completed and returned to the audit group. Instead the committees tended to rely on less formal means of finding out what was happening. The reports of local medical audit support staff about their work with specialty audit groups proved a useful source of information.

The failure to develop a formal reporting structure can be explained by the nature of the relationship that consultants have with one another. Reporting the results of audit to a committee of consultants had the potential to give rise to a hierarchical situation where one group of consultants was placed in the position of supervising or inspecting the work of another, thereby breaking the long established social order where consultants previously considered themselves as equals. So although local audit committees could be seen as being made up of a consultant's peers, in practice their peer authority was rejected.

Local managers too had difficulties in observing audit and overseeing the process. Through their membership of local audit committees, they were expected to have some input into the planning and oversight of the process. But the committees themselves had difficulty in planning and overseeing audit, and managers had little opportunity for input through this channel. Although at some of our sites there were management representatives on audit committees, they did not appear to be in senior positions. It may have been that senior managers were too preoccupied with other aspects of the NHS reforms to be able to attend meetings where they could obtain little information or have much effect on shaping the process. Indeed, given the technical nature of the majority of audits, even if information had been available, it is doubtful what contribution most managers would have felt able to make.

Clearly with the present organisational arrangements for audit and the current nature of the organisation of medical work there are many obstacles to exercising accountability through audit whether this is by peers, audit committees or local managers. But there is one group for whom audit does appear to work as a method of increasing managerial accountability; namely, junior doctors. As the scope of audit concentrated mainly on the technical aspects of inpatient care, junior doctors' work was made clearly visible at audit meetings. Similarly, consultants were prepared to criticise and take action, usually in the form of exhorting junior doctors to comply with existing policies. The one strong message that came over from the way in which meetings were conducted was that while all present were members of a common profession – and could relate, doctor to doctor – there was nonetheless a strong managerial relationship, with very real properties of authority and accountability, between a consultant and his, or her, junior staff.

In responding to our survey, junior doctors emphasised audit meetings as a means of learning about local policies and consultants' expectations. Very few saw them as a source of information about new developments or of material for professional examinations. This is compatible with a view that audit meetings provide an important means of socialisation, demonstrating the expectations of behaviour held by senior professionals to the juniors. From our experience, this has been a rather successful aspect of the implementation of audit. However a word of caution is necessary. In the absence of agreed criteria based on the literature or good data, changes in practice can only be based on the views of consultant experts. Clearly as medicine is a subject in which much learning must take place through trial and error, the implicit knowledge of those with experience will always play an important part in the education of doctors. But a problem with this approach was strikingly illustrated in one particular audit meeting. A geriatrician was auditing the general medicine team's care of the elderly. Although the findings were that medical management was good, many practices which were standard in the care of the elderly had not been carried out. Recording of social history, mobility and mental state were poor. It seems likely that junior doctors would have had no problem in giving appropriate answers should such a question be posed in an examination, but their attention was directed towards what they perceived to be the expectations of the consultant they were working for, a chest physician. The moral of this is that through audit junior doctors may learn good practices from one consultant but then have to give these less priority when they move on to the next.

Given that there are those among the medical profession who would not accept that audit is characteristically a management activity, but that a strong case can be made for seeing audit as an educational activity, what assessment can be made of audit as an educational enterprise?

Audit and Education

In practice it was difficult for audit to fulfil its educational objective for a number of reasons. First, the educational needs of doctors participating in audit were very different. The consultants required the opportunity to reflect upon their considerable professional experience. The junior doctors likewise required the opportunity to reflect upon, and extend their, in some cases, very limited experience. But what was of interest to the former could well be beyond the latter. Topics relevant to junior doctors would be boring to consultants, who might well feel that they were learning nothing from audit meetings, and particularly so if the topics had to be repeated every six months to cater for a fresh intake of junior staff.

A second problem was that unless the audit cycle was very short, junior doctors, in their six month and sometimes shorter rotation, would not see its conclusion let alone its effects. At many of our sites, as mentioned previously, the audit cycle was very compressed, and often this was to the detriment of reaching a consensus on criteria to be used or developing policies.

Third, although medical audit illuminated issues which had implications for formal medical education, the mechanisms for using it in such a way appeared haphazard. It was unlikely that any of the issues raised by audit would result in formal training either directly or through being raised at a local audit committee. This conclusion was confirmed both at our study sites and through our survey which suggested that, in general, formal education or training was unlikely to be an outcome of audit. In practice the connection between postgraduate medical education and audit appeared to be weaker than envisaged in the policy statements. Reasons for this may lie with the inability of postgraduate medical education to respond to the potential demands of audit. Recently research has emerged (Grant, 1992) which suggests that postgraduate medical education also requires greater planning and organisation. The techniques used, the organisational arrangements and its educational value are all being questioned.

Whither Audit?

The problems with the audit process outlined above will add weight to the arguments of those who wish to see a fundamental change in the nature of the process. In this connection, the way funds are allocated in future will play a large part in shaping the nature of audit. The current funding arrangements whereby audit funds are earmarked or ring-fenced and clinicians are not faced with having to justify the benefits of audit against other priorities for spending, have contributed to a situation where audit is currently marginal in terms of time, commitment and priority. Unfortunately past experience provides little reason to suppose that the existing framework will change. In each year since the initial implementation of audit, it has been rumoured that the way in which money is allocated will be changed fundamentally, with monies being allocated either to commissioners of services or to provider units. Such an arrangement would undoubtedly give commissioners or local managers much more say in the process. But every year the money has continued to be allocated through existing local medical audit committees. Clearly, the Government is caught between the fears of the medical profession, that any external involvement in audit will destroy the process completely, and demands for the activities of audit to take other interests into account.

Nevertheless much could be done to improve the functioning of the existing process. In our view attention could be fruitfully paid to a number of areas. A programme of audits could be better planned with more consideration given to who should be involved in each part of the cycle and when different parts of it should be timetabled. Moreover, different audits may require different audiences. For example, the audit of the microbiological urine analysis might usefully involve the junior doctors who requested the test, nurses who organised it, the porters who transported the sample, the laboratory staff who analysed it and the consultants who judged whether action as a result of the test was appropriate. All or some of these people might usefully be involved in planning audits, collecting data, analysing results and deciding upon action. In contrast, an audit of prescribing might just involve doctors.

Similarly, there is no reason why the whole audit cycle should be crammed into one meeting, with insufficient time being given to discussion or to reaching a consensus about the subject, the guidelines to be used, and the methods, let alone the important question of subsequent action.

The presentation of many audits could be improved. Basic weaknesses of presentation which reduce the impact on participants, such as mumbled delivery, speaking facing away from the audience and presenting overheads containing, or reporting verbally on, masses of data could have been avoided with a little preliminary advice.

Among the methodological problems facing audit, some, such as the availability of information, are difficult to resolve; others could be improved by education. It would appear to us that many doctors have difficulty in constructing problems in such a way that they can be usefully investigated, and in confidently interpreting and drawing conclusions from the data they have collected. Although much effort has been put into courses to teach doctors about audit, these tend to be didactic rather than experiential. It may be difficult to acquire the appropriate skills in this way; possibly these would be better acquired through some form of supervised practise.

Finally, more attention needs to be given to following up the results of audit. Problems identified which relate to other hospital departments or the organisation of the hospital in general need to be taken up and pursued; progress or otherwise needs to be reported back to the audit group. The identification of problems, sometimes serious, without subsequent attempts at action leads to disillusionment with audit in general.

Three other considerations relate to changes in the direction of the audit process, the way in which it is conducted and different funding arrangements. First there are pressures on audit to become more integrated with other aspects of the institution in which doctors work. Clearly, the allocation of funds to managers may provide them with the leverage required for this to occur. If such monies were not ring-fenced then audit would have to prove its value against other provider projects. With resources allocated to provider units, audit should have a clear local managerial focus, with active involvement of the clinical director and a much greater emphasis on inputs and outputs. Thus audit might be geared towards the management of a clinical directorate and its scope would include both clinical and managerial elements. Alternatively it could have an entirely clinical emphasis accepting that in reality much medical work takes place in multi-disciplinary teams. Thus medical audit should involve other professional groups and become clinical audit. If such groups broadened their horizons to look at all aspects of care which impinge on the outcome for patients, then the process may come to be called total quality management. However in terms of increasing the accountability of the medical profession there are dangers in this approach. Previous research evidence (Goldie, 1977; Dingwall and McIntosh, 1978; Kerrison, 1990) suggests that in any multi-disciplinary group, the differences in authority, status, knowledge and education between different professions means those in a subordinate position would be reluctant to challenge or openly criticise consultants or even junior doctors. This being the case, clinical audit or quality management may prove an even less effective mechanism for reviewing a doctor's work than medical audit.

A second scenario would be for audit to be directed towards the commissioning process. This too implies a shift in the nature of medical audit with the various aspects of the process including the scope, the standards used, the outcomes and the amount of money 'surcharged' in contracts for audit, all being a matter for negotiation between the purchaser and those who commission the service. There may be demands for this from commissioners who will wish to monitor the services they are purchasing, but whether or not this will increase accountability in practice is a complex and open question. Evidence from the USA, where many such formal standards are implemented, is equivocal. Experience suggests that the process has the tendency to develop into a very noisy argument with each side using ever increasing amounts of costly data to justify its position (Berwick, Enthoven and Bunker, 1992). As a consequence there are many doubts about the effectiveness of this mechanism for influencing medical decision making (Stone, 1980).

A final possible scenario is that the profession itself, in the form of Royal Colleges and other professional bodies, will increase oversight of the audit process and receive an enhanced allocation of money for this purpose. These bodies are, in fact, already involved in audit in a number of ways. For example, they are involved in the production of guidelines and in undertaking national or regional audits, such as the Confidential Enquiry into Peri-Operative Deaths, but as yet they have been reluctant to apply pressure to audit at the grassroots. If they choose to do so, they would be in a far better position than other agencies to effect change to the process and to give it more direction. They have insider knowledge of which rules or guidelines are most appropriate and stand most chance of being adhered to, they know when rules can and should be broken, and when and how rules are illegitimately avoided. In addition they have a range of powerful incentives and sanctions which can be applied to doctors. Accreditation for training posts, merit awards, and research grants can and are used to reward or sanction members.

On the other hand, if professional bodies choose not to see audit as an exercise in increasing accountability, they could still be involved in developing audit formally as a process of educational or professional development. In this case the processes required would be different for junior doctors and consultants; the former linked to competencies acquired through the postgraduate education system and the latter looking towards Royal Colleges for formal review of attainments. The subject matter, too, would have to be given a different emphasis from hitherto, encompassing an assessment of a consultant's ability to organise medical work, manage and train junior doctors and deliver a safe, efficient service according to the current consensus on professional standards.

The problem, of course, with these professionally determined scenarios for audit, is that they are unlikely to satisfy those who wish to place greater constraints on the profession by bringing societal or institutional interests to bear on the shape of medical practice. Only time will tell which of these paths medical audit will follow. They are not of course mutually exclusive options and it may be productive for medical audit to develop processes which relate to each of these three.

Wider Implications

The preceding discussion has indicated how the implementation of medical audit relates at several points to wider issues of social and public policy. These are briefly considered as a postscript to our work.

First, medical audit tells us something about how, as a profession, medicine runs its affairs and makes aspirants aware of what is expected. Mention was made earlier as to how junior doctors felt that one of the main functions of audit meetings was to clarify the expectations of their consultants. The expectations they had in mind were largely concerned with task performance, but audit meetings also relate to other desired attributes of the medical role. They give positive or negative messages regarding willingness to question one's practice, to learn from evidence, to be open to the possibility of change but also able to 'stand one's own corner' when the occasion demands, and to relate to colleagues as fellow professionals, while recognising gradations of authority, expertise and seniority. Perhaps most important, participation in medical audit has a symbolic quality; visible proof of the 'clinicians'' commitment and vocation. As Bosk wrote with reference to the participation of senior medical staff in mortality and morbidity conferences in the United States:

> *he has demonstrated that he is dedicated above all to the improvement of patient care (Bosk, 1979).*

But if audit meetings are important in socialising expected behaviour, their message as to the expected knowledge base that doctors should draw upon proves less sure than might be imagined. Certainly some stress is placed upon the traditional, positivist, scientific, experimental method of enquiry; measuring phenomena against agreed criteria and producing objective and generalisable knowledge. But in our experience this was flawed in practice by small samples, lack of time for inquiry and lack of agreement on desirable standards. This is hardly surprising. Since medical audit is concerned with the quality of current practice, it is not identical to medical research. It is as concerned with the art of medicine as with the science; with the idiosyncratic application to the individual as well as with the more regular patterns displayed by populations. In this context, as Henkel nicely expresses it in discussing evaluative models, 'the analogy of experiment was replaced by that of argument' (Henkel, 1991).

In the commercial sphere, knowledge, of course, carries a price; as opposed to the professional scientific sphere, which traditionally saw knowledge as a commodity which should be freely available for the general good. As a regulated market, the health service sits, rather uneasily, between the norms of the commercial and public worlds, and medical audit well illustrates some of the ambiguities that result. We have seen that knowledge gained from medical audit is restricted both to the medical profession and within medical specialties and sub-units of provider institutions. As information relating to audit is passed to managers, up organisations or over to purchasers, so it becomes increasingly aggregated, abbreviated and general in character. This would be compatible with a commercial model, where performance data is not freely available and is normally carefully packaged before being publicly released, but it makes it difficult for public bodies to use audit as a means of evaluating their wider legitimate concerns with social costs and benefits. As a result the latter may have to rely upon less direct evidence (Levacic, 1991).

Writers such as Harrison *et al* (1990) and Flynn (1992) have drawn attention to the increase of monitoring and evaluative activity in the NHS during the 1980s, and medical audit can be seen as a particular example. Indeed there was considerable speculation that medical audit would represent one of the means of at last extending managerial controls over clinical activities (Pollitt, 1993). Our experience is that, as yet, this has not proved to be the case. As a form of evaluation, medical audit appears restricted in both its membership and in its focus. The undertaking of medical audit is sanctionable, both by professional and local managerial requirements, but if sanctions are applied on the results of undertaking audit, they are largely informal and internal. In other words, medical audit is a formative type of evaluation, focused around the objectives of the participants for their work and aiming to induce change through education and argument. As such, it is increasingly out of step with other forms of evaluation in the health service, which are summative in their character, 'top down' strategies, delivering authoritative judgements which will be backed-up by managerial sanctions, and this, perhaps, partly explains the reluctance of clinicians to become involved in wider clinical audit and other forms of quality assurance and control.

Finally, what about incentives? Is participation merely a matter of form, complying with requirements to satisfy the consultant, local managers, the purchasers or the Royal Colleges? Our evidence suggests that for most clinicians the time costs are low, and that they are lowered by keeping audit outside the working day. But, and always excepting the enthusiasts for audit who have proved so important in getting it up and running, clinicians appear to feel that the benefits are also low; the knowledge gained from audit could be gained by other means without creating a formal process. If audit is to take on a greater significance within medical work, it would appear to require both a closer integration into day-to-day medical management, the clarification of purpose we have urged above and to produce clearer evidence of beneficial change.

8

THE CHANGING ROLE OF THE NHS PERSONNEL FUNCTION

James Buchan and Ian Seccombe

Personnel is a second rate function in the NHS. Personnel Officers are not second rate, but they have never had a fully-rounded job to do. Very few of them are within hailing distance of being chief executives. (Eric Caines, NHS Personnel Director, (*The Health Summary*, November 1992.))

The 1988 review of the National Health Service, which led to the NHS and Community Care Act 1990 and the implementation of the reforms in 1991, was a political reaction to a series of high profile NHS resourcing problems. A number of these problems relate to staffing, such as the shortage of specialist nurses at Birmingham Sick Children's Hospital. Solving the problems of skills shortages, real or apparent, and securing improvements in employee productivity have been central tenets of the NHS reforms.

Any radical attempt to reform the management of NHS services and finances had to address issues of the management of the NHS workforce. The NHS is a labour-intensive service industry; it is estimated that salaries and wages of staff directly employed by the NHS in England represented 76 per cent of health authorities' net revenue expenditure in 1990 (Office of Health Economics, 1992). The workforce is large – more than one million are employed in several hundred units – far from homogeneous and is heavily unionised, with several powerful professional and generalist unions.

Our study reviewed key developments in the management of the NHS workforce since the implementation of the reforms. This chapter examines the extent to which the pace and direction of these developments has reflected the direct effect of the reforms or of other factors, and assesses the likely future shape of the NHS personnel function.

Two main research methodologies are being used in the study, to achieve the stated objectives of describing and monitoring changes in the role of the human resource management function in the NHS as the *Working for Patients* strategy is implemented.

Postal surveys in autumn 1991 and summer 1993 have provided national data on changing employment patterns, the implementation of new and novel personnel policies, the assessment of the effects of change, and indicators of future priorities. These national surveys are complemented by a small number of case studies, which will 'follow through' in greater detail the changing role, and context, of the personnel function by regular group and individual interviews with personnel practitioners in NHS trusts and directly managed units. These case studies began in the spring of 1991.

This chapter presents material from a number of sources including semi-structured interviews at unit level with both personnel directors and senior managers outside the personnel function and from the 1991 benchmark survey of the NHS personnel function at district health authority (DHA) level in England and Wales, and at health board level in Scotland. The survey involved all 190 authorities in England, the nine in Wales, and the 15 Health Boards in Scotland. Despite the additional workload which the personnel function had to cope with at that time, the survey achieved a satisfactory usable response rate of just under 50 per cent. At the time of writing the follow-up surveys of NHS trusts, District Health Authorities/Boards and Family Health Service Authorities are under way.

The Pre-Reform Personnel Function

Although the NHS is labour intensive, the pre-reform NHS personnel function was limited in scope and often fragmented in responsibility. There was heavy reliance on centralised national negotiations of terms and conditions of employment, with local activity primarily being 'hiring and firing' and dealing with individual grievances. Other activities, for example training and development and manpower planning, varied markedly in depth and effect in different health authorities. In the early 1970s, the most senior personnel 'manager' was of officer status, with responsibilities for giving advice to line managers (Department of Health and Social Security, 1973) and was usually accountable to the district administrator, one of four senior officers (administrator, doctor, treasurer and nurse) who practised 'management by consensus' in each authority.

The role of the pre-reform NHS personnel function was caricatured in a recent National Association of Health Service Personnel Officers: Scotland (NAHSPO) document as:

> *Traditionally personnel management in the Service has had both operational and strategic dimensions. The main thrust of its contribution, however, has been operational — providing support services and 'fire fighting' problems and issues as they arise . . . the true strategic functions of human resource planning, organisational development and facilitating performance have been relatively under-developed . . . the capability to effectively create, integrate and implement a comprehensive human resource management agenda has not been developed (NAHSPO, 1991).*

The Griffiths reforms in the early 1980s replaced consensus management with general management, and the team of four senior officers with a single general manager who had overall accountability and responsibility for the management of services in the health authority. Griffiths also marked the beginning of an increased role for the personnel function:

> *Devolution in personnel matters will imply a strengthening of the personnel function at each level and its close support of line management* (Griffiths, 1983, para 24).

Personnel also secured a voice at the centre with Griffiths' recommendation that a personnel director be appointed to the new NHS Management Board whose main responsibility would be:

> *. . . to ensure that personnel relations support the . . . more thrusting and committed style of management which are implicit in our recommendations* (para 22).

The new personnel director was charged with, amongst other things, reviewing remuneration systems and conditions of service . . . *so as to overcome the lack of incentives in the present system,* to ensure the operation of policies for performance appraisal and career development, to review recruitment and selection procedures and to examine staffing levels.

Personnel 'officers' became 'managers' or 'directors', the human resource planning of medical and nursing staff, previously often dealt with by separate functions, began to be amalgamated and integrated with planning other staff groups and the focus of the personnel function began to shift from a primarily advisory role to one that was part of a corporate business team. Just as Griffiths signalled the importation of private sector business management principles, it also represented the beginnings of the establishment of private sector human resource management practices (Lloyd and Siefert, 1992). In sum, Griffiths provided the structural changes necessary to enable the organisational and cultural changes implicit in the reforms of the 1990s. Devolution of responsibility in the personnel function did not begin with the reforms of the 1990s; the Griffiths restructuring had already begun the process by the mid-1980s.

The Post Reform Personnel Function

The process of change in the role of the NHS personnel function, begun with the implementation of the Griffiths recommendation, was accelerated by the publication of *Working for Patients* in 1989. The three central elements of the reform – decentralisation of responsibility, the establishment of self-governing NHS trusts, and the introduction of the purchaser/provider split – all have significant implications for the management of labour costs and of NHS personnel. One of the driving forces behind the reforms was improved cost containment and, with labour costs representing the major element of expenditure, was an obvious area for improvement in terms of 'value for money'. Whilst there were major challenges for the personnel function in the thrust of the reforms, there was little specific guidance in the content of the 1990 Act as to how the function should meet these challenges. There was little mention of non-medical employment issues, and few considerations of employment practice. Beyond the general assumptions built into the reforms that devolution, decentralisation and flexibility should be articles of faith in the post-reform management of NHS personnel, there was no detailed blueprint for change. Indeed, such an approach would have cut across the grain of the reforms, which places the emphasis on local management's right and responsibility to manage.

The collective impact on the personnel function of decentralisation, the establishment of NHS trusts, and the introduction of the purchaser/provider split can best be assessed by examining in turn three central requirements of the function: to maintain effective staffing levels and skill mix; to establish appropriate employee relations policy and procedures; and to become increasingly involved in pay determination. These are clearly not the only issues involved but the benchmark survey of the NHS personnel function in 1991 revealed that these were, together with training and development, the main areas in which new initiatives were being planned by the personnel function: see Table 1.

Table 1: Initiatives Planned by the NHS Personnel Function	% Respondents
Training and development	29
Pay and reward strategy	27
Skill mix reviews	15
Employee relations	14
Improved staff communications	11
Equal opportunities	9
Information technology	8
Job evaluation	6
Workforce planning	5
Unit labour costs	4
Performance appraisal	2
Women into management	2
Succession planning	2

Source: Institute of Manpower Studies Survey 1991

The following sections review these three key challenges: staffing levels and mix, employee relations and pay determination. We then examine the NHS personnel function's response to these challenges.

Staffing Levels and Mix

The post-reform creation of provider units – directly managed units and self-governing NHS trusts – established several hundred employing units which had greater freedom, in theory at least, in employment practice than had the pre-reform district health authorities and boards. NHS trusts in particular, were given quasi-autonomous status.

It is important, however, not to overstate either the lack of freedom and flexibility in the pre-reform NHS, or the extent to which new freedoms exist, or have been grasped in the post reform NHS. Whilst the national Whitley system established terms and conditions of employment in the pre-reform NHS, there was little in the way of centralised planning of non-medical staffing levels or staff mix in that period.

In relation to staffing levels and staffing mix at local level, the effect of the reforms is less about dismantling bureaucracy than about stimulating management to review custom and practice and historical staffing patterns, with a view to achieving better value for money. The perpetuation of historical staffing levels and working patterns all too often results as much from a lack of unambiguous management responsibility as from the absence of appropriate competences. In this context the personnel function has been caught up in the continuing tension between those health care professionals focusing on patient care, and those managers responsible for cost-effective use of resources but constrained by a lack of clinical knowledge. In combative language, this has sometimes been characterised by managers as 'taking on the professions', or ending 'professional tribalism'. Recent comments by Roy Lilley, Chair of Homewood Trust, may reflect those of the more radical trusts. On professional boundaries he has written:

> *How much health care can be delivered by a nurse? It would appear that the only limits are to the imagination of the doctors who may or may not go into partnership with the nurses . . . Medical professionals, always pushing at the leading edge of technology and medical knowledge, are curiously shy about real, radical change (The Health Summary, November 1992).*

In the new market for health care, providers' income no longer derives from regional budgets but from purchasers choosing to buy their services. Competition in this market will, initially at least, be based largely on cost comparisons. The key requirement for management in provider units will be to achieve reductions in their costs, so that they remain competitive. The importance of labour costs has focused attention on staffing levels, mix and unit labour costs. Attempts are being made to devise and implement appropriate measures of unit labour costs which would provide local management, and external auditors, with a mechanism to map changes in cost-effectiveness over time and between providers (Harper, 1992). Increased use of temporary staff, contracting out of some hotel services, and shift pattern changes, are occurring as the NHS explores methods of saving on the pay bill.

The personnel function is increasingly involved in reviews of skill mix or grade mix, undertaken to identify the most cost-effective level of staffing, and mix of different grades or occupational groups. For example, the re-profiling exercise in the diagnostic imaging department of Bradford Hospitals Trust led to proposals for revising the proportion of clerical workers and radiography helpers, a new grade of associate radiographer, and far fewer, but more highly trained, graduate radiographers (NHSME, 1992a). In many cases skill mix exercises are instigated and conducted by clinical managers.

These activities sometimes lead to conflict with the representative organisations of staff being scrutinised in these reviews. There is increasing debate about the impact on the quality of care provided of some of the skill mix changes which are occurring. Latest national figures indicate a downturn in the numbers of staff in some groups, for example, qualified nurses, which have been the subject of skill mix reviews. If the recommendations of some reviews, such as the NHS Management Executive Value for Money Unit reviews of staffing in outpatients and in district nursing, were to be applied nationally, there would be a further significant proportionate decline in the number of qualified nursing staff, to be replaced by care assistants. Eric Caines, the former NHS personnel director, has argued that in nursing 'if we get the skill mix right, we could bring the number of qualified staff down from 80 per cent to 40 per cent which would bring our costs down astronomically' (The Health Summary, November 1992). More recently, (*The Guardian*, May 1993) he has claimed that overall staffing levels in the NHS could be reduced by 20 per cent with no effect on patient care.

Health care assistants (HCAs) are beginning to be employed in some units. These generic support workers are not linked to any one profession; their training is not profession-specific, but related to National Vocational Qualifications (NVQs). They are envisaged as being deployed flexibly, and – crucially, for the development of local pay determination – they are not bound by Whitley Council rates or other national terms and conditions of employment.

Directly managed units have been able to set local pay for HCAs since

1990, though many continue to place new HCA posts on nursing auxiliary rates. West Cumbria Health Authority is one example where new HCAs are starting on lower pay than the bottom of the national pay scale for nurses but, unlike the latter, they have a career structure with job descriptions based on NVQs. When the new pay and terms were offered to existing nursing auxiliaries in 1991, just under two thirds accepted them (Industrial Relations Services, 1992).

HCAs are likely to be in widespread use in the NHS by the mid or late 1990s working in support of and in some situations instead of, clinical professionals in nursing and the therapy professions. New initiatives in the development of patient focused hospitals described below are also likely to lead to the blurring of traditional professional boundaries and lines of demarcation, with the likely development of multi-skilled care workers. Personnel practitioners will be centrally involved in the local planning and implementation of these changes.

There has been surprisingly little attempt to conduct a proper evaluation of the cost effectiveness of skill mix changes. Whilst the cost savings, in terms of reduced pay bill can be readily demonstrated, little attention has been paid to evaluating the broader impact on costs and quality, in terms of employee productivity and effectiveness of care provided (Buchan and Ball, 1991). Some research has indicated that there is a direct relationship between the grade mix of nursing staff used and measures of the quality of care provided – the lower the average mix, the lower the quality of care (Carr-Hill *et al*, 1992).

One possible constraint on further developments towards a less skilled or qualified, but cheaper NHS workforce, could be the parallel drive towards lowering costs of patient care by reduced average length of patient stay. The achievement of higher turnover of patients, with a higher average acuity level may place a limit on such skill mix changes, as there will be a requirement of highly skilled staff to treat high dependency patients.

It is in the area of achieving change in staffing levels and mix that the NHS personnel function has made the most obvious impact during the course of the reforms. Early assessment of the likely impact of the reforms on personnel have, however, focused on the effects of trusts and local pay bargaining, and often underestimated the less high profile (because more transitional) results of staffing reviews. Research on the impact of the reforms on the personnel function has tended to be based on snapshot studies examining the issues of pay determination and employee relations policies, often focusing specifically on trusts (*eg* Industrial Relation Services 1991; Corby, 1992). These studies have therefore often underestimated the impact of less high profile, and more incremental developments occurring as a result of staffing changes and workforce re-profiling. In this context, case studies can provide a more revealing insight into the approach of management. Based on case studies in eight trusts and 15 directly managed units in 1991, Buchan (1992) noted:

> *In general, rather than focusing directly on pay levels, managers were look-ing to skill mix alterations and skill substitution as the main source of costs savings in the short term. There was a recognition that this focus on more effec-tive deployment of staff, and on altering the mix of staff employed (usually by reducing the number of comparatively 'expensive' trained staff) was likely to prove a less problematical source of immediate cost savings than would a con-centration of effort directly on the pay bill.*

It should be stressed that staffing reviews and staffing changes are not solely, or mainly a characteristic of self-governing trusts – indeed some of the most radical changes in approaches to managing staffing levels are occurring in directly managed units. The reforms, by creating the purchaser/provider split, have focused management attention on labour costs, and have stimulated change. However, some alterations in the profile of the NHS workforce would have been occurring even without the NHS reforms. The implementation of Project 2000, the new system of nurse education would, in any event, have altered significantly the skill mix of the nursing workforce.

Whilst most of the activity of the personnel function in relation to achieving changes in staffing levels and costs has been in relation to skill substitution, particularly in increasing the proportion of healthcare assistants and other cheaper support staff operating in clinical areas, or to alterations in shift patterns, some units have adopted a more radical approach to re-profiling the workforce, attempting to replace traditional working patterns, work practices and organisational structures. 'Patient focused care' is the label attached to a variety of new methods of organising the delivery of care, originating in the USA (Brider, 1992), which involve patient and ward centred care delivered by multi-skilled care teams. It is claimed that patient focused care will enable significant savings in labour and administrative costs through changes in skill mix, working patterns and staffing levels. Andersen UK, one of the management consultancies involved in patient focused care in the NHS, also claim that US experience shows that patient focused care can improve staff morale, reduce sickness absence and turnover (Andersen, 1992).

Whilst some doubts have been raised about the claimed potential cost savings (Davies, 1993), it is clear that the introduction of the patient focused approach, so far restricted to a number of pilot hospital sites in the UK and with little evaluation, will also have far reaching implications for training, for trade union/professional bodies and for collective bargaining (Fuchter and Garside, 1992).

Such ambitious exercises are comparatively few in number at present but represent a much more radical departure from conventional personnel practice in the NHS, involving in some cases the possible de-recognition of trade unions, the creation of new grades and employee categories, the establishment of new working practices and the introduction of performance or skill based pay.

As yet the overall impact of changes in staffing patterns and levels is difficult to assess, both in terms of changes in employee numbers and in terms of their effect on the level, cost and quality of service being provided. Change is incremental with different units moving at a different pace. In terms of overall effect on the NHS pay bill, it is apparent that ancillary staff have been reducing in significance since the 1970s as a result of contracting out, that the nursing pay bill peaked in comparative importance in 1988 because of clinical grading, and that the administrative and general management pay bill is increasing: see Figure 1.

Employee Relations

Employee relations in the pre-reform NHS were heavily unionised, with policy and procedure determined nationally and interpreted and applied locally. As with much else in the public sector, the employee relations system in the NHS was a post war development of the welfare state, with Whitley Councils being established for the various staff groups.

The Whitley system of National Councils was comprised of management and union representatives. Little changed from the inception of the NHS in 1948 until the implementation of the reforms in the 1990s. At the time of writing, the Councils remain in place and with much of their centralised power intact. Often characterised as unwieldy, unresponsive and overly bureaucratic, the Whitley Council system has been a major target for criticism and has occasionally been the target for reform (see for example, McCarthy, 1976). The whole thrust of the current reforms, with their emphasis on local management's right and responsibility to manage, the anti-bureaucratic language, and the freedom given to self-governing trusts to establish their own local employee relations machinery, reflected political and managerial frustration with the lack of national political control and

Figure 1   Breakdown of the NHS Wages Bill

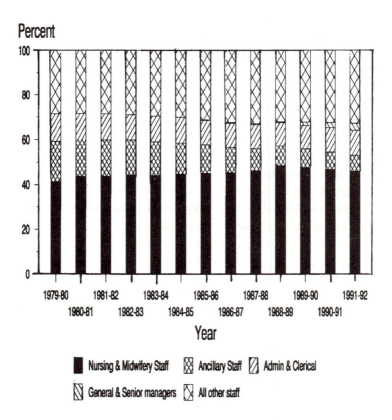

local managerial influence over the Whitley system.

Whitley is an easy target for criticism and jibes about bureaucracy, yet the implementation of the reforms has seen no rapid move away from its sphere of influence. This is perhaps unsurprising, given some of the checks incorporated in the NHS Act: for example NHS employees whose workplaces become self-governing trusts have the right to remain on Whitley terms and conditions. But it also reflects a pragmatism at local level which is not required by national level politicians and civil servants. If the influence of Whitleyism is to be reduced, or ended, some alternative system for employee relations has to be in place.

In an organisation where centralised negotiations are institutionalised, and where there has been little requirement to develop local level collective representation skills (see Lloyd and Siefert, 1992), such changes cannot happen overnight, even if all the parties involved were to regard them as desirable. Initial opposition to such developments from trade unions, and a 'wait and see' approach by some managers prior to the results of the 1992 election, also acted to slow the pace of change.

The transfer of undertakings regulations provide for the transfer of all collective agreements including those covering union recognition. New employers are obliged to recognise trade unions to the same extent as former employers. However, as Corby (1992a) has noted, the pre-reform employers, the district health authorities, had:

> . . . not recognised trade unions in respect of negotiations over pay and other terms and conditions as these are almost entirely determined at national level . . . so if the Trust wishes to seek changes to union recognition arrangements after the transfer . . . it is free to do so.

In the self-governing trusts, there have been few examples of attempts to de-recognise trade unions (COHSE, 1991) although some trusts are attempting to set up alternative in-house staff associations. According to Corby (1992b), two trusts, United Bristol Healthcare Trust and the Lincolnshire Ambulance and Health Transport Service Trust, have refused all union negotiating rights.

The main effort of personnel management in employing units has been directed at determining simplified and viable mechanisms for conducting employee relations. This activity has mainly been directed at establishing 'single table' recognition agreements, where all employee relations activity is conducted in one forum, with a limited number of union representatives, in some cases full time officials being excluded or having observer status only. Often it has been left to the unions themselves to decide which of their representatives will sit at the table. For example, Table 2 shows the staff side representations at Manchester Central Hospitals Trust which followed discussion with the 22 staff organisations previously recognised. The apportionment of places on the new 12 person joint negotiating and consultative committee was determined by the staff organisations.

A move to function based negotiating structures with representatives drawn from different clinical directorates rather than unions, is also said to be being widely considered at, for example, Mount Vernon Hospital, Cornwall Community Healthcare Trust, North Devon Health Care Trust, Newcastle Mental Health Trust.

Even with political and labour market conditions weakening the stance of the unions, most local managers are tending to adopt a pragmatic and long term approach, rather than going for radical short term change. New recognition agreements tend therefore to reflect Whitley in terms of the number of staff groups recognised. The most significant changes in approach to employee relations have tended to occur in trusts which are smaller and simpler in terms of staffing numbers and mix – for example, the ambulance

Table 2: Manchester Central Hospitals Trust Staff Side Representation on the JNCC

	No. of Places
NUPE	2
NALGO	2
RCN	2
MSF	1
Fed. of Professional Organisations	1
Fed. of Craftworkers	1
COHSE	1
BMA	1
RCM	1

Source: Industrial Relations Services, Employment Trends 518

service trusts and community or priority service units. The Northumbria Ambulance Service Trust's single union deal gave sole negotiating rights to the Association of Professional Ambulance Personnel, while Homewood Trust's agreement is said to be a virtual no-strike deal through the use of conciliation and binding pendulum arbitration.

It is important however, not to characterise the current employee relations situation in the NHS as being a 'steady state'. The comparative absence of radical short term change should not be taken as an indication that personnel managers do not have radical plans for change – it reflects rather their pragmatism in adopting an incremental approach which can more flexibly respond to changes in the political and labour market climates. Reporting on plans for change in case study units and trusts prior to the reforms, Buchan (1992) noted that:

> *No Trust or directly managed unit is a green field site on which a new industrial relations culture and pay determination process could be set up on April 1st 1991. Organisational status may have changed on that date, but the organisational politics, the personalities and the local industrial relations custom, practice and history remain.*

However, most managers were planning for change:

> *Main stated objectives of {personnel managers} was to reduce the number of recognised trade unions, to simplify local procedures, and to limit the bargaining rights of unions. Some managers stated that their long term aim was to end collective representation of the workforce and to deal with employees on an individual basis* (Buchan 1992).

Pay Determination

Paralleling the general employee relations structure of the pre-reform NHS, the pay of NHS employees was determined nationally, either within Whitley Councils, or by independent Pay Review Bodies. The Review Bodies which, from 1983, made recommendations on pay for doctors, dentists, nursing staff and the professions allied to medicine – in total, about half the NHS workforce – presented a particular problem to pre-reform governments and NHS management. As independent bodies, their recommendations were not, in theory at least, cash limited. As such, they could, and sometimes did, make recommendations for increases in the pay bill which were higher than governments wished to fund, or management thought were required.

The centralised system of pay determination was criticised by some in language similar to that used to deride the Whitley system – it was 'wasteful', 'unresponsive', 'lacked flexibility'. Various attempts to provide local supplements had been tried, or suggested, in the 1970s and 1980s, such as the establishment of local incentive payments for ancillary workers (Lloyd and Siefert, 1992) and the introduction of flexible pay supplements for senior staff and for administrative and clerical staff. The flexible local pay supplements, managed centrally, were by no means universally successful, and were not welcomed by all managers (Buchan, 1992). Some regarded the schemes as neither local nor particularly flexible.

Such schemes were tinkering at the margins of the centralised system. The NHS reforms of the late 1980s raised the prospect of a more fundamental move away from centralised pay determination, both as a result of the setting up of self-governing trusts, and because the focus on labour costs stimulated by the purchaser/provider split was bound to increase demands from local management to have greater control of pay bill size and allocation. Further stimulus came from the Patient's Charter, which emphasised the need for the pay of NHS employees to be more closely linked to local performance (Department of Health, 1991b).

As with NHS employee relations systems in general, the post reform pace of change in the ways NHS pay is determined has been slow – probably slower than those responsible for the reforms would have envisaged. A minority of trusts have begun to establish performance pay schemes, or move towards a single pay spine for all groups of employees, but most units – both trusts and directly managed units, continue to pay Whitley and Review Body rates. Generally change has been most evident where trust managers have concentrated on discrete areas of operation (for example hotel services, medical secretaries) which are not at the core of direct patient care. Only a handful of trusts departed from national pay setting in the first year of the reform and these were all ambulance or community care trusts with smaller and less complex organisational structuring than acute units: see Table 3. For the most part their 1991/92 settlements were between 5 and 5.75 per cent compared to the 4.75 per cent rise for most NHS staff. A further six trusts were reported to have departed from national pay setting in 1992/93.

A number of factors can be identified which explain this evolutionary rather than revolutionary change. Some have argued that a looser labour

---

Table 3: NHS Trusts Departing from National Pay Setting

1991/92
Homewood Trust
Lincolnshire Ambulance Trust
Northumbria Ambulance Trust
West Dorset Community Health Trust

1992/93
New Possibilities NHS Trust
Norfolk Ambulance Trust
Pembrokeshire Trust
West Dorset General Hospital Trust
West Dorset Mental Health Trust
Essex Ambulance Trust

Source: Industrial Relations Services, Pay and Benefits Bulletin 311 (September 1992); Incomes Data Services, Report Supplement (February 1993)

---

market, and the increasing flexibility being incorporated into Whitley and other NHS pay settlements already enables trusts to respond effectively to local pay pressures, thus mitigating against any immediate need to depart from national pay settlements.

In examining the stimulus for change in nurses' pay determination, Buchan (1992) identified two major constraints on rapid change – funding limitations and the absence of in-house capabilities in many local personnel management departments to manage the complexities of local pay determination. Table 4 reports additional constraints which were recognised by the Personnel Director at Manchester Central Hospitals Trust.

Similarly, the paucity of wage cost and related information was claimed to have forced Mid-Cheshire Hospitals Trust to restrict plans for local pay negotiations to health care assistants and hotel services in 1992/93 (Workman and Turnbull, 1993). Any attempt to establish a new pay structure, separate from Whitley can be an expensive exercise, particularly if there is an attempt to consolidate the pay of all NHS occupations on a single pay

---

Table 4: Manchester Central Hospitals NHS Trust

A first wave trust with over 6,000 employees has the long term aim of setting pay and conditions locally. Three constraints were identified by the Personnel Director in the short term:

- the trust had decided not to change the terms and conditions of staff on transfer to its employment;
- management time to implement local pay determination was not available;
- the appropriate information systems were not in place.

Source: Industrial Relations Services, Employment Trends 518

---

spine. Performance pay can also raise both employee expectations and the overall pay bill. The Government has argued that performance pay should be funded out of efficiency savings and without recourse to additional central government money. However, with continued funding constraints, and with a Government imposed pay limit of 1.5 per cent in 1993/94, there has been little room for manoeuvre in the shape of pay determination. Any continuation of pay restraint in the public sector, either directly or indirectly, is likely to limit the scope for pay flexibility.

In the pre-reform NHS, there was no requirement for local NHS personnel departments to have significant capabilities to determine pay locally. The radical policy changes signalled by the 1990 Act were not achievable in the short term, in practical terms. Pay determination at local level requires an expertise in negotiating, planning and maintaining pay and grading structures which was not evident in most NHS personnel departments – for the simple reason that such expertise had not been needed in the pre-reform NHS (Haywood and Vinograd, 1992).

These skills are now being rapidly developed, or acquired and it would be a mistake not to anticipate that the pace of change will now accelerate. Not only will practical expertise be increasingly available, and labour market conditions favourable to management, but the momentum to depart from standard, nationally determined, pay and conditions will increase as a greater proportion of NHS units achieve trust status. Ironically, the greatest change in payment systems has been in the pay of trust personnel managers and other senior management colleagues, who are now paid on individual contracts with performance related supplements.

The key skills being acquired by NHS personnel managers as they prepare for a greater degree of local pay determination are in employee communication, negotiation, job evaluation, financial modelling and labour market analysis. In particular, a number of job evaluation schemes are being developed by different consortia of NHS personnel managers and management consultants. Trade unions are also preparing for the mid-1990s by training local stewards and representatives to have similar skills.

At the time of writing, changes in pay determination as a result of the NHS reforms are more apparent than real. This may reflect the fact that existing trust employees have the right to retain their national pay and conditions, and the fact that recession has curtailed labour market pressure to set local rates at a higher level. There is little doubt, however, that the pace of change is likely to accelerate rapidly through the mid-1990s, as personnel departments acquire the skills to manage pay locally, as labour costs are increasingly the focus for management action, and as trusts become the norm. The structures and skills required for local pay determination are being developed. When they are in place, activity may focus increasingly on the core areas of the service.

The Changing Face of the NHS Personnel Function

The previous sections have highlighted the key challenges for the NHS personnel function arising out of the decentralisation, an increasing focus on cost control, and the establishment of self-governing trusts. Three main challenges were identified: achieving changes in staffing level and mix; establishing local employee relations policy and procedure; and managing local pay determination. Table 5 summarises these challenges.

In examining each of the challenges it became apparent that there was little evidence of rapid and radical change in most trusts and units. It was noted that a fundamental part of the NHS reform was the devolution of control to trust and unit level, and that the devolution of personnel responsibilities from district to unit level had already begun as a result of the mid-1980s Griffiths reforms. The Institute of Manpower Studies' survey reveals that almost a fifth of district health authorities/health boards had devolved at least some personnel responsibilities before 1990: see Table 6.

Table 5: The Changing Face of the NHS Personnel Function

	From	To
Managing Staffing Levels	historical norms	skill mix reviews re-profiling zero-based staffing unit labour costs
Managing Employee Relations	national power base many unions influential local interpretation multi-table	local power base fewer unions recognised local management and consultation single table
Managing Pay	national negotiation national grading criteria incremental progression national agreements on shift pay etc	local negotiation or determination local pay spine performance based progression buy out national supplements

Source: Institute of Manpower Studies

Table 6: Devolving the District Personnel Function

	% districts with devolved or partly devolved personnel function
Pre 1989	7
1989	12
1990	40
1991	41

Source: Institute of Manpower Studies Survey 1991

Significantly, the survey also reveals that the main thrust of devolution has been in terms of the more routine aspects of personnel management – recruitment and selection, employee relations, health and safety, welfare. More high level and strategic elements – pay, management development, manpower planning – were, at the time of the initial survey, more likely to be retained at district level. This probably reflects the availability and development of skills, and the potential for economies of scale. Overall, nearly a quarter of district personnel functions claimed to have fully devolved all aspects of personnel management to units or trusts. In contrast, 13 per cent had not fully devolved any of the personnel functions' activities. There was a marked geographic pattern to this, with the Welsh districts and Scottish health boards having devolved the least. Scotland in particular is generally a year behind in the pace of change.

Many trusts have a stated aim, at least in the long term, of taking managerial devolution one stage further – to line managers at, where that exists, clinical directorate level. This would leave the central personnel function, where that exists, with responsibility for developing strategy and providing line managers with the relevant information to implement that strategy. Some respondents to the survey commented that this devolution and decentralisation of the function could reduce and obscure its role and influence.

In early 1993, the NHS personnel function was in an interim phase, with some personnel departments making considerable progress towards meeting the main challenges of staffing levels, employee relations and local pay. But the majority having only just begun to face up to the demands of managing employee relations and local pay determination. In many ways, the significant changes so far have been in organisational culture and individual attitude. Approaches to personnel management practice, in employee relations and in managing staff levels, which would have been unthinkable in the pre-reform NHS are now accepted, albeit grudgingly by some, as the way forward. The first years of reform have been more about the personnel function accepting the need for change and arming itself with the expertise required to achieve that change, the next few years will be more about practical attempts to secure change. The pace of reform will accelerate as the broad-brush aims set out in the 1990 Act are adapted into locally achievable targets and objectives.

The pace of change has varied markedly in different units, partly as a result of variations in the level of resources and expertise available to personnel departments, and partly as a result of variations in the choice of approach to change. A minority of units – mainly trusts – have adopted a 'big bang' approach, going for rapid and radical change. Most units, because of lesser resources or greater pragmatism, are adopting a more incremental approach.

Labour market conditions and the general political climate have been conducive to these changes. General economic recession and a loose labour market have markedly reduced the effect of the skill shortages which were such a feature of the immediately pre-reform NHS. The re-election of the Conservative Government in 1992 has also provided NHS management with the likelihood of a five year planning cycle, and the continued series of employment legislation, begun in the early 1980s, has reduced the effectiveness of the trade unions.

Despite variations in the pace of, and approach to change, there is little disagreement amongst personnel managers as to what they envisage the final objectives to be – a personnel function operating in association with line and general management in determining and realising the unit business plan. To this end, the personnel function will have key responsibilities in managing labour costs, through periodic reviews of staffing levels, mix, and deployment, and through participation in local pay determination with a 'slimmed' down group of trade unions, or, in some cases, with no trade unions.

Many local personnel functions are some way short of realising this perceived 'ideal'. Whilst new skills and expertise are being acquired, through extensive use of training, much of it organised by the NHS Management Executive and by Regional Health Authorities, and by the import of skills from other sectors – either temporarily, by the use of management consultants, or permanently, through the recruitment of managers with experience in local negotiations, labour market analysis etc – there remains an expertise shortfall in many departments.

The Institute of Manpower Studies' survey of the personnel function in 1991 revealed that, at that time, pay and planning issues were secondary to more operational 'hire and fire' duties, but that extensive use was being made of external consultants and other professional support. Significantly, 45 per cent of respondents had used external consultants to advise on aspects of their changing role in the last year: see Table 7. The main reasons for using external support related to irregular demand (56 per cent), lack of in-house expertise (20 per cent) or both (22 per cent).

The survey also revealed a lack of confidence about the personnel function's ability to deliver the new NHS, coupled with an anxiety to demonstrate the function's worth in terms of cost-effectiveness. Asked about their key concerns for the function over the next two years (1992/93), three of the four most frequently raised issues concerned the skills and calibre of NHS personnel professionals – see Table 8 – and the anticipated pace of change.

The survey also revealed fears over job security and a sense of low morale

Table 7: NHS Personnel: Use of Other Professions

	% Respondnts
Information technology	82
Human resource consultants	45
Occupational psychologists	37
Labour market analysts	29
Operational research/statistical staff	24

Source: Institute of Manpower Studies Survey, 1991

Table 8: NHS Personnel Professionals: Key Concerns

	% Respondents
Slowness in developing new skills	29
Insufficient high calibre staff	27
Need to develop new skills	23
Resourcing the function	21
Recruitment and retention	14
The amount of change needed	24

Source: Institute of Manpower Studies Survey, 1991

within some district personnel functions. At best these would provide an inevitably smaller personnel service to the purchaser (district health authority) level or would disappear entirely as purchasers buy into consortium personnel services; for example, the West London Human Resource Consortium – a distant arm of the Hillingdon District Health Authority – provides agency support to more provider units across three West London districts. Some respondents commented that servicing purchasers inevitably means the loss of professional development opportunities for the personnel function.

In a recent report, the NHS personnel function in Scotland highlighted the challenge it faced (NAHSPO, 1991) identifying shortfalls in competences in seven key areas: see Table 9.

In a previous section it was noted that 'the reform agenda and direction of change had been set nationally, whilst the pace of change owed more to local capabilities'. It was also stressed that as trusts become the norm, in terms of local organisational structure, the implementation of change at local level is likely to accelerate, and what remains of the pre-reform national structure (Whitley Councils, Review Bodies) will come under greater pressure.

For some at the centre the lack of rapid progress has led to a deal of frustration. Eric Caines, Personnel Director, speaking at a conference in the summer of 1990 stated his hope that the Pay Review Bodies and Whitley Councils would have '. . . come to the end of their natural life within 18 months to two years'. Two years later, in November 1992, both were still in place, causing Caines to comment:

> *Somebody needs to kick the crutches away and tell trusts to stand on their own two feet on pay. The central systems – Whitley Councils and Review Bodies – should be buried without delay. But Ministers do not want to upset the professions or cause trouble with the unions . . . The professional organisations are the great problem of the next five years; it's time to kill them off (Times Health Supplement, November 1992).*

There is likely to be increasing organisational tension in attempting to maintain discrete but overlapping national and local employee relations policies and pay determination practice. As Buchan (1992) noted:

> *Government ministers may express public commitment to the existence of the Review Body, but they are also presiding over organisational changes which are likely to, at the very least, undermine its role.*

Table 9: The Preparedness of the Personnel Function

Key Area	Level of Preparedness
Corporate and strategic issues	'. . . the capability to effectively create, integrate and implement a comprehensive human resource management agenda has not been developed'.
Employee relations	'. . . the function's competence in such skill areas as communications and developing genuine staff participation are not high'.
Employee services	'. . . Personnel Directors will have to ensure that their support staff at an appropriate level develop these skills so as to free the more senior personnel staff. . .'
Manpower utilisation	'This is an area which is relatively new to those in the personnel function and, generally, the appropriate skill and experiences are scarce'.
Organisational development	'Skills in this area are patchy and there is an urgent need to build on development and share what experience exists'.
Regional rewards	'Experience of local pay determination is . . . limited and the function will have to develop organisational, planning and negotiating skills . . . There is an absence of meaningful information about pay markets or about unit labour costs and there is not a developed facility to assess the costs and implications of particular initiatives or to review their effectiveness'.
Training and development	'Those in the personnel function have varying experiences in this area. The disaggregation of specialist Board training departments and the devolution of this aspect of personnel work to units and Trusts must not be allowed to happen without those working in the personnel function at provider level acquiring and developing such skills'.

Source: National Association of Health Service Personnel Officers: Scotland (1991)

Table 10: Regional Pay and Labour Market Intelligence Units

Region	Name	Date	Comments
Northern	Remuneration + Development Section	–	Part of human resources strategy division
Yorkshire	Pay and Labour Market Information Unit	1990	Salary database; analysis of travel-to-work areas. Quarterly bulletin
Trent	–	–	Under consideration
East Anglian	Pay and Benefits Information Unit	1989	Quarterly bulletin; pay workshops; developing database
North West Thames	Regional Pay Unit	1990	Monthly newsletter and other publications. Database being developed
North East Thames	Personnel Research Unit	1990	Newsletter; Local salaries database; salary surveys and other research
South East Thames	–	–	Under consideration

South West Thames	Reward Section	1990	Section with human resources division. Pay information on senior posts. Runs seminars for unit personnel
Wessex	–	–	Under consideration
Oxford	Pay Strategy and Research Unit	1987	Part of human resources; change of role since 1990 to assist units develop own reward strategies
South Western	Pay and Information Research Unit	1989	Bulletin. Local salaries database; pay workshops
West Midlands	Reward Information Unit	1990	Bulletin. Database on local labour market and salaries
Mersey	–	–	Under consideration
North Western	–	–	Under consideration
Scotland	Pay Intelligence Unit	1993	Contract to be awarded March

Source: Incomes Data Services/Institute of Manpower Studies

Prior to the re-organisation announced in October 1988, most regions carried out a new role providing units and trusts with information and guidance on manpower planning and labour market analysis, developing reward strategies and pay negotiations. Specifically, at least six of the 14 English Regional Health Authorities have established stand-alone regional pay and labour market intelligence units, while others have strengthened or modified existing pay information functions within the personnel or human resources divisions: see Table 10. In March 1993 Yorkshire RHA's pay and workforce information unit was awarded a three year contract with the Scottish Office to provide a similar service to local managers in Scotland. The main activities of the various pay intelligence units focus on: interpretation and dissemination of Whitley information; development of salary databases; provision of pay research; collection and analysis of external pay and labour market information; workshops and seminars. However, at the time of writing a number of these units are apparently being wound down or closed – leaving questions about who, if anyone, will be carrying out a strategic planning role in relation to staffing numbers and levels.

There will continue to be a need, in the post-reform NHS, for some co-ordination of provider activities and collaboration between provider units in the field of personnel management. If these activities are not conducted by region in the shape of a formally constituted department or grouping within an intermediate tier of NHS organisation they may be undertaken by more *ad hoc* and informal groupings of trusts and units sharing labour market and/or planning requirements.

One particular labour market with a strong requirement for pan-unit strategic planning is London. The likely changes in the profile of the London NHS workforce as a result of the Tomlinson report (1992) are likely to present particular challenges to the NHS personnel function, in terms of co-ordinating activity and in co-operating on restructuring and re-profiling. Tomlinson comments that:

> *For all those who wish or need to move . . . arrangements should be made to minimise the disruption to individuals and the service. It is important that these arrangements are seen to be fair and consistent across the Thames regions. We therefore recommend that measures to facilitate the possible re-deployment and relocation of staff should be explored* (para 222).

In particular, Tomlinson highlights the need to facilitate consultant mobility in the light of a possible reduction of between 450 and 680 consultant posts.

These challenges are likely to be repeated in other major urban areas such as Belfast, Birmingham, Tyneside and Glasgow, often, in proportionate terms, with bigger changes in service delivery and staffing levels than are occurring in London, but without the associated help or hindrance of independent reviews and national media attention.

Another unknown, in terms of organisational shape and structure, relates to the future control of staffing information. The thrust of resource management, and the need to develop computerised personnel information systems to underpin change, is creating an overlap between two traditionally discrete functions in the NHS – personnel and finance. In the pre-reform NHS, the finance function controlled the pay bill, which was the main and sometimes the only source of staffing data. The post reform need to integrate data on costs with data on staffing, and with data on service provision, to provide information on labour costs and productivity is moving the personnel function into 'traditional' finance territory. Greater co-operation between the two disciplines will be required in many NHS units; power broking and conflict resolution will be required in some.

The 1991 survey of the personnel function asked personnel directors to identify major changes for the function over the next two years. The responses, analysed in Table 11, confirm the anticipated devolution of personnel responsibilities to line management. They also indicate that the personnel function was seeking a more influential, pro-active and strategic role in terms of local pay determination, workforce planning and performance management. In addition, the survey reveals a concern with the professionalism, profile and cost effectiveness of the personnel function. Significantly, a fifth of respondents stated that managing the function itself actually consumed the most time of senior personnel staff.

A recent study of the effectiveness of the NHS personnel function (Guest and Peccei, 1992) has confirmed that the function is well short of the influential and strategic role it seeks. The objective of the study, which was commissioned by NHS Personnel, a Regional Personnel Directors working party, was to develop and validate a qualitative measure of personnel management effectiveness and to explore the influence on effectiveness of a range of personnel practices. The study showed that personnel management is rated by NHS managers as most effective in traditional areas of personnel administration – recruitment and selection, employee relations

– rather than in human resource management areas such as performance management and reward strategy. Even in trusts the personnel function was rated more for its administrative role. Interestingly, this study demonstrated that personnel managers think that they have more influence over major and day-to-day personnel decisions than line managers were willing to acknowledge.

Where Next for Personnel?

This chapter has reported on the first phase of the Institute's study, which has been to monitor the reforms as they were being introduced to the NHS. The general thrust of the chapter has been two-fold:

- the post reform pace of change in human resource management practices has, with some well-publicised exceptions, been slow and incremental, rather than revolutionary;
- the first years of reform have been largely about scene setting, as the personnel function has recognised the need for change and has begun to gear up with appropriate skills and competences.

The cost driven nature of the reforms has meant that the personnel function has become involved in implementing significant changes in staffing levels

Table 11: Major Changes Facing the Personnel Function

	% Respondents
Local pay determination	59
Completing devolution to unit level	27
Improved workforce planning	22
Performance management	22
Relating staffing levels to business plan	21
Greater professionalism	17
Devolution to line managers	16
Raising the profile	16
Cost effectiveness	8

Source: Institute of Manpower Studies Survey, 1991

Table 12: The Changing Face of the NHS Personnel Function

Less	More
Welfare oriented	Business oriented
Generalist service	Specialist function
Training	Appraisal and development
Collective	Individualised
Negotiation	Consultation and communication

Source: Institute of Manpower Studies

---

and staffing mix. This is the area in which the personnel function has so far secured the greatest degree of change – mainly because it has been the line of least resistance to the implementation of reforms. The greater challenge to the personnel function over the next few years will be to ensure that the short term cost savings so far secured are transferred into longer term productivity and quality benefits.

In general, the changes in the NHS personnel function can be characterised as the adoption and adaption of private sector human resource management techniques to meet the challenges of public sector reform: see Table 12.

This is not the first time, and will not be the last, that the public sector looks to the private sector for solutions. There are dangers in an over-reliance on importing off the shelf solutions – partly because these may be inherently inappropriate for a public sector context, and partly because 'fashionable' ideas may have become unfashionable by the time they are established and acted on in the public sector: developments in the importation of performance related pay into the NHS may fall into this trap (Thompson and Buchan, 1992). The appointment of a new NHS Personnel Director in 1993 may perhaps signal the move to a more pragmatic style of human resource management in the NHS and an acceleration in the pace of real change as personnel takes on the fully-rounded role that Caines identified.

9

IS IT FAIR?: EVALUATING THE EQUITY IMPLICATIONS OF THE NHS REFORMS

Margaret Whitehead

The National Health Service was founded on equity principles. It is therefore extraordinary that in the current mammoth upheavals so little official attention has been paid to monitoring and ensuring the protection of these principles. Debate was generated when various alternative proposals were made in the late 1980s, but nothing concrete was put in place to test any of the predictions in any systematic way. In consequence evidence from a variety of sources has to be pieced together from a very inadequate information base.

This chapter makes a start at assessing the equity implications by looking at what equity means in relation to the NHS and outlining the potential dangers and benefits in the current reforms. It then goes on to comment on the evidence available so far on whether any of these predicted effects have materialized, before discussing how these early results could be followed up on the research and policy development fronts.

Equitable Components of the NHS

Equity means different things to different people (Whitehead, 1990). It is a nebulous concept and consequently difficult to measure, though perhaps no more so than some of the terms abounding in current mission statements. However, there was a considerable degree of consensus when plans for the NHS were formulated about what would constitute a fairer, more equitable system than the previous one (Webster, 1988, 1992).

The NHS is built up of at least eight components that could be said to be equitable or fair, though no single measure would capture these different dimensions:

- Universal entitlement: Everyone is entitled to healthcare. There are no eligibility hurdles or means tests to overcome before being able to claim that right. Being universal also means there is no stigma attached to using it, as there sometimes is with systems designed just for the poor. At the same time it saves on the bureaucracy found in other systems where entitlement has to be checked.

- Pooling of financial risks: Funding of the system through general taxation means that financing is linked to ability to pay, and indeed has recently been shown to be one of the most progressive systems of ten OECD countries (van Doorslaer *et al*, 1993). It seems to be accepted as fair that people who need less health care share the costs of those who have greater needs for care.

- Free at the point of use: Detaching the use of the service from the ability to pay for it, removes financial barriers to access. Coupled with the pooling of financial risks it also removes the fear of being burdened with overwhelming costs if serious illness or disability occurs. Some see this as the chief benefit brought about by the NHS.

- Equality of access to a comprehensive range and geographic spread of services: It was decided right from the beginning that a broad range of services would come under the scheme, covering primary, secondary and tertiary care, chronic as well as acute episodes, so that the health care needs created by a much wider spectrum of conditions and people would be catered for. It also represented a commitment to improve the spread of such services around the country so that no community faced unreasonable time and travel barriers to access when in need of care. As a result of these decisions we now have one of the most highly developed primary care services in the world, delivered to people in their own homes or close by, supported by a network of emergency, secondary and planned tertiary care in most parts of the country.

- The same high standard of care for all: The notion of a two-tier service – basic for the poorer sections of the population and a superior level for those with more power and influence – was rejected. It is expected that people from all social groups will be treated with the same degree of respect and consideration and have access to the same quality of care.

- Selection on the basis of clinical need: This recognises that publicly-funded services should be available to all on the basis of need, rather than social or financial status and that when resources are scarce allocation will be on an equitable basis. Queue-jumping by less sick but more influential patients would be considered unacceptable by many professionals and public alike.

- The non-exploitative ethos of the service: The high degree of integrity and altruism of those working for the NHS has been noted (Schwartz and Aaron, 1984; Godber, 1988; Light, 1990b). The perception that they do not have overt financial incentives to exploit patients for profit can provide health professionals with a source of pride in their work and heightens the respect and trust given to them by patients. One indication that something of this nature might be operating in Britain comes from surveys of the perceived trustworthiness of different professionals, like lawyers, doctors, accountants etc. British doctors consistently come out well while American doctors come out badly in such ranking exercises (Higgins, 1988).

- Bevan's 'feel-good factor': Some go further and suggest that a benevolent 'feel-good factor' is important in continued popularity and public approval of the NHS, first articulated by Aneurin Bevan:

Society becomes more wholesome, more serene and spiritually healthier, if it knows that its citizens have at the back of their consciousness the knowledge that not only themselves, but all their fellows have access, when ill, to the best that medical skill can provide (Bevan, quoted in Foot, 1975).

The last two aspects would seem particularly elusive to tie down and measure. Nevertheless, it may be that some of the factors least amenable to precise measurement are ultimately the most important in maintaining an equitable system. They should certainly not be left out of the analysis.

It is, of course, debatable how far these fundamental objectives of the NHS have been achieved. After 40 or so years, we certainly still have inequalities in access to care, for example, Julian Tudor Hart's *Inverse Care Law* (Hart, 1971), is still evident in deprived areas (Whitehead, 1992). There has been erosion of some of the principles over the years; for example, prescription and dental charges have whittled away at the notion of 'free at the point of use'. But what seems to be accepted by a wide spectrum of commentators is that the system is far more equitable than the one it replaced (Webster, 1988; Godber, 1988; Black, 1991; Le Grand, 1992) and considerably more equitable than systems in many other developed countries (Radical Statistics Health Group, 1987; Barr *et al*, 1988; Ham *et al*, 1989).

Any major changes to the NHS should therefore be required to show that the gains outweigh the costs in terms of equity, as well as efficiency and effectiveness. This is particularly important at this critical time for the NHS, when the series of white papers and national initiatives are unfolding and have the potential to interact in a variety of ways – some unforeseen.

Potential Dangers

Much of the concern about various proposals for change in recent years has centred on the possible effects of increased competition and market forces on the distribution of resources and quality of services. The following exchange actually took place between two senior managers at a presentation I was making in Wales in 1993:

> *I fear that equity and the market are irreconcilable.*
>
> *No, I don't agree. The market is our servant. It is a means, not an end in itself. If equity is what we want, then the market should be required to deliver it.*

Clearly some see more dangers than others, but both the pessimistic and the optimistic in that exchange would agree that careful monitoring and control of the situation were necessary, because there are potentially major pitfalls.

In general, by the very nature of competition, there are both winners and losers, and in a health care market, not just the weakest services, but also the chronically sick and economically weaker members of society could be the main losers.

As far as services were concerned some have postulated that the less profitable, but not necessarily less efficient ones, might go to the wall (Parker, 1988; Whitehead, 1988; Williamson, 1989). This might erode the comprehensiveness of the NHS if, for example, services for the chronically sick were neglected in favour of rapid throughput services for acute conditions. Geographic spread and access might decline if services became concentrated in localities where it was easier to compete and make a profit. In any situation where there is competition for patients, under certain conditions some patients will be more attractive to providers than others. Patients could end up competing for the services rather than the other way round (Quam, 1989; Light, 1990a). For example, patients from disadvantaged groups and neighbourhoods can be more costly to treat than the average, because they have a higher prevalence of illness including 'expensive' chronic conditions. They may also take longer to recover, owing to malnutrition or poorer living conditions and lack of social support. If services are funded on some variant of average cost per case, then losses will be made on deprived patients. Providers may therefore try to avoid disadvantaged patients and communities, concentrating on serving more prosperous, healthier populations. Alternatively, the services provided for a set price may be of lower quality in a deprived area to keep within a capped budget (Dahlgren and Whitehead, 1992).

Purchasers in a market system may also seek to restrict the range and quality of services that they contract for in order to make savings and may be more selective about the cases in the population for which they agree to pay (Le Grand, 1992).

If patients are judged on their economic value to providers then such principles as selection on the basis of need, high standards of quality for all, equality of access and comprehensiveness are all threatened.

Health economists are quick to point out that true market conditions do not prevail in any health care system (Appleby *et al*, 1990; Le Grand, Propper and Robinson, 1992). All are regulated to a greater or lesser degree to restrict the consequences outlined above. There is, therefore, no question of giving market forces free rein. However there are specific details of the current British reforms which continue to raise concern.

In primary care it was predicted that the already apparent 'quality divide' would widen with the combined effects of *Working for Patients* and the 1990 GP contract (Pringle, 1989; Drummond *et al*, 1990). This was because the higher income, innovative practices mainly based in affluent surburban areas, would be in a better position to respond to the incentives on offer and improve their services to patients (Bosanquet and Leese, 1988; Leese and Bosanquet, 1989). With the GP fundholding scheme, only the most well-organised, larger practices, mainly in affluent areas, were eligible to take advantage of the generous development money on offer (King's Fund Institute, 1989; Glennerster *et al*, 1992; Ham, 1993). As originally formulated, the scheme was open to the charge that it would channel resources to those areas least in need (Coulter, 1992).

There were however, further concerns about the scheme creating a two-tier service. In the early days, opinion was split on whether it would be patients of the fundholder who would get the poorer deal. Some pointed to the incentives for fundholders to reduce hospital referral and prescribing for their patients in order to save money. This could have perverse effects if, for example, doctors delayed referral until the patient's condition turned into an emergency, as emergency treatment is paid for by district purchasers (Bevan *et al*, 1989). There was a related risk that fundholding would damage the doctor-patient relationship if patients perceived there was a conflict of interest (Drummond *et al*, 1990). On the other hand, the rules which allowed GPs to set up their own companies to supply some of the budgeted services to their own patients raised the possibility that referrals for those particular company services would be increased over and above the needs of their patients. The temptation for fundholders to 'cream-skim' – to drop 'expensive' patients from their list and attract healthier ones – was also noted (Scheffler, 1989; Bevan *et al*, 1989; Mullen, 1990b; Le Grand, 1992; Weiner and Ferris, 1990).

Others suggested that the patients of non-fundholding practices would be disadvantaged as their doctor's freedom of referral would be limited by the contracts set by the district (King's Fund Institute, 1989; Mullen, 1992) and that gains for fundholders' patients might be made at the expense of patients from non-fundholding practices (Coulter, 1992).

At the secondary care level, some predicted that the purchaser/provider split and the granting of trust status to selected hospitals and services would lead to some local specialties disappearing (IHSM, 1992). Trusts would pick and choose the work they found the most profitable and some patients might be forced to travel further to obtain treatment. This would particularly affect the elderly and those on low income relying on public transport (Robinson, 1990). Patients might have to travel greater distances also as a result of purchasers selecting cheaper contracts out of the district (Mullen, 1990a). There was speculation that hospitals would make more income from attracting out-of-district patients than from local residents, reducing access for local people and involving selection of patients on other than clinical grounds (King's Fund Institute, 1989; Mullen, 1990b).

Predicted Advantages

Some aspects of the reforms were heralded as good news in relation to equity, as being beneficial to the public health in general and to disadvantaged groups and underserved communities in particular. The advantages related to the components of the reforms that were not primarily concerned with introducing competition, but related to the assessment of needs, of standards, and of effectiveness. Explicit health promotion strategies were also seen as a positive development.

First, having purchasers who were to be 'champions of the people', with the responsibility to access the health needs of the population and use this assessment as the basis for planning services and allocating resources, was seen as advantageous (Scott-Samuel, 1990; Ham and Mitchell, 1990; Jacobson *et al*, 1991). The second manager quoted on page 211 certainly felt that the market could be used as a positive tool to achieve greater equity. If assessments examined the socio-economic distribution of ill health, of risk factors and determinants of health, then they would highlight inequalities in health and in provision and hence could lead to a more equitable allocation of resources. Switching to a system based on residents' needs requires the development of resource allocation formulae which could also lead to more equitable distribution of resources than in the past.

Second, the emphasis on the use of contracts to specify quality and access standards, and to monitor those standards was considered as a possible way to bring up standards of care for the most disadvantaged areas, which had in the past suffered poorer quality services (Hoskins and Maxwell, 1990; Appleby *et al*, 1990).

Third, contracts were seen as potentially useful because of their ability to reveal which services were *not* being purchased so that health authorities could use the information to press government for more resources for unmet need (Heginbotham and Ham, 1992).

Fourth, the schemes for auditing activity – medical and public health – could encourage a greater emphasis on health outcomes and the effectiveness of interventions in improving health and wellbeing.

The need for a national health strategy encompassing the wider determinants of health and dimensions of health beyond sickness and death has been advocated for many years. The decision to prepare strategies for the four countries of the UK therefore was seen as a step in the right direction and one which could ultimately help to tackle the substantial social inequalities in health in this country. Public health organisations believed that 'improving the population's health overall depended largely on the reduction of inequality among its constituent groups' (Faculty of Public Health Medicine, 1991). The reduction depended on tackling the causes of inequality such as poverty, poor housing, unemployment and social conditions.

Turning to the evidence to support or refute any of these claims, three subject areas have been selected in this chapter, where possible challenges to the principle of maintaining an equitable health service are coming to a head, to illustrate the sorts of questions that need to be asked of the new system:

- General practice fundholding: bringing in questions of two-tier services and queue-jumping.
- Assessing need and allocating resources: raising issues of equality of access and the fair distribution of available resources.
- Provision for non-acute health care: touching on the issues of entitlement to free care, the pooling of financial risks and the provision of a comprehensive range of NHS services.

The rest of this chapter looks at each of these in turn.

Fundholding: the Question of a Two-tier Service

The GP fundholding scheme has brought equity issues into sharp focus, particularly worries about the development of a two-tier service. It is also one of the few areas in which several major research projects have been carried out, though unfortunately they still leave many questions unanswered.

First, there have been several studies of a largely qualitative nature documenting the process of setting up fundholding and the perceptions of the GPs involved concerning the effects it has had on the service. The aim of such studies is 'to capture the experience through the eyes of the participants' (Duckworth et al, 1992). These qualitative studies – see Table 1 – have covered first wave fundholders in the West Midlands

Table 1: Recent Research on GP Fundholding

Investigators	Region	Study Period	No. of Fundholders	No. of Non-Fundholders	Data Collected
Duckworth, Day & Klein 1992	West Midlands	1st wave Nov 1991 – Jan 1992	All 26 in region	0	Qualitative experience of fundholders and interviews with related Managers.
Glennerster, et al, 1992	3 regions in SE England	Prelim year from Jan 1990, 1st wave onwards	10	0	Mainly qualitative, fund-holders and some related managers.
Corney, 1993	SE Thames	1st wave	All 15 in region	0	Qualitative; fundholders.

Study	Region	Period			Methods
Newton et al, 1993	Northern	1st wave March–July 1992	10 of 28 in region	0	Qualitative perceptions; GPs and GPs and practice Managers.
Coulter and Bradlow 1993. Bradlow et al, 1992	Oxford	Prelim year (Oct 1990) 1st wave April 1991 onwards	10	7	Qualitative and quantitative on referral and prescribing rates, facilities. Also practice managers.
Howie et al, 1992, 1993	Grampian & Tayside	Pre-'shadow', 'shadow', real funds	6	6*	Qualitative and quantative; GPs, practice managers, consultants and patients.

* Prescribing and referral only

(Duckworth *et al*, 1992), three regions of South East England (Glennerster *et al*, 1992), South East Thames Region (Corney, 1993), and the Northern Region (Newton *et al*, 1993). Individual fundholders have also published their reflections on the experience (Bain, 1991 and 1992; Wisely, 1993). Common findings from these studies include:

- While some fundholders went into the scheme for positive reasons, a substantial proportion gave defensive explanations – to protect the previous right to refer their patients anywhere. There was a perception that non-fundholders would lose that right and have to place patients where the district had contracts.
- Communication with secondary care providers had improved, with consultants and hospital managers much more responsive to GPs' views, leading to process improvements such as speedier reporting back and discharge letters.
- Improvements in direct access services such as pathology and radiology had been secured, mainly in terms of speed of service. Sometimes this led to an improved service for all residents of the district.
- Improvements in secondary care services were achieved for fundholding patients, for example shorter waiting times, specifications that patients would be seen by the consultant, and numerous examples of consultants agreeing to hold clinics in GP surgeries. Again, examples were cited of improvements spreading to non-fundholding patients. For example, a practice with a predominantly Asian population persuaded the local hospital to subscribe to a telephone interpreting service, which then became available to all visitors to the hospital (McAvoy, 1993).
- More services provided by GPs within the practice setting, especially health promotion clinics, management of asthma and diabetes and minor surgery sessions.
- Commom problems cited by the GPs included a heavy administrative load and the need for additional accommodation and staff to cater for expanded services in practice settings.

However, such studies do not provide information on whether the GPs' perceptions matched reality, or whether they were seeing their efforts through rose-tinted spectacles. They also fail to differentiate between the effects of the fundholding scheme *per se* and the influence of other changes. For example, the 1990 GP contract introduced financial incentives for setting up health promotion clinics, minor surgery sessions and disease management clinics for asthma and diabetes. Was the increase observed in such services the result of fundholding or the 1990 contract?

Nor could these studies shed much light on the wider effects of fundholding on non-participants in the scheme, for example, the effects on services available to non-fundholding practices, on district purchasing and strategic planning, on ethical and commercial decisions made by providers, and changes in the geographical spread of various services and resource allocation. There have been very few studies which touch on these wider questions. One study which has been able to test specific hypotheses concerned with referral and prescribing behaviour is the Oxford Region study listed in Table 1 (Coulter and Bradlow, 1993). This compared 10 first wave fundholding practices in the Oxford Region with seven controls (non-fundholders) in the preparatory year before fundholding and at intervals subsequently. Qualitative data were collected from GPs, NHS staff and patients, as well as quantitative data on use of hospital services, prescribing patterns, and investments in facilities.

On the subject of referral to outpatient clinics, three hypotheses were tested in the Oxford study. First the fundholders would be less restricted than non-fundholders in their ability to refer outside district boundaries. Second, referrals from fundholders would decline, partly because they could make savings on their budget by referring less and partly because budgets had been set on rates for the pre-fundholding year, providing an incentive to inflate rates in that year and reduce them once fundholding began. Third, referral to private clinics might increase, partly because some of these would be paid for from patients' private insurance rather than be a charge on the GP's budget.

The evidence ran contrary to all three hypotheses. There was no change in out-of-district referral in either group, referrals to NHS outpatient clinics showed a slight increase for both fundholders and controls (though this was complicated by government waiting list initiative activity at the time of data collection), and referrals to private clinics declined for fundholders and stayed the same for controls. On the facilities and services provided by GPs within their own surgeries there had been increases in both fundholding and control practices in health promotion and preventive care. With prescribing, two-thirds of fundholders in the region made savings on their drug budgets, but this was difficult to interpret as the cost of drugs went up in all practices and the number of items prescribed also increased. However, there was some evidence that fundholders' prescribing costs did not increase as steeply as in control practices.

Coulter and colleagues concluded that the finding on lack of change to referral patterns in the first year of fundholding was not surprising, given that there was an explicit regional policy to maintain a 'steady state' for this first year. Oxford Region had secured agreement from fundholders that 80 per cent of their referrals would go to the same hospitals as before. There had also been encouragement from national level for regions to be generous with their budget setting for fundholders and to allow non-fundholders freedom of out-of-district referral to ensure a smooth transition period. It was therefore too early to draw conclusions for the long term from these first year's experiences (Coulter and Bradlow, 1993).

The Oxford findings do, however, illustrate some degree of discrepancy between GP perceptions and reality. For example, the fundholders in this study felt that they had achieved service improvements similar to those in the qualitative studies listed above, such as shorter waiting times for their patients. However, the data for the first year of the scheme showed that there was no difference in outpatient waiting times for patients of fundholding and control practices. There was no difference for inpatient waiting times either for the first nine months of the year, though it was anticipated that this picture may change when the data for the fourth quarter of the financial year are analysed, following reports of some districts' budgets for elective surgery running out at the end of the year (A Coulter, personal communication, July 1993). A separate analysis by Oxford Region using 1992/93 data on inpatient and outpatient waiting times confirmed the finding that there were no differences between patients of fundholders and non-fundholders on these measures (Peeke, 1993).

However, an analysis of 1992/93 data in an adjacent region found evidence of differential funding for hospital activity in at least one district, with fundholders having greater purchasing power than non-fundholders. In addition, the main provider's waiting list for patients of non-fundholders increased by 24 per cent, while those for first wave fundholders had decreased by 35 per cent and for second wave fundholders had decreased by 41 per cent. This district was keen to promote the fundholding scheme on an equitable basis. The problems revealed by this study are therefore being addressed for 1994/95 to ensure that fourth wave fundholders are not given greater purchasing power than non-fundholders. A plan is being drawn up, to be agreed by all parties, to tackle current inequities between earlier waves of fundholders and non-fundholders.

In Scotland, a more cautious approach to the introduction of the scheme led to the setting up of an experiment in one part of the country, before full-scale implementation (Howie *et al*, 1992, 1993). Six practices in Grampian and three in Tayside agreed to organise themselves into six 'shadow' fundholding practices for one year from April 1990 and to collect extra data needed for the evaluation. Both qualitative and quantitative data were collected including prescribing and referral patterns, content of consultation, patient satisfaction, administration of the funds, the structure of services provided by the practices, consulting patterns of patients and use of the doctors' time. Full controls for these experimental practices were not available, but six Grampian practices agreed that their prescribing data and some referral data could be used for comparison where appropriate. An important condition stipulated at the beginning of the experiment was that fundholders were not allowed to negotiate contracts which would disadvantage other purchasers, to avoid a two-tier service.

Comparison of prescribing patterns with control practices showed that fundholders managed to control the increase in cost of drugs slightly better than controls. Referrals for outpatients went down slightly overall, but there were huge variations within individual practices. For example, the practice ranked highest for referral rates before the 'shadow' period, became the practice with the lowest rates in the 'shadow' fundholding period. Over the same period the practice ranked lowest became the highest referrer. However, when questioned, the doctors had no perception that they had altered their referral patterns, providing a further example of discrepancy between perception and reality (Heaney, 1993). The Scottish study also documented that health service personnel had to work at a level of intensity on the scheme which was not sustainable over the long term with the current resources (Howie *et al*, 1993).

Turning to the impact of the scheme on other purchasers and providers, very few studies have covered this aspect in any detail. A relatively small scale study in North West Thames Region carried out in December 1992 and January 1993, interviewed the purchasing teams from three districts and senior management in three provider units in these districts (Dixon, 1993). All three purchasing teams perceived that fundholders had secured 'process' improvements, such as prompt discharge and pathology reports for their patients and sometimes for all patients. There were also examples of collaboration between fundholders and district purchasing teams in contract setting, and a feeling that a better debate about rationing had been stimulated. On the negative side, all the district purchasers felt that the fundholders had been allocated too much money from the district funds and cited examples of 'windfall' savings by fundholders. For example, they claimed that fundholders had been allocated money for all their outpatient referrals, but were not billed by hospitals for patients who did not attend the appointment. The money was gained by the fundholders at the expense of the providers and the district. One district stated that 85 per cent of its budget for the following year was to be spent on emergency and urgent cases, leaving only 15 per cent for elective work, so that the perceived overpayment of fundholders was a particular cause of resentment. All the purchasers also perceived that a two-tier service was operating in terms of the types of operation patients of fundholders had access to and the time they had to wait. One purchaser reported that they had managed to quash an attempt by fundholders to set contracts specifying shorter waiting times for their patients. Some fundholders were said to show little interest in planning for a wider community beyond their practices and risked de-stabilising some services for non-fundholders by 'short-termism'.

Providers mentioned most of the positive and negative points listed above, but were able to provide more specific examples of a two-tier service developing. For example, in one provider unit waiting times for elective work were 15 months for non-fundholders and six months for fundholders, with a predicted reduction to two months by the end of the financial year. They all confirmed that some contracts had been set with waiting times, differential pricing of contracts and quality of reporting favouring fundholders. One indicated that the notes of fundholding patients were clearly marked to be able to distinguish them. Transaction costs to provide information and billing for fundholders were perceived as high by another provider. The ethical dilemma faced by consultants being asked to select fundholder patients in preference to others was also mentioned in several interviews. Some had resisted, though it was not clear if they had eventually given in to arguments about saving the hospital if they favoured fundholders.

This was only one study in one area, but there is some evidence from national surveys that some of the views expressed in it are more widely held. For instance, in the NAHAT 1992/93 financial survey of district health authorities, 41 out of 82 stated that GP fundholding budgets had been excessive while 41 thought that they were correct (NAHAT,

1993). A survey of budgets allocated to fundholding practices in the first wave, revealed considerable variation in budgets both within and between regions, with the highest spending fundholders having twice as much to spend on each patient for hospital services than their lowest spending colleagues (Day and Klein, 1991). When the audited accounts of the first wave practices were published in October 1992, an average surplus of £44,000 – four per cent of budget – had been made. Very few had overspent, and some had achieved savings in six figures. In addition, first and second wave fundholding practices received an average of £20,000 per practice in computer reimbursements – approximately four times the amount for non-fundholding practices – and £25,753 per practice in special management allowances, adding weight to perceptions of generous allocations (House of Commons, 1993a and b).

Other published accounts provide evidence to support the purchasers' and providers' concern that fundholders, acting without regard for district plans, could de-stabilise services for other patients. For example, one case was reported of ophthalmology services for a whole district being lost and patients then having to travel up to 50 miles because the sole consultant in the specialty had switched to providing his services to fundholding practices in their surgeries on a full time, private fee basis (McAvoy, 1993).

Formal evaluations of the perception and experiences of non-fundholding GPs seem to be singularly lacking. But individual GPs have recorded their experiences in medical journals and press. The overriding comment from non-fundholders in these reports is that patients of fundholders have been given preference in terms of admission for elective treatment, as well as generous practice allocations for computers and management costs (Samuel, 1992; Wright, 1993; Pulse, 13 Feb. 92; GP, 12 Feb. 93; Guardian, 26 Jan. 93 and 13 Feb. 92; Doctor, 23 Jan. 93; British Medical Journal, 18 May 91; Scott, 1992; Fisher, 1993).

At the same time there is also evidence of considerable inventiveness and service development among non-fundholding practices. For example, there is growth in provision of health promotion clinics and various experiments in collaboration between non-fundholding GPs and districts to provide a greater GP input into purchasing decisions and quality monitoring (Bowling et al, 1991; Eve and Hodgkin, 1991; Tower Hamlets DHA/GP Forum, 1993).

To sum up; in the first year of fundholding there were no signs of fundholders in general cutting back on referrals or prescribing in a way which might be detrimental to their patients. There were, of course, exceptions to this and at least one practice has been removed from the scheme for making large profits from running companies to which they referred their own patients. But this was an isolated case. Predictions about fundholding patients being disadvantaged by the scheme have not been borne out so far. Indeed, rather the reverse has happened, with non-fundholding patients at a disadvantage in certain respects. For example, some fundholders have pressed for and achieved specifications in contracts giving their patients preferential treatment over other patients. In other cases the hospitals and consultants have gone out of their way to attract fundholders' custom by offering preferential terms which would be impossible for them to offer to everyone. There is evidence of hospitals in financial difficulties pressing consultants to select patients on financial grounds, and consultants refusing to do so in some, but not all, cases. There are increasing numbers of consultants offering to hold clinics in fundholders' surgeries, sometimes on a private fee basis, thus increasing access for those patients but sometimes decreasing it for other patients in the district. Against these can be set reports of improvements achieved by fundholders for patients beyond their own practices.

The evidence suggests that a two-tier service has developed in places, almost by default. What is not clear is how widespread these findings are and how exceptional the conditions in the first two years of the scheme were. It has been suggested that the development of a two-tier service between fundholders and non-fundholders may merely be a transitional aspect of the scheme which will disappear as the vast majority of practices become fundholders or as district purchasers flex their muscles and demand equal terms for non-fundholders in contracts with providers. This scenario sees fundholders leading the way to improved services for the whole community and an eventual reduction in the two-tier effect. It is hard to see how this could come about without some expansion in funding to finance across-the-board improvements in services. The contrary view is that the more likely scenario is a contraction in public spending in the next few years, in which case gains by fundholders might only be possible at the expense of other parts of the system. Some go further and predict that fundholding will now be used to bring about drastic cost containment throughout general practice, reducing quality and quantity of services for all sections of the population (Hughes and Dingwall, 1991; Melzer, 1992; Keeley, 1993).

Some question why the two-tier issue in fundholding is so important, when there was plenty of anecdotal evidence before these latest reforms that some patients and health professionals manipulated the system to obtain preferential treatment. The main objection is that under the new arrangements, far from being condemned, a two or multi-tier system is openly condoned or even encouraged. If allowed to continue, it would mean that principles of equity such as equality of access and selection on the basis of clinical need were officially being abandoned.

To counteract this tendency, much closer monitoring is required in the immediate future of the extent of various developments, such as differential contracts and waiting times. Also, more effective ways of preventing a two-tier service need to be investigated: the joint guidelines to consultants issued by the NHS Management Executive and the Joint Consultants Committee in 1991 are clearly not sufficient as reports of differential service continue (Dobson, 1993). Much firmer strategies are needed to maintain a universal equitable service.

Studies also need to go beyond the experience of fundholders to investigate much more thoroughly the impact of the scheme on non-fundholders, purchasers, providers and the community at large.

A third major issue is resource allocation in primary care. Are the effects of the different components of the reforms increasing the quality divide between deprived and affluent areas? If so, what can be done about it? This issue is discussed in greater detail below.

Assessing Need and Allocating Resources

The stated intention of some of the reforms is to base health and social care policy and health promotion strategies on:

- assessment of health of the population and the needs they have in relation to improving their health;
- assessment of effectiveness of different policy and service options for meeting those needs;
- devising ways of allocating resources efficiently to meet identified needs.

As these developments were seen as potentially among the most beneficial aspects of the reforms in relation to social inequities in health care, and even health status, it is important to examine how these aims have been put into operation, if at all. As with the other topics, the evidence is sketchy and indeed it may be too early to expect much development work to have taken place. Nevertheless, some initial indications of areas for closer inspection have emerged.

Strategies for Health: The long-awaited national health strategies for the four countries of the UK have now materialised and show a varied approach by the different countries. The Welsh have based their health promotion and health service strategies very much on WHO 'Health for All' principles, in which concern for equity figures strongly (Health Promotion Authority for Wales, 1990; Welsh Health Planning Forum, 1991). Tackling social inequalities in health is therefore a stated objective in the published reports and they have started to set some targets which specify action to improve the health of the most disadvantaged sections of the population with the poorest health.

The Welsh are said to have invented the phrase 'health gain' to describe the notion that policy, whether in the health service or beyond, should be focused on interventions that have been shown to have an impact on health. And health is seen not only in terms of prolonging life but also improving its quality. The Welsh Health Planning Forum has started to develop protocols for purchasing for health gain in the NHS and is about to embark on an equity audit of its policy development so far. However, they are faced with a common problem of a tight financial situation, in which it is difficult to find the resources to allocate to the identified needs and effective interventions without withdrawing funds from services with competing claims.

The other three countries in the UK have not taken this approach. In the case of England, when the green paper proposing a national health strategy was first unveiled, many expressed great disappointment that the issue of tackling social inequalities in health had been practically ignored (Jacobson, 1991; Health Visitors Association, 1991; Ham, 1992). This has not stopped local initiatives seeking to assess social and economic factors and incorporating them into plans for tackling the five priority areas chosen in the national strategy. However, the position still remains that there is no national commitment or lead apparent on tackling inequalities in health in England. This means that the contribution that the NHS could make to ameliorating the health effects of social disadvantage is not being given due emphasis in local and national policymaking.

Purchasing for Health Gain: With health needs assessment and the development of 'purchasing for health gain', it is difficult to get an overall picture of what is happening in different parts of the health service. Compared with the massive injection of funds to develop financial information systems, only modest resources have been allocated to work on assessing health needs and outcomes. But it is clear that some useful support systems have been put in place to aid local initiatives on these issues. For example, the NHS Management Executive has commissioned a series of epidemiologically-based assessments of health needs on various diseases and conditions requiring surgery, and has set up a clearing house at the University of Birmingham to collect and disseminate details of local assessments. In a similar vein, the UK Clearing House for Information on the Assessment of Health Outcomes has been set up at the Nuffield Institute in Leeds, to establish a resource centre on outcomes assessment materials, as well as acting as a focal point for information exchange and training on the subject. At the regional and district level, departments of public health have been set up in each purchasing authority in response to the Acheson report of 1988, with varying complements of staff. Some, but not all, regions fund public health research and resource centres to provide expertise and support to local agencies assessing health needs.

What is not clear is what status is accorded these functions and what improvements in matching services to needs have taken place as a result of the changes. Expectations of the ability of public health departments and others to undertake health needs assessment overnight have perhaps been counterproductive.

One of the few published studies to document perceptions of what is happening in this field at the local level has been a qualitative interview survey of chief executives, directors of planning and contracting and directors and consultants of public health in eight purchasing organisations in the Northern Region in 1992 (Freemantle *et al*, 1993). The assessment of health needs and how it related to other functions of purchasing authorities was perceived as problematic for many of the respondents in this survey. There were divergent stances taken on the subject, for example, at one extreme, a director of contracts dismissed the activity altogether:

> *I leave all that health needs nonsense to public health . . . it's irrelevant . . . I just place contracts and try and get more out of them than they are giving us at the moment.*

Others were said to use it just as a 'fig-leaf' to justify cuts in services. On the other hand, in another district an active project was underway to survey the needs of a very deprived area – assessing health needs in broad terms, rather than from a narrow health care perspective. This had led to an allocation of 70 per cent of the development budget to primary care in response to identified needs. Another was working closely with GPs to help identify needs in the population.

The study concluded that progress and attitudes towards health needs assessment were linked to the financial position of the organisation. Those with development money were sometimes using it in innovative ways – one had secured an extra £1 million for primary care developments following assessment procedures. But in organisations which had been allocated a reduced budget there was little prospect for development work and a much more restricted view of the value and relevance of health needs assessment – a luxury they could ill afford.

These findings illustrate new resource allocation anomalies discussed in the next section, but they also highlight what is a growing concern among several commentators: that divergent interpretations of health needs assessment and health gain are developing (Scott-Samuel, 1992; Hunter, 1992 and 1993; Radical Statistics Health Group, 1991; Mooney et al, 1992). These point to some positive but also some potentially negative activities as far as equity is concerned. Some agencies appear to use health needs assessment as part of purchasing for health gain, as intended by the Welsh Health Planning Forum, to focus on effective interventions to improve health. However, many are facing pressure to meet short term targets, for example, those stemming from the Patient's Charter, coupled with pressure to balance the books with a shrinking budget. Under such conditions, the concern is that local policymakers may feel the need to focus on quick and easy benefits that can be achieved with sections of the population who find it easier to respond, or simpler, easier to treat conditions to demonstrate that they have 'delivered health gain'. The notion of health gain then equates with the quickest, or easiest, benefit at least cost. Groups for whom improvements may take longer to achieve may be seen as worthy of less priority and little attention.

There are only anecdotal reports that this interpretation is gaining ground, but it poses a potentially serious challenge to the principles of providing an equitable service to all sections of the community, treating everyone as worthy of equal respect and consideration.

The Flow of Resources: Questions also need to be asked about resource allocation linked to the process of assessment of need. For example, are the methods of allocating resources efficient and equitable? Are they based on assessment of need and are funds going where intended? How do resource allocations policies in the different components of the reforms interact to affect the overall distribution of resources around the country and in different types of community?

These are complex questions to address, but there are indications of major issues for the future arising out of the patchy evidence available. Evidence on weighted capitation formula, on community care funding, and on primary care resources all point to results at variance with stated policy intentions and show the importance of taking an overview.

The attitudes of purchasing authorities to needs assessment discussed above seemed to depend on their financial position. How have new methods of resource allocation introduced in 1991 affected their position and their purchasing power? From 1976 to 1991, allocations to regions in England were based on the RAWP formula which aimed to channel extra resources to those parts of the country which showed poorer health status but had historically received less funding than healthier regions in the country. Standardised mortality ratios were used as a proxy for need for health services, and as these are highly correlated with social deprivation, the effect was to start to shift resources towards the less prosperous and higher mortality regions generally in the north and north-west of the country (Mays and Bevan, 1987).

The Department of Health's new weighted capitation formula introduced in 1991 to fund regions, and recommended for use in resource allocation to district purchasing authorities, weights the age-adjusted population in each region by the square root of its all-cause, under 75 years, standardised mortality ratio, giving a reduced weighting for the level of mortality in each region. The effect of this is to channel more resources back towards the south-east of England and away from the north, reversing the effect of the RAWP formula (Royston et al, 1992). When regions use the same formula to allocate budgets to districts, some deprived districts, particularly in inner cities, with high mortality and morbidity are net losers of resources, and conversely, more prosperous districts with better health profiles are relatively better off. The result has been that some of the most deprived districts in London, Birmingham and Manchester have faced the threat of substantial cuts in budget (Jacobson, 1990; Appleby, 1992a). There have also been claims of unfairness stemming from the age weighting in the formula, resulting in money moving away from younger populations, mainly in deprived inner city areas, to retirement areas (Williams *et al*, 1992).

Once the perverse effects of the new formula began to emerge, regions started experimenting with a range of alternative weightings, but these produce problems of their own (Sheldon *et al*, 1993). The situation is now in a state of flux, with the Department of Health reviewing the formula as the 1991 census data become available. Whatever formula is chosen, it will have a profound effect on the level and quality of service different districts can fund in response to their needs assessment work.

The effects of changes in funding for community care policies add a new complication to stated policy objectives for the NHS. As early as 1986, the Audit Commission identified a conflict in funding arrangements, with the growth of social security funding for private residential care creating a flow of resources from the poorer to the richer parts of the country, at the same time as the RAWP formula in the NHS was trying to create a flow in the opposite direction (Audit Commission, 1986). The way the funding for the new community care arrangements has been distributed to local authorities still seems to favour the same areas (House of Commons, 1993c). Where there is a low density of private beds there will be less money to pay for any type of provision for local people, residential or domiciliary. The situation is particularly acute in some parts of London which have relatively little local community care provision coupled with understaffed and undeveloped primary health care services. This represents a new manifestation of the Inverse Care Law.

If the distribution of funds in primary care through the GP fundholding scheme and 1990 contract are added to the equation, an even more distorted pattern of resources emerges. It has already been noted that the first and second waves of fundholders were mainly the large, well-organised practices in suburban neighbourhoods (Coulter and Bradlow, 1993, Glennerster *et al*, 1992). They received substantial grants to improve their computer facilities still further and to help with management costs. If, as has been suggested by purchasers quoted above, they also received generous budget allocations to buy hospital services and staffing, then this is another instance of funds flowing to the healthier, better serviced areas of the country. The same has been said for some of the financial incentives built into the 1990 GP contract (Waller *et al*, 1990). Deprivation payments in the contract worked in the opposite direction, providing funds to GPs serving the poorest 5 per cent of the population, though some suggest that provision should have covered 9 per cent of the population (Jarman, 1991). What the net effect of these two policies was in terms of funds available for patients' services is a matter for further study.

What Should be Done?: On the issue of needs assessment and resource allocation, evidence to build up a national picture is not available. Some of the evidence does, however, show where vigilance is needed over the next few years. If purchasing for health gain comes to mean concentrating on patients who can show a rapid return on investment, then there will be serious implications for equity; the NHS will be failing to achieve equal access and quality of care for all. There needs to be careful monitoring of how purchasers are dealing with this aspect of the reforms and how the concepts such as health gain are put into operation. It is also important to document the positive ways in which health needs assessment can provide more equitable distribution of services.

There is sufficient evidence to show that some resource allocation formulae work against stated policy objectives concerned with distributing funds equitably. Obviously the effects of the formulae chosen on the resources provided for different sub-groups in the population need to be carefully researched. But, as Sheldon and colleagues argue; 'there is also a need for studies aimed at producing clearer understanding of the variations in the need for health services and in the use of services to provide a better basis for deciding how resources can be used equitably and efficiently' (Sheldon *et al*, 1993).

Clearly, it is very difficult to get an overall view of how resource allocation through one set of policy initiatives is distorted or enhanced by interaction with other schemes. Studies of distribution at this macro level are, however, very important for assessing the wider implications of policy changes.

Non-acute Health Care: Who is Entitled to What?

The rights to universal and free health care for a large proportion of the population are being removed.

(Henwood & Wistow, 1991)

Melanie Henwood, in her report *Through a Glass Darkly* (1992), makes a compelling case to support the above statement. The charge specifically relates to changes throughout the 1980s in the rights and provision made for frail elderly people requiring non-acute health care, including what are known as continuing care beds. The crucial question now is whether this erosion of free NHS care will be exacerbated or halted by the combined effects of the *Working for Patients* and *Caring for People* arrangements. In this case it is crucial to consider how the two white papers will interact together in practice because the topic under discussion is at the boundary between health and social care, where there are many overlaps and considerable potential for dispute over responsibilities. New factors were introduced into the equation in 1993 with the decision to devolve community health service purchasing to GP fundholders and the granting of trust status to increasing numbers of community health service units, separate from acute care trusts.

To understand the current policy dilemmas, it is necessary to look at how the situation had developed before the latest reforms. The numbers of elderly people in Britain increased substantially over the last decade and will continue to do so well into the next century. Whilst the vast majority will live independent lives right up to the end, significant numbers will experience disabilities and chronic ill-health, requiring varying degrees of help, and these numbers will increase as the elderly population, particularly the very elderly, increases.

Despite this rise in need for care, there has been a decrease in the provision of NHS long-stay geriatric beds from 58,000 in 1978 to 53,000 in 1988. There has been no corresponding increase in contractual arrangements for NHS patients to receive private care at the NHS's expense. The decline in geriatric beds is just one indicator of the shedding of services – geriatricians point to a reduction in comprehensive NHS geriatric services in each district, including day and respite care since the beginning of the 1980s (Lancet, 1992). The provision was far from adequate and quality varied greatly as it does in both the private and public sectors today, but experiments in developing NHS nursing homes had proved successful and cost-effective (Bond *et al*, 1989).

However, these experiments have since been largely abandoned and NHS responsibility, not only for providing care, but also for funding it has continued to decline. A survey by the Association of Community Health Councils for England and Wales (ACHCEW) in 1990 found that 77 per cent of Councils reported a reduction in provision of NHS continuing care beds over the previous three years. The Association concluded that 'some elderly people, their relatives and carers are faced with the discovery that there is no NHS provision for non-acute nursing needs' (ACHCEW, 1990).

This shedding of responsibility for continuing care was made possible by a change to the social security regulations in 1980, allowing social security payments to be made to support people living in private residential and nursing care. Private homes sprang up in many parts of the country and the social security budget covering this type of provision sky-rocketted from £10 million in December 1979 to an estimated £2.4 billion in 1992/93. In the ten years from 1982 to 1991, the numbers of independent sector nursing beds for elderly people increased five-fold, from 18,000 to 109,000 (House of Commons Health Committee, 1993).

At first sight, it might appear as though there was a straightforward change of provider with independent provision rising to fill the gap left by the decline in NHS care, with little overall impact on patients. However, from the patient's point of view the change has had profound effects. The situation reached in 1993, just before the implementation of *Caring for People* involved three different categories of patient facing different financial consequences:

- Some elderly people were cared for by the NHS – either in NHS facilities or through contracts with the private sector – and received free care, free ancillary services such as chiropody and free appliances. However, they may have found difficulty in gaining access to local services of this nature because of NHS reductions in this type of care.
- Some elderly people with the same level of need for continuing care would be placed in private nursing care not financed by the NHS. These patients would probably have undergone a means test and those with low income and capital assets below £8,000 would be entitled to social security payments to help with the cost of care. Benefit levels have been found to be too low in many cases to cover the full fees of the nursing homes (Price Waterhouse, 1991). Consequences of this included patients and their relatives having to top-up fees, having to travel out of their area to find a cheaper home, and having to accept a lower quality of care in a two-tier service.
- The third category of patient was in private nursing care, but would not qualify for social security benefits because the value of their capital assets, including their house, was above £8,000. They were responsible for the full fees for their care, which may have involved running

down their resources to pay for the fees, selling their houses so that they had nowhere to return to should they get better.

There is evidence from ACHCEW and charities such as Age Concern of the hardship these funding arrangements have caused patients not supported by the NHS (ACHCEW, 1990; Age Concern, 1991). No national survey has been carried out to ascertain the extent of these effects. However, the evidence of financial hardship and distress was on a sufficient scale for the House of Commons Social Security Committee to express grave concern and state that the Members failed to see why many people should now be put into the situation where they had to pay all or part of the fees (House of Commons Social Security Committee, 1991).

Reports in the press of people being pressurised by hospital staff to move out of NHS beds into the independent sector were sufficiently disturbing to trigger Department of Health guidance to health authorities:

> No NHS patient should be placed in a private nursing or residential care home against his or her wishes if that means that he or she or a relative will be personally responsible for the home's charges (Circular HC(89)5).

Regular data on this issue have not been collected since the guidance was issued, but anecdotal reports from charities and relatives suggest that the practice is still continuing. When the implementation of the *Caring for People* changes was delayed from 1991 to 1993, there was further incentive for health authorities to shed patients from their responsibility on to the social security budget before this source of funding dried up. No record has been kept of the number of beds transferred in this way and no information was available to the House of Commons Health Committee in March 1993 on the current continuing care bed commitments of each health authority (House of Commons Health Committee, 1993). As a result, there is not even a reliable estimate of the diminished level of NHS commitment for continuing care, never mind what the level would have been if health authorities had not shed their responsibilities during the 1980s.

Since April 1993, new funding arrangements have come into force, triggered by the urgent need to curb the almost exponential rise in the open-ended social security budget and to tackle the perverse incentive in the system to place people in residential care rather than support them in their own home. The uncontrolled rise in social security spending is tackled by capping the budget transferred from social security funds to local authorities. Local authorities then have the responsibility for assessing the needs of each individual presenting for care and devising care packages to satisfy those needs, with patient preferences taken into account. The cost of the services in the package is retrieved from the patient on a means-tested basis, apart from services accepted as the responsibility of health authorities.

In theory, this should be a better system than before in terms of matching the services provided to the needs of each person and avoiding inappropriate placement. Unmet needs may also be documented for which new services may be devised, although guidance on this matter has been confused. Authorities are having to record 'unmet preferences' rather than 'unmet need' if they wish to avoid the possibility of judicial review. Even so, the new arrangements do not ease the patient's burden of payment for health services which the system over the last ten years has created.

It should also be noted that there is an added barrier to gaining access to the non-NHS funded care under the new system. Patients under NHS care have no means test or eligibility criteria to satisfy. Patients funded by the pre-April 1993 social security arrangements did have to undergo a means test, but if a person met the income rules, there was no eligibility test for the service itself. Post-April 1993, a patient has to undergo a needs assessment by the local authority, with locally devised eligibility criteria for services. If successful, there is then a means test if they wish to claim exemption from any of the charges.

Whether the new arrangements now in place under the two white papers lead to more or less hardship for people needing non-acute health care depends crucially on the adequacy of local authority and NHS funding. For example, if funding is set at an inadequate level then local authority eligibility criteria are likely to be more stringent and may exclude people who previously received services. A debate on whether the local authority funding is adequate is now in full swing (Jowell, 1992; House of Commons Health Committee, 1993).

Diagram 1 illustrates two potential pressure points at the interface between NHS and local authority responsibility, which may exacerbate the situation for this group of vulnerable patients. The first is at the point of discharge from hospital. In order for the NHS to shed its responsibility for provision and funding of long term nursing care, it has relied on patients having access to the open-ended social security budget to allow them to move into private nursing beds and release the hospital beds they were occupying.

Figure 1 Pressure Points from 1 April 1993

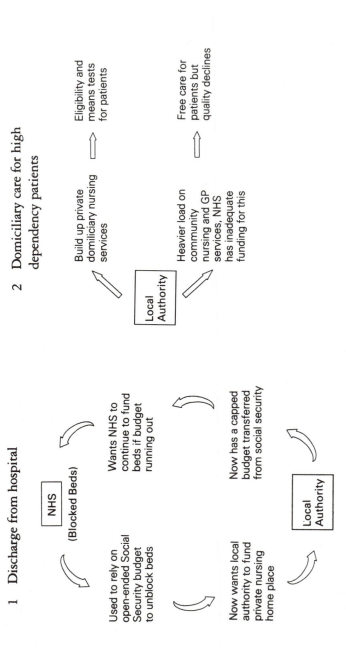

1   Discharge from hospital

NHS

(Blocked Beds)

Used to rely on open-ended Social Security budget to unblock beds

Wants NHS to continue to fund beds if budget running out

Now wants local authority to fund private nursing home place

Now has a capped budget transferred from social security

Local Authority

2   Domiciliary care for high dependency patients

Build up private domiciliary nursing services

Eligibility and means tests for patients

Local Authority

Heavier load on community nursing and GP services, NHS has inadequate funding for this

Free care for patients but quality declines

Under the new system, health authorities will want the local authorities to take over responsibility for funding patients who would previously have been supported by the social security budget, so that they can still move into a nursing home or intensive domiciliary support. On the other hand, the local authority now has a capped budget to fund nursing home and residential care beds and domiciliary services. If the local authority budget is in danger of running out, the authority will be reluctant to accept responsibility for the patient and will insist that the health authority has responsibility. In that case the patient may stay in the hospital bed, with a knock-on effect on the beds available for acute conditions. The effects are potentially devastating for NHS purchasers (districts and GP fundholders) and providers alike in terms of keeping within budgets and meeting various service targets. The patient would still be placed in a free versus fee-paying situation.

By June 1993, there were already some reports that bed-blocking was occurring. One chief executive of a 1,000 bed acute trust reported that 40 to 100 patients were stuck in wards waiting for the social services department to arrange assessments for them. Another had 40 to 60 people in the same situation in an 800 bed unit (Eaton, 1993). These managers warned that waiting lists would start to rise and trust contracts with health authorities about the number of acute episodes that they could treat might be broken. They also flagged up the issue of means testing as staff had to fill in lengthy and detailed forms before the social services department would accept responsibility for the patient. These included information on the financial resources available to relatives, which many families were unwilling to give.

The second pressure point concerns the development of domiciliary care for high dependency patients. It is an explicit objective of the *Caring for People* changes that local authorities will encourage more services to be developed to allow people to stay in their own homes and that the independent sector will be stimulated to offer more domiciliary provision. In the longer term, there are incentives for local authorities to offer to maintain some patients in their own homes possibly at higher dependency levels than previously, requiring nursing care on a continuing basis. In this case, local authorities may wish to draw on the existing community nursing and GP services, assuming that this type of care is the NHS's responsibility. Such services will then have a much heavier workload. Either the district and GP purchasers will have to find additional funds to maintain the free service at the previous standard, or the quality of service offered is likely to decline.

Alternatively, the local authority may encourage residential nursing home owners and others to diversify into providing private domiciliary nursing services. These would be financed from the local authority budget, with charges reclaimed from patients following eligibility and means tests. This scenario suggests that we could end up with the same anomalous categories of NHS and means tested patient in the community that are already evident in residential nursing care. Some community health service trusts are financially vulnerable and are looking at tendering for social care contracts from local authorities, blurring the free/means tested service boundary still further. The long term consequences of letting this situation develop do not appear to have been thought through, but could involve a firmer hold for the notion of means testing, new forms of cost shifting between agencies, and possibly even the abandonment of the principle of free NHS services at the point of use.

Future Action on Continuing Care: This potentially explosive interaction between *Working for Patients* and *Caring for People* policy changes needs to be monitored much more closely. The House of Commons Health Committee has noted the absence of information about health authority responsibility for continuing care beds (House of Commons Health Committee, 1993). It has asked the Department of Health to monitor the level of long term NHS care across the country and the NHS Management Executive to instigate regional level monitoring of community care plans for these services and what actual services are being delivered. This will help in the monitoring of any further re-drawing of NHS boundaries though it does nothing about the services already lost.

From the patient's point of view, it will be crucial to monitor the hospital discharge pressure point. Studies are needed of what actually happens to patients when they move from the requirement for acute to continuing care. It will be essential to find out their experiences, their interaction with various agencies and the services offered to them. The costs to individual patients and their families of the care they are offered need to be taken into consideration. Every area is supposed to have plans to deal swiftly with patient discharge arrangements, but how well do these plans work in practice? The hospital discharge procedures are probably the most critical test of the new arrangements: if this interface collapses, the failure will be immediately evident in blocked beds, re-admissions and community service crises.

With domiciliary care, the same type of careful qualitative studies are required to document the experience of patients as they go through assessment procedures, how their needs are met and at what cost to themselves and their families. The help offered to patients and their carers by community health services needs continuing monitoring. Evidence of a change in the intensity or quality of service provided to such patients and the workloads of community health staff needs to be collated.

The realities of the needs assessment systems need to be investigated to obtain a national picture. What criteria of eligibility are different local authorities using? What types and extent of unmet need are being documented? How do the criteria and the services offered differ with the financial circumstances of the authorities? How does assessment and provision vary with measures of area deprivation? Are acute and community health service providers documenting unmet need and patient distress?

Going back to the quote at the beginning of this section, as the charge of loss of entitlement to free NHS services appears to be supported by the evidence, it is crucial to ask how the NHS reforms are going to address the issue. At the moment, we have an inequitable situation for some of the most vulnerable members of society.

Conclusion

This chapter has tried to draw together the available evidence on the equity implications of three aspects of the changes taking place in the NHS: fundholding; the linked processes of needs assessment and resource allocation; and changes in responsibility for non-acute health care. Although these cover only parts of the very complex set of reforms, they touch on most of the components of an equitable health service listed on page 209 and illustrate both research and policy issues for the immediate future.

What does the research evidence show? First, there is no overall picture of what is actually going on. Above all, it shows how painfully incomplete our information is, particularly in relation to equity, and that the studies so far have covered only fragments of the total package of policy interventions and even then from only certain angles. For example, there are more studies covering the perceptions of managers and the doctors most closely involved in leading specific aspects of the reforms than other groups of health workers in more direct contact with patients. Studies of the perceptions and experience of nurses, for instance, are almost totally lacking. There are even fewer studies that move from perceptions of what is happening to examining if these perceptions bear any resemblance to day-to-day practice. There are isolated reports of specific effects of the reforms, but no indication of how widespread these effects are.

Second, examination of these fragments and individual pieces of evidence indicates that there are reasons to be concerned about whether an equitable service can be maintained under the new conditions set in place under *Working for Patients*. Yet there are also some rays of hope.

On the negative side, there is evidence that situations have developed in which the will to succeed financially, or even just survive, has overriden the concern to ensure that everyone has access to the same high standard of service. In the new contract culture, deals have been struck which deliberately give preference to some patients above others, on financial rather than clinical grounds. This has come to a head with contracts between fundholders and hospitals or consultants, but it is more pervasive than that.

There are also instances of decisions being made for short term gain, which threaten long term plans and provision of services for a wider community. Access to a comprehensive range and geographic spread of services could be reduced if this process went unchecked. Then there are instances of policy making by default. When was the policy debated and the decisions made that health authorities would reduce their responsibility for funding long term non-acute health care for elderly people? The fact that, whether intentional or not, it removes entitlement and access to certain NHS services for particularly vulnerable groups in the population and puts them in danger of financial hardship, should cause disquiet in many circles. There are also suggestions that some resource allocation mechanisms may be increasing inequalities in provision rather than decreasing them.

On the more positive side, there are reports of people striving very hard to adapt to the new structures and ways of working to make sure the new arrangements are still based on equity principles. Co-operation between some FHSAs, DHAs and fundholders, for example, has resulted in contracts being set that do not contain clauses giving preferential treatment to one set of patients over another. There are examples where consultants have resisted pressure to choose patients on financial grounds. Health needs assessments have been developed for the benefit of communities which have been neglected in the past. It is clear, even from the sparse evidence available, that there are people working in the service who want to do all they can to protect the fundamental principles.

Apart from the specific suggestions for studies mentioned throughout this chapter, there are more general considerations. To gain more understanding of what is going on and what could be done about it, a mix of research and policy analysis is required on four broad fronts:

- **Ethical purchasing and providing:** At every level of the service, people are liable to be faced with ethical dilemmas thrown up by the greater financial incentives and market pressures in the new system – pressures to select patients and offer differential service, for instance. The situations health workers face in their day-to-day contacts need to be investigated much more thoroughly. What are the problems people face, how extensive are these and how are they being resolved? Are there examples of good practice that could be developed further? There have already been some discussions about 'purchasing for equity', but there are two sides to any contract. Managers as well as health professionals in provider settings need to be drawn into discussion of the ethics and practicalities of providing equitable services.

- **Distribution of human costs and benefits:** Much more needs to be known about the way the human costs and benefits are distributed among different groups in the population. For example, on the issue of choice, which many of the reforms claim to improve, more choice for whom? What groups of patients receive improved services, and at what cost to themselves? At what cost or benefit to other users of the service? How are people affected by the policy changes in personal and financial terms? Are any of these changes causing hardship?

    Studies of the distribution of costs and benefits across different parts of the service and different categories of staff would also give a fuller picture of the implications of the reforms. Have the reforms altered the ethos and morale among those who work in the service? This is a neglected area of research, yet it has been a time of great insecurity for most of the workforce as purchasing authorities merge or slim down and trusts are formed. At the same time, the values on which their work is based may have changed drastically, altering the ethos of the service. Has this helped or hindered the maintenance of an equitable system?

- **Modelling longer term implications of policy:** The long term implications of some of the current reforms do not seem to have been worked through in any great depth, nor have the interactions with other policies been studied. For example, how will having different proportions of fundholders in a district affect strategic planning for the district's resident population? transaction costs of providers? management time from Family Health Services Authorities? and so on. How will the requirement for local authorities to encourage the proliferation of private domiciliary care affect the provision of free community health services? How are different policies influencing the distribution of resources geographically and by socio-economic status of area, and what do the long term trends look like with various policy combinations?

- **Assessing policy options:** Situations have been reached, for example in the case of non-acute care for elderly people, where NHS boundaries have been redrawn without consultation. There is a clear need for this problem to be more publicly debated and this process would be aided by examining the options available in much greater depth. Which solutions would be more equitable? Which would cause the least distress? Already some proposals are being put forward which the proposer admits would 'make those who require nursing care through no fault of their own shoulder the cost' (Kellett, 1993). Each option needs to be carefully tested against the equity principles of the NHS and alternatives put forward if necessary.

So can the NHS remain an equitable service under the reformed arrangements? The evidence so far does not provide an answer, but it does provide plenty of indications that there are grounds for concern. People will have to work very hard and actively manage the situation, rather than leaving it to the whims of the new and evolving system. If left to drift, without active promotion of the fundamental principles, then we stand to lose much more than we gain.

10

EVALUATING THE NHS REFORMS

Julian Le Grand

Anyone who has come to this book hoping to find a definitive answer to the simple question as to whether, overall, the NHS reforms have had a positive or negative impact will be disappointed. This is partly because, even in an ideal world, there are rarely simple answers to apparently simple questions – usually because, as in this case, the questions are not actually simple. The reforms embrace a wide variety of organisational changes, each of which involves different aspects of the NHS, affects different players and agents within the service and, ideally, should be subject to its own evaluation process.

There are also reasons specific to the process of the reforms' implementation which makes their evaluation particularly difficult. One is a consequence of the fact that when the reforms were introduced no governmental system of monitoring and evaluation was set up alongside them. Nor was research into their progress by other organisations or researchers in or outside government officially encouraged. This in turn derived from a perhaps understandable reluctance by the Government to countenance the delays and equivocations that often accompany policy experimentation and evaluation. But it has had the undesirable consequence, at least from the Government's point of view, that policy makers have been unable to counter the inevitable rash of hostile anecdotes that have emerged as the reforms progressed with hard evidence concerning that progress.

A second problem is spelt out by a number of the contributors to this book. It is that there have been other major changes in the NHS during the period, changes which undoubtedly have had a significant impact on any indicator that might otherwise have been used to monitor the progress of the reforms. Obvious examples are the changes in the GP contract, the Patient's Charter and the parallel set of reforms into community care, all of which have induced significant changes in behaviour by the key players in the system that overlay any changes induced by the reforms.

Perhaps more important than any of these, there was a dramatic increase in resources going to the NHS in the run up to the last general election: 6.1 per cent in real terms in 1991/92 and 5.5 per cent in real terms in 1992/93. In Chapter One, Butler points to a number of factors, changes in which could be taken as indicators of the reforms' success, including falls in waiting lists and the provision of a greater range of services; and political debate over the reforms has indeed centred on these issues. But, with increases in resources of this magnitude, it would be astonishing if there were no changes in waiting lists or improvements in the range of services offered, quite independently of any changes in the delivery system of health care, such as those induced by the reforms. On their own, therefore, such indicators can tell us nothing about the progress of the reforms.

Is the task of evaluation therefore hopeless. Not quite – as the results of the King's Fund research projects reported in this book indicate. As explained in the Introduction to the book, the projects do not in themselves constitute anything like a complete evaluation exercise; they were relatively small in scale, and they were selected on the basis of proposals in specific areas defined by the researchers themselves. Nonetheless, they have yielded results that enables something to be said about the progress of the reforms, even if that something is far from definitive. That is the task of this chapter.

The chapter begins with a short discussion of the criteria for evaluation, specifying a number of broad areas where, if the reforms are to be judged a success, changes in the appropriate direction might be expected. It then briefly summarises such 'direct' evidence as is available from the projects reported in earlier chapters concerning changes in these areas. It continues with a review of the 'indirect' evidence from the projects and elsewhere concerning the reforms' ability to meet certain conditions for their success. There is a brief concluding section. It should be emphasised that all the interpretations made are the author's and are not necessarily representative of the views of other contributors to the book.

Criteria for Evaluation

As noted in Le Grand and Bartlett (1993, Chapter Two) it is easy to spend a good deal of time discussing evaluation criteria. There are issues concerning their scope, their definition, their operability and their ownership, detailed treatment of any of which could take up a chapter on its own. However, it is possible to identify a set of broad criteria that seem to capture the principal interests of all those concerned with the progress of the reforms. They may be summarised under the headings of *quality, efficiency, choice, responsiveness* and *equity*.

Whether or not they yield a better *quality* of health care is perhaps the most obvious criterion against which the reforms should be judged. The original white paper outlining the reform programme, *Working for Patients*, gave as one of its two key objectives for the reform programme 'to give patients . . . better health care' (p. 3), and it is hard to imagine this being seriously challenged as a policy goal.

However, this is not to say that the criterion is unproblematic. The principal difficulty is, of course, to decide exactly what constitutes 'better health care' or, more generally, an improvement in quality. One obvious interpretation would be an increase in the 'effectiveness' of care: that is, improvements in health attributable to the changes in care that themselves are attributable to the reforms. But changes in health outcomes may take a long time to appear, and in any case are often heavily determined by factors outside the remit of the National Health Service. Alternatively, the focus could be on aspects of performance, such as numbers of hospital patients treated, or on aspects of process, such as waiting lists. But this says nothing about the effectiveness of the treatments being provided.

For obvious reasons these issues cannot be resolved here. Instead we accept that quality is multi-dimensional and report below on those dimensions that have been investigated by the projects that form the basis for the book.

Efficiency is often identified with cost-cutting regardless of the impact on the quality of service, and as such efficiency concerns are often resisted in health policy circles, particularly professional ones. However, a more sophisticated approach would acknowledge that quality on its own cannot be the only concern and that it is necessary also to examine the efficiency by which *service of a given quality* is delivered. Other things being equal, a high quality, low cost service is to be preferred to one that delivers the same quality but at a higher cost. Again, this seems relatively unobjectionable as a goal, although again there are problems of definition and measurement to be resolved.

As noted above, *Working for Patients* indicated that better health care or quality is one of its two objectives for the reforms. The same statement referred to the importance of giving patients 'greater choice of services available' (p.3) and a concern for *choice* obviously underlay much of the government's motivations for the reforms. Greater choice may be seen as a desirable aim in and of itself; and/or it may be viewed as an instrument for achieving other ends, such as efficiency and responsiveness. The aim of improving the *responsiveness* of the system to users needs and wants was also explicitly flagged in the white paper, where it stated that its second principal objective was for those in the NHS who successfully respond to local needs and preferences' to be appropriately rewarded (p.4).

It is perhaps not surprising, given its provenance, that *Working for Patients* was relatively weak on the language of equity or social justice. Nonetheless equity considerations were not ignored entirely. There were several references to the importance of tailoring services to need; indeed, in so far as there was any conception of equity underlying the white paper, it was probably that services should be related to need rather than, for example, to desert or to ability to pay.

But, even if there were no governmental concern, given that a desire to promote social justice was undoubtedly one of the major motivating factors behind the creation of the National Health Service in the first place, no evaluation of the reforms would be complete without some consideration of their impact on equity. Again, as can be seen from Margaret Whitehead's discussion at the beginning of Chapter Nine, the problem lies more in defining and operationalising the term; and again in what follows several different aspects of the concept are used.

Direct Research

How successful have the reforms been in improving quality, efficiency, choice, responsiveness and equity. For the reasons spelt out at the beginning of this chapter, this is not an easy question to answer directly and one that may never be answered in its entirety. However, some of the projects have tried to address aspects of it.

Quality: The study of 2,400 elderly people discharged from hospital by Jones, Lester and West reported in Chapter Six found little significant improvement between 1990 and 1992 in the aspects of the quality of non-clinical hospital services that they investigated. On average patients waited longer for their hospital treatment in 1992 than in 1990, while fewer patients received information about their hospitals before admission. There were no improvements in food quality or cleanliness. On a more positive note, there were signs that staff at ward level were increasing their efforts to communicate effectively with patients, and there was some improvement in the amount of notice given to patients of admission. Paradoxically, however, patient dissatisfaction with the amount of notice they were given increased, perhaps indicating that expectations were rising faster than the improvements themselves.

The same team also used a different sample to investigate aspects of primary and community care. Here some changes were noted, including improved accessibility through appointments systems and telephone contacts, and some increase in consultations and in drug prescriptions for patients over 75. However, the authors attribute these mostly to changes other than the reforms, notably the GP contract and the Patient's Charter.

This study did not distinguish between the patients of GP fundholders and non-fundholders, perhaps because, in their sample, there were no fundholders in the first year and only relatively few in the second. The study undertaken by Glennerster, Matsaganis, Owens and Hancock reported in Chapter Four concentrated only on fundholders. The results suggest that the fundholding scheme has improved certain aspects of the quality of services. Communications with secondary providers improved significantly with, for example, more consultants being persuaded to come to the practice to do outpatient sessions. The boundary line between hospital outpatients and primary care was challenged, to the benefit of the fundholders' patients. Money was saved on drug bills with the savings being used to employ more practice staff of various kinds.

Care must be taken in interpreting these results. The early fundholders were a self-selecting group, and were probably already among the most dynamic and innovative practices. Also, the study did not investigate the experience of non-fundholding in the same way, to distinguish between the effects of the fundholding scheme and of other changes during the same period. Evidence from another study of fundholding by Coulter, reviewed by Whitehead in Chapter Nine, found little difference between fundholders and non-fundholders in Oxfordshire with other aspects of behaviour, such as hospital referral rates, at least in the first year of the scheme. However, in other parts of the country, there was evidence of differential funding for hospital activity, with fundholders having greater purchasing power than non-fundholders. There was also evidence that fundholders' patients were being selected from waiting lists ahead of non-fundholders. This raises questions as to how far gains in quality are a function of preferential resourcing.

Nonetheless Whitehead's review confirms that there are some significant changes that may be attributable to fundholding, with communications between GPs and secondary care providers improving, shorter waiting times, and improvements in direct access services such as pathology and radiology. If the gains really are a consequence of fundholding *per se* and not of preferential resourcing or of other changes, and if they are sustained as fundholding expands, then, at least in terms of impact on quality, the scheme may turn out to be one of the most positive aspects of the reforms.

All the aspects of quality considered so far are non-clinical. There is almost no evidence at all concerning changes in the quality of the clinical services that could be attributed to the reforms. This is not very surprising; the methodological difficulties already alluded to with reference to evaluating changes in the quality of non-clinical services are multiplied many times over when clinical services are concerned. For instance, an obvious measure of the quality of clinical services is the health gain that can be attributed to the use of those services. Yet not only is there no consensus on how to measure health gain, there is remarkably little evidence concerning the relationship between the provision of clinical services and any measure of health gain. Add to this the difficulty noted above of attributing changes in any service, clinical or non-clinical, specifically to the reforms, and it is clear why information on the reforms' impact on clinical services (and indeed on health outcomes) is scarce.

However, a study reported in Chapter Seven by Kerrison, Packwood and Buxton has investigated progress at four hospitals in one aspect of the reforms that was intended to monitor the quality of clinical services: medical audit. Audit is a contested term, with its interpretations ranging from a full cost-benefit analysis of the procedure concerned to a simple peer review of good practice. Despite this uncertainty, clinicians rapidly accepted the need to set up collective processes to examine the quality of care, and audit, of some sort, was quickly in place.

In their case studies, the researchers found a process much closer to the peer review of good practice than to the cost-benefit end of the spectrum. The process of audit consisted of meetings of consultants and their juniors. There was little involvement of other professional groups, and no involvement of purchasers or users. Good practice tended to be defined by reference to case-notes; there was very little consideration of cost, of systematic assessments of health gain or of user satisfaction. Some changes in practises and policies did emerge from the meetings. But the main outcomes of the process were case-driven policies or protocols developed by, and for, clinicians, with no reference to outside agencies.

Efficiency: In Chapter Three Bartlett and Le Grand report on a study that examined the pre-reform cost structures of the first and second waves of hospital trusts and compared them with a sample of non-trusts. They found that in many areas of hospital operations, trusts had significantly lower costs than non-trusts, particularly in ward unit costs and in areas associated with administration and management. However, these could not be attributed to the reforms, since the data were taken from the period immediately before the reforms were implemented. Rather, the results showed that the first, and, to a lesser extent, the second, wave of trusts were a selected group of units that were already among the more efficient providers.

The results of this study provide a warning to any one who wishes to use simple cost comparisons to make inferences about the efficiency consequences of the reforms, or indeed more generally to attribute observed differences of any kind exclusively or primarily to the reforms. It is not only important, as has already been pointed out, to try to strip out the effects of other changes going on at the same time; it is also necessary to control for pre-existing differences.

Buchan and Seccombe in Chapter Eight report on an investigation into personnel changes that could have an impact on the efficiency of running hospitals: changes in staffing levels and mix, managing local employee relations policy and procedure, and pay determination. The study was based on postal surveys of district health authorities in England and Wales and health boards in Scotland, and on semi-structured interviews with personnel directors and senior managers. They found some significant changes in staffing levels and mix in the first year of the reforms; however, there was little indication of the impact on the level, cost and quality of the service being provided. There were few changes with respect to employee relations policy or to pay determination. However, there were indications that the pace of change in these areas was about to accelerate rapidly, as personnel departments acquired the skills to manage pay locally, as labour costs became the focus of management action, and as trusts became the norm.

One way in which costs might *increase* as a consequence of the reforms, to which a great deal of anecdotal attention has been paid, concerns administration. The administrative and general management bill is definitely increasing, but there is controversy over the exact extent. Official estimates suggest that administrative and clerical staff increased from 116,842 in 1989 to 127,367 in 1991. General and senior managers increased over the same period from 4,609 to 13,338; however, this figure was affected by classification changes (Department of Health, 1993, pp.80–1).

Glennerster and colleagues discussed the administrative costs issue with respect to the comparative costs of GP fundholding and district purchasing. They concluded that the costs of the former were undoubtedly higher, but they believed the efficiency gains from fundholding would outweigh these extra costs. However, they emphasised this was only a judgement.

Finally, a note of caution. There may be a Hawthorne effect from the reforms, with any improvement in efficiency resulting from the process of change itself rather than the specific form the changes have taken. With respect to this it is worth noting that, although the hostility of medical practitioners to the reforms has been widely noted, there has often been a positive attitude among NHS managers towards them. For instance, the study by Appleby and colleagues reported in Chapter Two investigated the attitudes of NHS managers towards the reforms at the beginning of the implementation process and found a very high level of approval. Eighty-five per cent of district general managers approved of the changes 'with some reservations' and 88 per cent believed they would make the NHS more business-like which was a 'good thing'. A survey of unit general managers showed a similar pattern.

Choice and Responsiveness: Chapter Five reports the results of a survey by Mahon, Wilkin and Whitehouse into GPs' and patients' views about the effects of the reforms on patients' choices of hospital and on choices exercised on their behalf by GPs. It focused on referrals for elective surgery in the specialties of general surgery, ophthalmology and orthopaedics, since it is in these areas where there is considerable potential for enlarging choice. The researchers found that the level of patient involvement in choice of hospital and consultant was generally low and that this changed little in the first year of the reforms. However, many of the patients interviewed would have liked to have had more choice of hospital and more information. Three-quarters of the GPs interviewed reported that the reforms had made no difference to the choices available to them; 17 per cent that choice had been reduced and five per cent that choice had increased. Fundholders were more likely to perceive an increase in choice, with 40 per cent reporting an increase, while 60 per cent reported no change.

Finally, it should be noted that the study of health services for elderly people by Jones, Lester and West reported in Chapter Six found no increase in patient choice of hospital between 1990 and 1992.

Equity: One of the dangers to equity arises from the possibility of cream-skimming. In a world where purchasers and providers are divided, both purchasers and providers have an incentive to be selective about the kinds of cases and social groups with which they deal. On the provider side, in dealing with districts or GP fundholders under block contracts, the incentive for trusts is to avoid accepting patients with conditions that require expensive treatment; even under cost-per-case contracts, they have an incentive to avoid patients for whom there is a risk that the marginal treatment cost will exceed the price as agreed in the contract. On the purchaser side, if they are funded on a basis that is not appropriately adjusted for risk, GP fundholders have an incentive not to accept patients on to their list who are likely to require expensive treatment and therefore contribute to the possibility that the fundholders will over-run their budget.

In these circumstances purchasers or providers have an incentive to select cheaper patients and to exclude, if they can, expensive ones. Treatment becomes *inversely* related to need, rather than directly as a needs-related interpretation of equity would require.

As noted by Glennerster and colleagues, cream-skimming was widely predicted to be a potentially serious problem in Chapter Four, particularly in GP fundholding practices. This fear was to some extent supported by US experience of health maintenance organisations which have a number of similarities to fundholders (Weiner and Ferris, 1990). However, Glennerster and colleagues found no evidence of cream-skimming among the fundholders they were investigating. Indeed, another study actually found indications to the reverse: one of the benefits of the scheme as perceived by fundholders was an improvement in their ability to 'voice the needs of poor patients' (Duckworth, Day and Klein, 1992, Summary).

Glennerster and colleagues point out that there is a simple explanation for this: fundholders do not have to bear the costs of a patient's treatment above £5,000 and hence the incentive to cream-skim has been removed, at least for patients with treatment costs above that limit. The down-side of this provision is that it also removes all other incentives for fundholders treating these patients, notably that of economising on their treatment. If the limit were raised to cope with this difficulty, then incentives for cream-skimming could re-emerge.

In her review of the consequences of the reforms for equity in Chapter Nine, Whitehead drew attention to a number of other areas of possible concern. One again referred to GP fundholders and the possible development of a two-tier service, with fundholder patients either losing out in hospital referrals, or, the opposite, receiving preferential treatment. That fundholder patients would be referred less frequently to hospital was again widely predicted before the reforms came into operation; but this appears not to have happened. Instead the principal concern is the opposite: the development of a two-tier service, with fundholders' patients in the higher tier. Although this has not been systematically researched, Whitehead refers to growing evidence that a two-tier service is indeed developing, with hospitals and consultants offering services to the patients of fundholders that are denied to the patients of non-fundholders. This could be reduced in future if DHAs used their buying leverage: also, as Glennerster and colleagues argue, to the extent that the phenomenon is occurring, it may be a transitional one, and hence, if most or all GPs became fundholders, it would disappear.

Whitehead also points to the possibility that some district health authorities are interpreting health gain in a way that discriminates in favour of those for whom such gain can be easily obtained – again a form of cream-skimming. She also notes that some resource allocation formulae are working against stated policy objectives concerned with distributing funds equitably. More generally, neither the formulae nor the purchasers themselves in making their purchasing decision appear always to show a great concern for equity considerations *per se*, and this may lead to disadvantaged groups losing out.

Finally, Whitehead points out that the combined effect of the NHS reforms and those being introduced in community care may result in elderly people previously in receipt of free NHS non-acute care now having to pay for their care in 'the community'. Again, this could lead to inequity, although this time of the payment structure rather than of the delivery systems.

Indirect Research

As explained above (Bartlett and Le Grand, Chapter 3; see also, Le Grand and Bartlett, 1993, Chapter 2) the indirect approach to evaluation has two steps. First, it uses economic analysis to specify the conditions which quasi-markets of the kind brought in by the NHS have to meet if they are to meet certain goals (specifically, efficiency, choice and responsiveness). Second, it examines whether there is evidence that the conditions are being met in practice. Of these, the most important for our purposes relate to market structure, information, transactions costs, and motivation. The theoretical basis for these conditions is discussed in some detail in Le Grand and Bartlett (1993, Chapter 2); hence what follows simply summarises the relevant arguments.

Market Structure; For the allocation of a service by a quasi-market to be efficient, to offer choice to users and to be responsive to users' needs and wants, the market concerned has to be *competitive* on both the purchaser and the provider side. The problems that a lack of actual or potential competition among providers can create are obvious. A few dominant providers can use their monopoly power to raise prices and to lower the quantity and/or the quality of the services they provide. They offer little choice and have no great incentive to be responsive. Only if there are economies of scale in service provision, might a provider monopoly be more efficient than a competitive market; and there is not much evidence of such economies in medical care, particularly with the present trend away from large scale hospital procedures.

Large scale purchasers may be justified if there are large scale providers – although even then there may be difficulties if both sides become too dependent on each other. On the other hand a monopoly purchaser dealing with many small providers could be harmful, driving down the returns to providers below acceptable limits. Also, monopoly purchasers have fewer incentives to respond directly to users than competitive ones. If purchasers are to be properly responsive to users, it is desirable that users have a choice of potential purchasers to act on their behalf.

What is happening with respect to competition on either the purchaser or the provider side in practice? On the provider side, the potential for competition may be greater than is commonly thought. Chapter Two reports on a study by Appleby and colleagues concerning the extent of potential competition among hospital providers in the West Midlands. This suggested that only one quarter of the providers studied operated in areas where there was a significant degree of monopoly or oligopoly power (as measured by the Hirschman-Herfindahl Index), although these hospitals accounted for 38 per cent of patient episodes. Three quarters of the hospitals concerned therefore had the potential for competition.

In any given situation the extent of competition will depend in part on the willingness of patients to use alternative, perhaps more distant providers and on the willingness of GPs to refer them there. The study by Mahon, Wilkin and Whitehouse in Chapter Five explores the views of both patients and GPs with respect to choice of hospital for referrals. The results for patients suggest that there may be some reluctance to travel, with over a third of the sample not being prepared to travel at all to be seen more quickly, and less than a quarter prepared to travel up to or more than 30 miles. This in part conflicts with the results of earlier surveys which generally indicated a considerable willingness to travel among patients; as the authors point out, this may be because there are special features for the sample for this study who were older than the general population and suffering from conditions that may well have affected their ability to travel.

With respect to GPs, the study found a reluctance to refer patients far afield among non-fundholders, with 64 per cent not prepared to refer more than ten miles for general surgery, 56 per cent for ophthalmology and 53 per cent for orthopaedics. However, fundholders were more adventurous; one third said they would be prepared to refer their patients more than 50 miles for elective surgery for all three specialties, compared with less than one in ten of non-fundholders.

Finally, it is worth noting that even if there is provider competition in the short run, problems may develop over time. A review of experience in US human services markets, which offer some parallels with UK health care quasi-markets, suggests that as these markets evolve competition may be of limited effect (Propper, 1993). The long term evolution of a competitive environment appears to lead to a limiting of competition for contracts, a lengthening of contractual relationships and domination by the incumbent of the provider side of the market.

On the purchasing side the situation is less hopeful, at least so far as health authority purchasing is concerned. In a case study of one health authority (Bartlett and Harrison, 1993), the market structure, so far from being competitive, was closer to a bilateral monopoly, with a single purchaser and a few large providers. There was little by way of bidding processes between purchaser and providers and little evidence that the health authority involved saw the stimulation of a competitive market as a high priority. In fact to describe the situation as a bilateral monopoly may be over-generous. Members with powerful positions in the old organisational structure found themselves in powerful positions in the new one and, in consequence, there were many non-market interactions between purchaser and provider.

Although there is no systematic evidence on a wider scale, this does not seem to be unrepresentative of the situation with respect to districts elsewhere in the UK. Indeed arguably on the purchaser side the situation is getting even less competitive, with mergers between purchasing authorities being actively encouraged. This is generally justified on the grounds of the savings possible in staffing; little consideration is given to the potential of a single purchaser distorting the market and creating inefficiencies.

Perhaps the best hope for a more competitive market to emerge, particularly with respect to purchasing, lies with the GP fundholding scheme. There is clearly the potential for competition of various kinds: between fundholders themselves and between fundholders and health authorities. There is considerable anecdotal evidence that fundholders are indeed engaging in competitive behaviour at least with respect to district health authorities, but no systematic studies of the phenomenon.

Information: The second condition that markets need to meet to function effectively concerns information. In markets, quasi or otherwise, accurate information about costs, prices, quality and other attributes of goods and services should be available to all participants. In particular, the monitoring of quality has to be an essential part of any quasi-market system. Otherwise providers may engage in what Williamson (1975, 1985) calls opportunistic behaviour, exploiting their informational advantage to reduce costs at the expense of quality.

The study by Appleby and colleagues reported in Chapter Two investigated the process of contracting. The researchers found that, for both purchasers and providers, a lack of information was perceived to be a major area of difficulty. Information systems were poor; there was a lack of data about current service provision and doubts about the accuracy of such data as were available; there was poor information about health needs and only crude information about costs and activity.

Other research has reached similar conclusions. A case study examining the process of reform implementation in one health authority initially found little evidence that the information structures necessary for quasi-market efficiency were being set up within the authority concerned (Bartlett and Harrison 1993). Individuals in the purchasing authority expressed hopes that they would continue to have physical access to trust facilities to witness the delivery of services and to talk with staff. They also assumed that the data generated within the provider unit would be available to the purchaser authority. But there was no indication at that stage of this going much beyond the levels of hope. If this is representative of the situation in other authorities, it seems inevitable that purchasing authorities will remain largely dependent on their own providers for its information: an outcome that is not likely to promote efficiency.

If medical audit were a more open and a more regular procedure, then this could provide a possible source of information to purchasers concerning the quality of care. However, the professional encapsulation of audit activity reported by Kerrison, Packwood and Buxton in Chapter Seven means that little information has emerged for monitoring quality in the market.

Moreover information problems do not seem to be confined to health authorities. The study by Mahon and colleagues in Chapter Five exploring the views of GPs on patient referrals found a surprising lack of information on such basics as waiting times for different providers.

However, the situation with respect to GP fundholders is rather different. GPs have ready access to one crucial piece of information: the condition of patients *before* they receive the treatment being purchased and the condition *after* they receive it. And, with their medical knowledge, they are in a good position to assess that information, so they can monitor directly the quality of the product.

Moreover, there is some evidence to suggest that fundholders are utilising their power in this respect. A study of 26 fundholding practices in the West Midlands found 'a significant change in the relationship between general practitioners and providers, as the former insisted on information about what was happening to the patients they had referred to consultants' (Duckworth, Day and Klein 1992, Summary). However, this study did not investigate non-fundholders.

GP fundholders therefore seem well-placed at least with respect to one important piece of information, individual patient outcomes. However, they are not in a position to do comprehensive studies related to outcomes at a hospital level; here a centralised purchaser like the district health authority has the edge.

Transactions Costs: The transactions which take place in quasi-markets are often quite complex and multi-dimensional, involving the provision of sophisticated service activities rather than the relatively basic provision of material commodities with which traditional markets deal. As a result, the creation and management of these markets may involve a relatively high burden of what have been termed transactions costs.

As developed by Williamson (1975, 1985), transactions costs can be usefully divided into two kinds: *ex ante* and *ex post* exchange. *Ex ante* transaction costs are those encountered in drafting negotiating and safeguarding an exchange agreement. These tasks can be done with a great deal of care, specifying as many contingencies as possible and detailing all the appropriate reactions in each contingency for all the contracting parties, in which case the associated costs are likely to be high; or they can be done in an incomplete fashion in which case the costs will be low. *Ex post* transactions costs are the costs of monitoring the outcomes of the exchange to check compliance with the exchange's terms after the transaction has taken place, and the costs of any haggling or other forms of dispute resolution if the terms have not been complied with. *Ex post* costs are likely to be greater, the less care has been taken in drawing up the terms and conditions of the exchange in the first place. Hence high *ex post* transactions costs may be associated with low *ex ante* costs and *vice versa*.

Here districts may have an advantage over GP fundholders as purchasers, at least in terms of *ex ante* costs. The study by Appleby and colleagues reported in Chapter Two found a very high level of use by health authorities of block or cost and volume contracts, which have low *ex ante* costs. If cost-per-case contracts are to be negotiated for each patient, as is often the case with fundholders, then, given their numbers, this is likely to prove expensive in terms of transactions costs for providers. And these costs will increase as the number of GP fundholders increases. However, as noted above, fundholders have an advantage in terms of *ex post* costs, since they are in closer touch with the patient and thus are better placed to monitor contract compliance.

Motivation: A fourth condition for markets to operate efficiently concerns the motivation for providers and purchasers. All providers should be at least in part financially motivated: that is motivated to minimise their costs. If they are not motivated in this way, they will not respond appropriately to market signals. So, for example, if prices rise, indicating a profitable opportunity, but providers are not interested in making surpluses, or in reducing their deficit, they will not increase the amount they provide.

On the purchaser side, the aim should be to maximise the welfare of the users of the service concerned, given the resources available. This condition is likely to be met if purchasers and users are the same people; however, under the NHS quasi-market reforms they are not. Health authorities purchase on behalf of the populations in their districts; fundholding GPs on behalf of their patients. In these situations, there is clearly a problem in ensuring that purchasers will act in the interests of users, and not pursue their own agendas. Hence it is important that there be some mechanism for ensuring that purchasers do take account of users' welfare and views in making their purchasing decision.

In the case study of an authority mentioned above (Bartlett and Harrison, 1993) the motivations of purchaser and provider were expressed in general, and indeed rather ambiguous terms. Statements about 'utilising available resources to optimise health status of the population' or 'committed to the continuing excellence of teaching and research' were offered to indicate the objectives of purchaser and provider respectively. Perhaps not surprisingly, neither referred to profit-maximisation as an objective, nor indeed to any form of financial aim. However, there was a strong motivation on both sides to keep within budget.

The study by Appleby and colleagues described in Chapter Two also produced some results relevant to this issue that space precluded including in their chapter. Their interviews with potential health authority managers found that GPs' preferences would count for more as a determinant of their purchasing decisions than a wide variety of other factors, including competitive prices and quality assurance, suggesting a concern for the welfare of users at least as perceived by GPs. The researchers also found that, when asked about their own priorities, they gave a high priority to 'purchasing the greatest quantity of health care for resources available' and 'moving towards equality of access', both of which seem to display a user-orientation: potential provider managers gave top priority to 'remaining financially viable', above, it might be noted, delivering efficient or high quality health care (Appleby *et al*, unpublished).

The GP fundholding study by Glennerster and colleagues did not address the question of motivation directly. Nonetheless, even in the first year of operation it was clear that practices are responding to market incentives in a way that suggests that the motivational structure on the provider side is appropriate. Also, some fundholders set up private companies so as to contract with themselves and profit thereby; these activities, perceived by the Government as violating the spirit of the purchaser/provider split, were stopped in 1993, but they did indicate a market-type motivation for the practices concerned.

Conclusion

Much of the direct research reported here indicates little actual change of any kind and even less that could be attributed to the reforms in key areas of quality, efficiency, choice, responsiveness and equity. However, given that most of the studies concerned took place in the first year or two of the reforms, this is not very surprising.

More positively, what some of the results of the direct and indirect research suggest is that, at least in some areas, there is potential for real gains arising from the reforms. Many hospitals are in competitive situations. Trust managers are looking for efficiency improvements. Fund-holders do appear to be obtaining quality improvements for their patients, although the extent to which this is the result of the fundholding scheme *per se* is not clear. Medical audit is leading to changes in behaviour by clinicians. There are equity worries, but as yet no evidence that some of the principal areas of concern, such as cream-skimming, are more than theoretical issues.

Inevitably, these conclusions have to be tentative. Moreover, the results may be subject to different interpretations. This author has taken the view that some of them at least lend support to a broadly positive view of the reforms; but others who have participated in the projects are more sceptical. What everyone would agree on is the necessity for more research; in particular, the importance of going back to the areas investigated after an appropriate interval to discover signs of change. Also, several aspects of the reforms were only explored indirectly, if at all – for instance, their impact on administrative costs – and these need serious research attention. In the debate over the NHS reforms, anecdote and prejudice have generally substituted for systematic evaluation; the projects reported in this book have attempted partially to correct this imbalance, but there is still a long way to go.

REFERENCES

Age Concern (1991), *Under Sentence: continuing care units for older people within the NHS*, Age Concern, London.

Andersen Consulting (1992), *Patient Centred Care: re-inventing the hospital*, Arthur Andersen & Co, London.

Anon (1991), 'Health and education reforms – half right', *The Economist*, 9 February, pp 43–4.

T Albert and S Chadwick (1992), 'How readable are practice leaflets?', *British Medical Journal*, 305, pp 1266–68.

J Appleby (1992a), 'NHS distribution of funds unfair', *British Medical Journal*, 304, p 70.

J Appleby (1992b), *Financing Healthcare in the 1990s*, Open University Press, Buckingham.

J Appleby *et al* (1990), 'The use of markets in the health service: the NHS reforms and managed competition', *Public Money and Management*, Winter, pp 27–33.

J Appleby *et al* (1993), *Implementing managed competition: second survey of UGMs*, Project Paper No 8, NAHAT, Birmingham.

J Appleby, V Little, W Ranade and J Salter (1991a), *How Do We Measure Competition?*, Monitoring the White Paper, Project Paper No 2, NAHAT.

J Appleby, V Little, W Ranade, R Robinson and M McCracken (1991b), *Implementing the Reforms: a survey of district general managers in the West Midlands Region*, Monitoring the White Paper, Project Paper No 4, NAHAT.

J Appleby, V Little, W Ranade, R Robinson and M McCracken (1991c), *Implementing the Reforms: a survey of unit general managers in the West Midlands Region*, Monitoring the White Paper, Project Paper No 5, NAHAT.

K Ascher (1987), *The Politics of Privatisation: contracting out public services*, MacMillan Education, London.

L Ashburner (1993), 'The Composition of NHS Trust Boards – a national perspective', unpublished, University of Warwick, Coventry.

L Ashburner and L Cairncross (1992a), 'Just trust', *Health Service Journal*, May 14, pp 20–22.

L Ashburner and L Cairncross (1992b), *Members, Attitudes and Expectations*, Research for Action: Authorities in the NHS Paper No 5, Centre for Corporate Strategy and Change, University of Warwick, Coventry.

Association of Community Health Councils for England and Wales (1990), *NHS Continuing Care of Elderly People*, ACHCEW, London.

Audit Commission (1986), *Making a Reality of Community Care*, HMSO, London.

J Bain (1991), 'Budgetholding: a step into the unknown', *British Medical Journal*, 302, pp 771–773.

J Bain (1992), 'Budgetholding in Calverton: one year on', *British Medical Journal*, 304, pp 971–973.

J H Barber and J B Wallis (1978), 'The benefits to an elderly population of continuing geriatric assessment', *JRCGP, 28*, pp 428–433.

N Barr, H Glennerster and J Le Grand (1988), *Reform and the NHS*, Welfare State Programme No WSP/32, London School of Economics, London.

W Bartlett (1991), 'Quasi-markets and contracts: a markets and hierarchies perspective on NHS reforms, *Public Money and Management*, Autumn, pp 53–61.

W Bartlett (1993), *A Comparison of the Development of Small Firms in Bulgaria and Hungary*, MOST, May, pp 73–96.

W Bartlett and L Harrison (1993), 'Quasi-markets and the National Health Service Reforms', in J Le Grand and W Bartlett (1993).

W Bartlett and J Le Grand (1992), *The Impact of NHS Reforms on Hospital Costs*, SAUS Studies in Decentralisation and Quasi-Markets No 8, School for Advanced Urban Studies, Bristol.

W Bartlett and J Le Grand (1993), *Cost and Trust*, SAUS Studies in Decentralisation and Quasi-Markets, School for Advanced Urban Studies, Bristol.

W Bartlett and M Uvalic (1986), 'Labour-managed firms, employee participation and profit sharing: theoretical perspectives and European experience', *Management Bibliographies and Reviews*, 20, pp 1–67.

E Bates (1983), *Health Systems and Public Scrutiny*, Croom Helm, London.

A E Beisecker (1988), 'Aging and the desire for information and input in medical decisions: patient consumerism in medical encounters', *The Gerontologist*, 28(3), pp 330–335.

D Berwick, A Enthoven and J Bunker (1992), 'Quality management in the NHS: the doctor's role – I', *British Medical Journal*, 304–p 235.

G Bevan, W Holland and N Mays (1989),'Working for which patients and at what cost?' *Lancet*, i, pp 947–949.

D Billis (1993), *Organising Public and Voluntary Agencies*, Routledge, London.

D Black (1991), 'Paying for health', *Journal of Medical Ethics*, 17, pp 117–123.

M Blaxter (1990), *Health and Lifestyles*, Tavistock/Routledge, London.

J Bond *et al* (1989), *Evaluation of continuing care accommodation for elderly people*, School of Health Care Sciences, University of Newcastle-upon-Tyne, Newcastle-upon-Tyne.

M Bosanquet and B Leese (1988), 'Family doctors and innovation in general practice', *British Medical Journal*, 296, pp 1576–80.

C Bosk (1979), *Forgive and Remember: managing medical failure*, University of Chicago, Chicago.

A Bowling *et al* (1991), 'GP views on quality specifications for out-patient referrals and care contracts', *British Medical Journal*, 303, pp 292–4.

J Bradlow, A Coulter and P Brooks (1992), *Patterns of Referral*, Health Services Research Unit, Oxford.

P Brider (1992), 'The move to patient focused care', *American Journal of Nursing*, September, pp 26–33.

D Brindle (1990), 'Waldegrave shuns business jargon', *The Guardian*, 13 December.

British Medical Association (1989), *BMA News*, February 3.

C Brown (1988), 'Family doctors get key role in reformed NHS', *The Independent*, 28 December.

J Buchan (1992), *Flexibility or Fragmentation: trends and prospects in nurses' pay*, Briefing Paper No 13, King's Fund Institute, London.

J Buchan and J Ball (1991), *Caring Costs: nursing costs and benefits*, Institute of Manpower Studies Report No 208, University of Sussex, Falmer.

J R Butler (1992), *Patients, Policies and Politics*, Open University Press, Milton Keynes.

L Cairncross and L Ashburner (1992), *NHS Trust Boards*: The First Wave,

Research for Action: Authorities in the NHS, Paper No 6, University of Warwick, Coventry.

R A Carr-Hill (1992), 'The measurement of patient satisfaction', *Journal of Public Health Medicine*, 14:3, pp 236–249.

R Carr-Hill, P Dixon, I Gibbs, M Griffiths, M Higgins, D McCaughan and K Wright (1992), *Skill Mix and the Effectiveness of Nursing Care*, Department of Health/Centre for Health Economics, University of York, York.

A Cartwright (1967), *Patients and their Doctors*, Routledge and Kegan Paul, London.

A Cartwright and R Anderson (1981), *General Practice Revisited: a second study of patients and their doctors*, Tavistock, London.

Centre for the Evaluation of Public Policy and Practice (1991), *Evaluation of Total Quality Management Projects in the NHS*, First interim report to the Department of Health.

COHSE (1991), *To boldly go? Report on the Personnel Policies of the First Wave NHS self-governing trusts*, Confederation of Health Service Employees, Banstead.

J Coope and T S Warrender (1986), 'Randomised trial of treatment in hypertension in elderly patients in primary care', *British Medical Journal*, 293, pp 1145–51.

S Corby (1992a), 'Industrial relations developments in NHS trusts', *Employee Relations*, Vol 14, No 6, pp 33–34.

S Corby (1992b), 'Swing of the pendulum', *Health Service Journal*, 24 September, special report on NHS trusts, pp 5–6.

R Corney (1993), 'General practice fundholding in South East Thames RHA: the experience of first wave fundholder', *British Journal of General Practice*, (forthcoming)

A Coulter (1992), 'Fundholding general practices: early successes – but will they last?', Editorial in *British Medical Journal*, 304, pp 397–8.

A Coulter and J Bradlow (1993), 'Effect of NHS Reforms on General Practitioners' Referral Patterns', *British Medical Journal*, 306, pp 433–437.

A Coulter, M Roland and D Wilkin (1991), *GP Referrals to Hospital: A Guide for Family Health Service Authorities*, Centre for Primary Care Research, University of Manchester, Manchester.

B Crump *et al* (1991), 'Fundholding in general practice and financial risk', *British Medical Journal*, 302, pp 1582–4.

A Culyer and J Posnett (1990), 'Hospital Behaviour and Competition' in A Culyer *et al* (eds) *Competition in Health Care: reforming the NHS*, Macmillan, London.

P Curley, G J A Brown and P M T Weston (1993), 'Effect of NHS reforms on GPs' referral patterns, Letter to the Editor in *British Medical Journal*, 306, p 716.

G Dahlgren and M Whitehead (1992), *Policies and Strategies to Promote Equity in Health*, World Health Organisation, Copenhagen.

P Davies (1988), 'The public speaks out on the NHS', *Health Service Journal*, May 19, pp 556–7.

P Davies (1989), 'Setting an example in New Zealand', *Health Service Journal*, 99, pp 68–9.

P Davies (1993), 'In focus', *Health Service Journal*, 22 April, p 12.

K Davis (1972), 'Economic theories of behaviour in nonprofit private hospitals', *Economic and Business Bulletin*, 24, pp 1–13.

R Day and R Klein (1987), *Accountability: five public services*, Tavistock Press, London.

P Day and R Klein (1991), 'Variations in budgets of fundholding practices', *British Medical Journal*, 303, pp 168–70.

W Decker (1987), *Bereidheid tot Verandering*, Commissie Structuur en Financiering Gezondheidszorg, Amsterdam.

Department of Health and Social Security (1973), *Operation and Development of Services: organisation for personnel managers*, HRC(73)37, DHSS, London.

Department of Health and Social Security (1979), *Patients First*, HMSO, London.

Department of Health and Social Security (1983), *Competitive Tendering in the Provision of Domestic, Catering and Laundry Services*, HC(83)18, DHSS, London.

Department of Health and Social Security (1986), *Review of the Resource Allocation Working Party Formula*, NHS Management Board, London.

Department of Health and Social Security (1986), *Promoting Better Health*: *The Government's programme for improving primary health care*, Cm 249, HMSO, London.

Department of Health (1989a), *More Trouble with Feet: a survey of the foot problems and chiropody needs of the elderly*, HMSO, London.

Department of Health (1989b), *Terms of service for doctors in general practice*, HMSO, London.

Department of Health (1989c), *Medical Audit Working Paper No 6, Working for Patients*, HMSO, London.

Department of Health (1989d), *Discharge of patients from hospital*, accompanying circular HC(89)5, London.

Department of Health (1989e), *Income Generation: A Guide to Local Initiatives*, HN(89)9, Department of Health, London.

Department of Health (1990), *Standing Medical Advisory Committee. The Quality of Medical Care*, HMSO, London.

Department of Health (1991a), *Medical Audit in Hospitals and Community Health Services*, HC(91)2, HMSO, London.

Department of Health (1991b), *The Patient's Charter*, HMSO, London.

Department of Health (1993), *The Government's Expenditure Plans 1993–94 to 1995–96: Departmental Report*, Cm 2212, HMSO, London.

Department of Health/Department of Social Security/Welsh Office/Scottish Office (1989), *Caring for People*, HMSO, London.

M Dean (1991), 'End of a comprehensive NHS?', *Lancet*, 337, pp 351-52.

R Dingwall and J McIntosh (1978), 'Teamwork in theory and practice', in Dingwall and McIntosh (eds), *Readings in the Sociology of Nursing*, Churchill Livingstone, Edinburgh.

J Dixon (1993), Impact of GP fundholding scheme in North West Thames RHA, NW Thames RHA, London.

J Dobson (1993), 'Tiers before bedtime', *Health Service Journal*, 103 (5337), p 15.

A Donabedian (1988), 'The quality of medical care', *Journal of the American Medical Association*, 260, pp 1743–48.

C Donaldson and G Mooney (1991), 'Needs assessment, priority setting and contracts for health care: an economic view', *British Medical Journal*, 303, pp 1529–30.

E van Dooslaer, A Wagstaff and F Rutten (1993), *Equity in the Finance and Delivery of Health Care: an international perspective*, Oxford University Press, Oxford.

P Draper (1993), 'Will radical surgery save the internal market?', *Pharmaceutical Marketing*, February, pp 18–21.

M Drummond *et al.* (1990), 'General practice fundholding', Editorial in *British Medical Journal*, 301, pp 1288–9.

J Duckworth, P Day and R Klein (1992),*The First Wave: a study of fundholding in General Practice in the West Midlands*, Centre for the Analysis of Social Policy, University of Bath, Bath.

L Eaton (1993), 'When bureaucracy is blocking beds', *Health Care Today: Journal of the NHS Trusts*, Issue No 9, June, pp 12–13.

R P Ellis and T G McGuire (1986), 'Provider behaviour under prospective reimbursement: cost sharing and supply', *Journal of Health Economics*, 5, 129–151.

M A Elston (1991), 'The politics of professional power: medicine in a changing health service',. in Gabe, Calnan and Bury (eds), *Sociology of the Health Service*, Routledge, London.

A C Enthoven (1985), *Reflections on the Management of the National Health Service*, Occasional Paper 5, Nuffield Provincial Hospitals Trust, London.

R Eve and P Hodgkin (1991), 'In praise of non-fundholding practices', *British Medical Journal*, 303, pp 167–8.

Faculty of Public Health Medicine (1991), *The Health of the Nation Cm 1523: Faculty Response*, Faculty of Public Health Medicine, London.

A Fisher (1993), 'Fundholding', British Medical Journal, 303, p 1003.

R Flynn (1992), *Structures of Control in Health Management*, Routledge.

N Freemantle, I Watt and J Mason (1993), 'Developments in the purchasing process in the NHS towards an explicit politics of rationing', *Public Administration*, (forthcoming).

J A French, C H Stevenson, J Eglinton and J E Bailey (1990), 'Effect of information about waiting lists on referrals patterns of general practitioners', *British Journal of General Practice*, 40, pp 186–189.

K French (1981), 'Methodological considerations in hospital patient opinion surveys', *International Journal of Nursing Studies*, 18, pp 7–32.

M Foot (1975), *Aneurin Bevan 1945–1960*, Paladin, London.

E Fuchter and P Garside (1992), 'Patient-focusing Central Middlesex', *The Health Summary*, September, pp 6–8.

A Gamble (1988), *The Free Economy and the Strong State*, Macmillan, Basingstoke.

H Glennerster, M Matsaganis and P Owens (1992), *A Foothold for Fundholding*, Research Report No 12, King's Fund Institute, London.

G Godber (1988), *The NHS: Origins and Early Development*, Green College lecture, Oxford.

N Goldie (1977), 'The division of labour between the mental health professions. A negotiated or imposed order', in M Stacey (ed), *Health and the Division of Labour*, Croom Helm, London.

J Grant (1992), *Formal Opportunities in Postgraduate Education for Hospital Doctors in Training*, Standing Conference on Postgraduate Medical Education.

D G Green and J Neuberger (1990), *The NHS reforms: whatever happened to consumer choice?*, Institute of Economic Affairs Welfare Unit, London.

R Griffiths (1983), *NHS Management Enquiry*, DHSS, London.

R Griffiths (1988), *Community Care: agenda for action*, HMSO, London.

R Griffiths (1988), 'Does the public service serve? The consumer decision', *Public Administration*, 66, pp 195–204.

T Groves (1993), 'Public disagrees with professionals over NHS rationing', *British Medical Journal*, 306, p 673.

Guardian (1991), *Increased suffering for the elderly on the NHS*, 10 October.

D Guest and R Peccei (1992), *The Effectiveness of Personnel Management in the NHS*, Department of Health, London.

D Haigh Smith and D Armstrong (1989), 'Comparison of criteria devised by government and patients for evaluating general practitioner services', *British Medical Journal*, 299, pp 494–496.

C Ham (1991), 'Revisiting the internal market and finding it's all gone slow', *British Medical Journal*, 302, pp 250–251.

C Ham (1992), 'Policy may fail without action to tackle poverty', *Independent*, 9 July.

C Ham (1993), 'How go the NHS reforms?, *British Medical Journal*, Vol 306, 9 January.

C Ham et al (1989), *Managed Competition: a new approach to health care in Britain*, Briefing Paper No 9, King's Fund Institute, London.

C Ham and J Mitchell (1990), 'A force to reckon with', *Health Service Journal*, 1 February, pp 164–5.

H Hansmann (1987), 'Economic theories of nonprofit organisation', in W W Powell (ed), *The Nonprofit Sector: A Research Handbook*, Yale University Press, Newhaven.

H Hansmann (1980), 'The role of nonprofit enterprise', *The Yale Law Journal*, 89, pp 835–98, reprinted in Rose-Ackerman (1986).

J Harper (1992), *Unit Labour Costs: a guide*, NHS Personnel Development Division, London.

J E Harris (1977), 'The internal organisation of hospitals: some economic implications', *Bell Journal of Economics*, Autumn, pp 467–482.

A Harrison (1992), 'Auditing Audit', in A Harrison and S Bruscini (eds), *Health Care UK 1991*, King's Fund Institute, London.

A Harrison (1993), *From Hierarchy to Contract*, Policy Journals, Hermitage.

L Harrison (1991), *Implementing the White Paper: Working for Patients*, SAUS Studies in Decentralisation and Quasi-Markets No 6, School for Advanced Urban Studies, Bristol.

S Harrison, D Hunter and C Pollitt (1990), *The Dynamics of British Health Policy*, Unwin Hyman, London.

J T Hart (1971), 'The inverse care law', *Lancet*, i, pp 405–12.

P Haywood and M Vinograd (1992), 'Taking local management responsibility for NHS pay', *Health Manpower Management*, Vol 18, No 1, pp 4–7.

Health Promotion Authority for Wales (1990), *Health for All in Wales*, Health Promotion Authority for Wales, Cardiff.

Health Visitors Association (1991), *Building a Healthy Britain: an HVA response to the Health of the Nation Consultative paper*, Health Visitors Association, London.

D Heaney (1993), *Evaluation of the Scottish Shadow Fundholding Scheme*, Paper presented to conference of Society of Social Medicine/King's Fund Institute, 31 March–1 April, London.

M Henkel (1991), *Government, Evaluation and Change*, Jessica Kingsley, London.

M Henwood and G Wistow (1991), Memorandum to the Social Security Committee (R74), Appendix 15, Fourth Report, Volume II, minutes of evidence and appendices.

M Henwood (1992), *Through a Glass Darkly: community care and elderly people*, Research Report No 14, King's Fund Institute, London.

J Higgins (1988), *The Business of Medicine: Private health care in Britain*, Macmillan Education, London.

C Heginbotham and C Ham (1992), *Purchasing Dilemmas*, King's Fund College, London.

R Hoffenberg, P I Todd and G Pinker (1987), 'Crisis in the National Health Service', *British Medical Journal*, 295, p 1505.

A Hopkins and R Maxwell (1990), 'Contracts and quality of care', *British Medical Journal*, 300, pp 919–22.

House of Commons (1983), Hansard, Vol. 47, col 1094, HMSO, London.

House of Commons (1987), Hansard, Vol. 24, cols 166–7, HMSO, London.

House of Commons (1993a), Hansard, *Computer budgets*, Written answer, 25 January, HMSO, London.

House of Commons (1993b), Hansard, *Fundholders' management fees*, Written answer, 16 January, HMSO, London.

House of Commons (1993c), Hansard, *Local Government Finances*, 11 February.

House of Commons Health Committee (1992), *NHS Trusts: interim conclusions and proposals for future inquiries*, First report, session 1992–93, HMSO, London.

House of Commons Health Committee (1993), *Community Care: funding from April 1993*, Third report session 1992/93, House of Commons papers 309–1, HMSO, London.

House of Commons Social Security Committee (1991), *The Financing of Private Residential and Nursing Home Fees*, Fourth report, HMSO, London.

House of Commons Social Services Committee (1988), *Fifth Report 1987–8. The Future of the National Health Service*, HC613, HMSO, London.

J Howie, D Heaney and R Maxwell (1993), 'Evaluation of the Scottish shadow fundholding project: first results', *Health Bulletin*, 51, pp 94–105.

J Howie *et al.* (1992), 'The Scottish general practice shadow fundholding project – outline of an evaluation', *Health Bulletin*, 50, 316–328.

D Hughes and R Dingwall (1991), 'Joe Stalin and the NHS Revolution', *Health Service Journal*, 101, pp 23–4.

D Hunter (1993), 'Rationing and health gain', *Critical Public Health*, 4, pp 27–32.

Industrial Relations Services (1991), 'NHS trusts: employment terms and bargaining survey', *Employment Trends*, No 991, July, pp 9–15.

Industrial Relations Services (1992), 'New skill based pay structure for healthcare assistants at West Cumbria Health Authority', *Pay and Benefits Bulletin*, 303, May, p 12.

Institute of Health Services Management (1992), Memorandum submitted by IHSM to House of Commons Health Committee, Minutes of evidence, 5 February.

B Jacobson (1990), *Health in Hackney*, Annual Public Health Report for 1990, City and Hackney Health Authority, London.

B Jacobson (1991), 'The gaps in the strategy', *Health Service Journal*, 101 (5257), 8, 20 June.

B Jacobson, A Smith and M Whitehead (1991), *The Nation's Health*, King's

Fund, London.

B Jarman (1991), 'General practice, the NHS review and social deprivation', *British Journal of General Practice*, 41, 76–9.

F Jebb (1991), 'Referrals under threat', *Medeconomics*, March, pp 37–42.

H Joseph (1975), 'On economic theories of hospital behaviour', *Journal of
Economics and Business*, 27, pp 69–74.

T Jowell (1992), 'Community care in London: the prospects', *British
Medical Journal*, 305, pp 1418-1420.

D Keeley (1993), 'The fundholding debate: should practices reconsider the
decision not to fundhold?', *British Medical Journal*, 306, pp 697–8.

J Kellett (1993), 'Long-term care in the NHS: a vanishing prospect', *British
Medical Journal*, 306, pp 846–8.

S Kerrison (1990), *A diplomat in the job. Diabetes nursing and the changing
division of labour in diabetic care*, Research Paper 4, Health and Social
Services Research Unit, South Bank Polytechnic, London.

S Kerrison (1993), 'Contracting and the Quality of Medical Care', in I
Tilley (ed), *Managing the Internal Market*, Paul Chapman, London.

S Kerrison, T Packwood and M Buxton (1993), *Medical Audit: Taking Stock*,
King's Fund, London.

King's Fund Institute (1989), *Managed Competition: a new approach to
health care in Britain*, Briefing Paper 9, King's Fund Institute,
London.

R Klein (1989), *The Politics of the NHS*, Longman, London.

R Klein (1990), 'The State and the Profession: the politics of the double
bed', *British Medical Journal*, 301, p 700.

R Klein and J Lewis (1976), *The politics of consumer representation*, Centre
for Policy Studies, London.

R Klein and S Redmayne (1992), *Patterns of Priorities: a study of the
purchasing and rationing policies of health authorities*, NAHAT Research
Paper No 7, NAHAT, Birmingham.

M Krashinsky (1986), 'Transactions costs and a theory of the nonprofit
organisation', Chapter 6 in Rose-Ackerman (1986).

Lancet (1992), 'Long-term care in the UK: do we need it?', Editorial in the
Lancet, 339, pp 96–7.

B Leese and N Bosanquet (1989), 'High and low incomes in general
practice', *British Medical Journal*, 298, pp 932–4.

J Le Grand (1991), 'Quasi-markets and social policy', *Economic Journal*, 101,
pp 1256–1267.

J Le Grand (1992), 'Market-orientated health care reforms: impact on equity and efficiency', Paper presented to conference *From economic analysis to health policies*, December, Paris.

J Le Grand and W Bartlett (1993),*Quasi-Markets and Social Policy*, Macmillan, London.

J Le Grand, C Propper and R Robinson (1992), *The Economics of Social Problems*, Third edition, Macmillan, London.

R Levacic (1991), 'Markets and Government', in G Thompson, J Frances, R Levacic and J Mitchell (eds), *Markets, Hierarchies and Networks*, Macmillan, Basingstoke.

D Light (1990a), 'Learning from their mistakes?', *Health Service Journal*, 100 (5221), pp 1470–2.

D Light (1990b), 'Bending the rules', *Health Service Journal*, 100 (5222), pp 1513–5.

S Little (1991), 'Will non-fundholders be left with the scraps?', *Pulse*, 2 March.

C Lloyd and R Siefert (1992),*Industrial Relations in the NHS: A study of four hospitals*, Centre for Industrial Research, University of Keele, Keele.

D Locker and D Dunt (1978), 'Theoretical and methodological issues in sociological studies of consumer satisfaction with medical care', *Social Science and Medicine*, 12, pp 283–292.

H Luft and R H Miller (1988), 'Patient selection in a competitive health system', *Health Affairs*, Vol 7(3), pp 97–119.

A Mahon (1992), 'Journey's end', *Health Service Journal*, 102 (5331), pp 21–22.

M Marinker (1984), 'Developments in primary health care', in G Teeling Smith (ed), *A New NHS Act for 1996?*, Office of Health Economics, London.

M Matsaganis and H Glennerster, Journal of Health Economics, (forthcoming).

R Maxwell (1984), 'Quality assessment in health care', *British Medical Journal*, 288, pp 1470–1472.

R Maxwell (1992), 'Gatekeepers and goalkeepers: general practice advice to purchasers', *British Journal of General Practice*, November, pp 450–1.

A Maynard (1986), 'Performance incentives in general practice', in G Teeling-Smith (ed), *Health Education and General Practice*, Office of Health Economics, London.

N Mays and G Bevan (1987), *Resource allocation in the health service*,

Occasional Papers in Social Administration No 81, Bedford Square Press, London.

B R McAvoy (1993), 'Heartsink hotel revisited', *British Medical Journal*, 306, pp 694–5.

McCarthy (1976), *Making Whitley Work: A Review of the Operation of the National Health Service and Whitley Council Systems*, HMSO, London.

S McIver (1992), 'Counting customers or making customers count', *Critical Public Health*, 3:1, pp 16–21.

G Melnick and J Zwanziger (1998), 'Hospital behaviour under competition and cost containment policies' *Journal of American Medical Association*, 260, 11 November.

D Melzer (1992), 'Supermarket fantasies', *Health Service Journal*, 102, (5306), p 17.

B Meredith (1993), *The Community Care Handbook; The new system explained*, Age Concern, London.

R A Miller (1982), 'The Hirschman-Herfindahl Index as a Market Structure Variable: an exposition for anti-trust practitioners', *Anti-trust Bulletin*, 27, pp 593–596.

G Mooney *et al* (1992) *Priority Setting in Purchasing: some practiced guidelines*, NAHAT Research Paper No. 6, Birmingham.

G H Mooney, E M Russell and R D Weir (1986), *Choices for Health Care*, Macmillan, London.

M Morrill and R Earickson (1968), 'Hospital variation and patient travel distances', *Inquiry*, 5, pp 26–34.

R Morris (1993), 'Community care and the fundholder', *British Medical Journal*, 306, pp 635–7.

P Mullen (1990a), 'Planning and internal markets', in P Spurgeon (ed), *The Changing Face of the NHS*, Longman, London.

P Mullen (1990b), 'Which internal market? The NHS white paper and internal markets', *Financial Accountability and Management*, 6, pp 33–50.

P Mullen (1992), *Waiting lists and the NHS review: reality and myths*, HSMC Research Report 29, Health Services Management Centre, University of Birmingham, Birmingham.

NAHAT (1987), NHS Pay: *Achieving Greater Flexibility*, King's Fund, London.

NAHAT (1991), *Implementing the Reforms: A National Survey of District General Managers*, Project Paper 4, NAHAT, Birmingham.

NAHAT (1992), *Implementing the Reforms: A Survey of Unit General Managers in the West Midlands Region*, Project Paper 5, NAHAT, Birmingham.

NAHAT (1993), *The Financial Survey: 1992/3*, NAHAT, Birmingham.

National Association of Health Service Personnel Officers – Scotland (1991), *The Role and Preparedness of the Personnel Function*, Edinburgh.

National Consumer Council (1992), *Quality Standards in the NHS: the consumer focus*, NCC, London.

Newchurch (1993), *The Third Newchurch Guide to NHS Trusts*, Newchurch and Company Ltd, London.

J Newhouse (1970), 'Toward a theory of non-profit institutions: an economic model of a hospital, *American Economic Review*, 63, 64–74.

J Newton *et al* (1993), 'Fundholding in Northern Region: the first year', *British Medical Journal*, 306, pp 375–78.

NHS Management Executive (1991), *NHS Reforms: The First Six Months*, HMSO, London.

NHS Management Executive (1992a), *Women in the NHS: An Action Guide to the Opportunity 2000 Campaign*, HMSO, London.

NHS Management Executive (1992b), *NHS Trusts: The First 12 Months*, HMSO, London.

NHS Management Executive (1992c), *Future Directions in Managing People in the Health Service*, Personnel Development Directorate, Leeds.

NHS Management Executive (1993), *The NHS Management Executive Business Plan 1993/4*, HMSO, London.

NHS Management Executive/JCC (1991), *Joint guidance to hospital consultants on GP fundholding*, HMSO, London.

North Western Regional Health Authority (1990), *A New Way of Thinking! Contract and planning guidance*, North Western RHA, Manchester.

A Odell (1983), 'A study of patient referrals', *Public Health*, 97, pp 109–114.

Office of Health Economics (1992), *Compendium of Health Statistics*, OHE, London.

R Oldcorn (1989), *Management*, Macmillan, London.

A N Oppenheim (1966), *Questionnaire Design and Attitude Measurement*, Heinemann, London.

T Packwood, S Kerrison and M Buxton (1992), 'The audit process and medical organisation', *Quality in Health Care*, 1, pp 192–196.

T Packwood, J Keen and M Buxton (1991), *Hospitals in Transition: the resource management experiment*, Open University Press, Milton Keynes.

P Parker (1988), 'A free market in health care', *Lancet*, i, pp 1210–1213.

M S J Pathy, A Bayer, K Harding and A Dibbie (1992), 'Randomised trial of case-finding and surveillance of elderly people at home', *Lancet*, 340, pp 890–893.

M V Pauly and M Redisch (1973), 'The not-for-profit hospital as a physicians' cooperative', *American Economic Review*, 63, pp 87–99.

A Peeke (1993), *Waiting times for GP fundholder procedures*, Performance Monitoring Department, Oxford Regional Health Authority, Oxford.

Perri 6 (1992), Non-profit organisations and competition policy, National Council of Voluntary Organisations, London.

A M Pettigrew (1990), 'Longitudinal field research: theory and practice', *Organisational Science, 3:1*.

N Pfeffer and A Coote (1991), *Is Quality Good for You? A critical review of quality assurance in welfare services*, Institute of Public Policy Research, London.

A Pike (1990), 'NHS – a new spirit lives', *Financial Times*, 29 January.

C Pollitt (1989), 'Consuming passions', *Health Service Journal*, 23 November.

C Pollitt (1993), 'The politics of medical quality', *Health Services Management Research*, 16, No 1.

A Pollock (1992), 'Local Voices: The bankruptcy of the democratic process', *British Medical Journal*, 305, pp 535–536.

J E Powell (1966), *A New Look at Medicine and Politics*, Pitman Medical, London.

Price Waterhouse (1990), Survey of Residential Care and Nursing Home Running Costs: a report to the Department of Social Security, Price Waterhouse, London.

M Pringle (1989), 'The quality divide in primary care: set to widen under the new contract', Editorial in *British Medical Journal*, 299, pp 470–1.

C Propper (1993), 'Quasi-Markets, Contracts and Quality', in J Le Grand and W Bartlett (1993).

L Quam (1989), 'Improving clinical effectiveness in the NHS: an alternative to the white paper', *British Medical Journal*, 299, pp 448–50.

Radical Statistics Health Group (1987), *Facing the facts: what really is happening to the NHS?*, Radical Statistics Health Group, London.

Radical Statistics Health Group (1991), 'Missing: a strategy for health',

British Medical Journal, 303, pp 299–302.

Radical Statistics Health Group (1992), 'NHS reforms: the first six months – proof of progress or a statistical smokescreen?', *British Medical Journal*, 304, pp 705–709.

W Ranade and J Appleby (1989), *To Market, To Market: a study of the current trading activities in the NHS and the implications of the Government's provider market proposals*, Research Paper 1, NAHAT, Birmingham.

A Richardson and C Bray (1987), *Promoting health through participation. Experience of groups for patient participation in General Practice*, Policy Studies Institute, 1987.

A Richardson, M Charney and S Hamner-Lloyd (1992), 'Public opinion and purchasing', *British Medical Journal*, 304, pp 680–682.

J Roberts (1990), 'Kenneth Clarke: hatchet man or remoulder?', *British Medical Journal*, 301, p 1383–6.

R Robinson (1990), *Competition and Health Care: a comparative analysis of UK plans and US experience*, Research Report No 6, King's Fund Institute, London.

R Robinson (1991), 'Who's playing monopoly?', *Health Service Journal*, March 28, pp 20–22.

R Robinson and K Judge (1987), *Public Expenditure and the NHS: Trends and Prospects*, King's Fund Institute, London.

M Roland (1991), 'Fundholding and cash limits in primary care: blight or blessing?' *British Medical Journal*, 303, pp 171–2.

M Roland and A Coulter (eds) (1992), *Hospital Referrals*, Oxford University Press, Oxford.

S Rose-Ackerman (1986), *The Economics of Nonprofit Institutions: Studies in Structure and Policy*, Oxford University Press, Oxford.

G Royston *et al* (1992), 'Modelling the use of health services by populations of small areas to inform the allocation of central resources to larger regions', *Socio-economic Planning Sciences*, 26, pp 169–80.

O Samuel (1992), 'Fundholding practices get preference', *British Medical Journal*, 305, p 1497.

R Scheffler 1989), 'Adverse selection: the Achilles heel of the NHS reforms', *Lancet*, i, pp 950–2.

W Schwarz and H Aaron (1984), 'Rationing hospital care: lessons from Britain', *New England Journal of Medicine*, 310, pp 52–56.

A Scott (1992), 'Commercialism in the NHS', *British Medical Journal*, 304, p 85.

A Scott-Samuel (1990), 'White paper blues', *The Public Health Physician*, 1 p 1.

A Scott-Samuel (1992), 'Health gain versus equity', *Health Visitor*, 65, p 176.

Secretaries of State (1989), *Working for Patients*, HMSO, London.

R Sheaff (1991), *Marketing for Health Services*, Open University Press, Milton Keynes.

T Sheldon, G Davey and G Bevan (1993), 'Weighting in the dark: resource allocation in the new NHS', *British Medical Journal*, 306, pp 835–9.

T Sheldon (1990), 'When it makes sense to mince your words', *Health Service Journal*, 100, 1211.

M Skeet (1970), *Home from Hospital*, Macmillan, London.

T Smith (1988), 'New year message', *British Medical Journal*, 296, pp 1–2.

M Stacey (1976), 'The health service consumer: a sociological misconception. The sociology of the NHS', *Sociological Review Monograph*, 22, pp 194–200.

N Starey, N Bosanquet and J Griffiths (1993), 'General Practitioners in partnership with management: an organisational model for debate', *British Medical Journal*, Vol 306, 30 January, pp 308–309.

M Stewart and L J Donaldson (1991), 'Travelling for earlier surgical treatment: the patient's view', *British Journal of General Practice*, 41, pp 508–509.

D Stone (1980), *The Limits of Professional Power*, Chapter 10, University of Chicago Press, Chicago.

P Strong and J Robinson (1990), *The NHS: Under New Management*, Open University Press, Milton Keynes.

G Teeling-Smith (1984), 'The Evolution of the NHS Debate' in G Teeling Smith (ed), *A new NHS Act for 1996?*, Office of Health Economics, London.

M Thompson and J Buchan (1992), *Performance Pay and NHS Nursing*, Institute of Manpower Studies Report No 235, University of Sussex, Falmer.

N Timmins (1988a), 'NHS region may test internal market plan', *The Independent*, 14 March.

N Timmins (1988b), 'Government aims to let NHS hospitals opt out', *The Independent*, 5 December.

B Tomlinson *et al* (1992), *Report of the Inquiry into London's Health Service, Medical Education and Research*, HMSO, London.

Tower Hamlets GP Forum (1993) *Partners in Commissioning*, Tower Hamlets District Health Authority, London.

J Vanek (1970), *The General Theory of the Labor-Managed Economy*, Cornell University Press, Ithaca.

N J Vetter, D A Jones and C R Victor (1984), 'Effect of health visitors working with elderly patients in general practice: a randomised controlled trial', *British Medical Journal*, 288, pp 369–372.

N J Vetter, D A Jones and C R Victor (1986), 'A health visitor affects the problems others do not reach', *Lancet*, pp 30–32.

B C Vladeck, E J Goodwin, L P Myers and M Sinisi (1988), 'Consumers and hospitals use: the HCFA 'Death List', *Health Affairs*, 7, pp 122–125.

D Waller *et al* (1990), 'Health checks in general practice: another example of inverse care?', *British Medical Journal*, 300, pp 115–118.

B Ward (1958), 'The Firm in Illyria', *American Economic Review*, 48, pp 566–589.

K R Waters (1987), 'Discharge planning: an exploratory study of the process of discharge planning on geriatric wards', *Journal of Advanced Nursing*, 12, pp 71–83.

I Watt, N Freemantle and J Mason (1993), 'Purchasing and public health: the state of the union', *Journal of Public Health Medicine*, (forthcoming).

R Webber and J Craig (1978), *Socio-economic classification of local authority areas*, Studies on Medical and Population Subjects No 35, OPCS, London.

C Webster (1988), 'Confronting historical myths', *Health Service Journal*, 98 (1501) Supplement, pp 2–3.

C Webster (1992), 'Beveridge after 50 years. Plus ça change', *British Medical Journal*, 305, pp 901–2.

J Weiner and P Ferris (1990), *GP Budget Holding in the UK: Lessons from America*, Research Report No 7, King's Fund Institute, London.

B Weisbrod (1988), *The Nonprofit Economy*, Harvard University Press, Cambridge, Mass.

Welsh Health Planning Forum (1991), *Protocols for investment in health gain (various diseases)*, Welsh Health Planning Forum, Cardiff.

M Whitehead (1988), *National Health Success*, South Birmingham District Health Authority, ACHCEW, Birmingham.

M Whitehead (1990), *Concepts and Principles of Equity and Health*, World Health Organisation, Copenhagen.

M Whitehead (1992), 'The Health Divide', 2nd edition, in *Inequalities in Health*, Penguin, London.

M Whitehead and G Dahlgren (1991), 'What can be done about inequities in health', *Lancet*, 338, pp 1059–63.

D Wilkins and M Roland (1993), *Waiting times for first outpatient appointments in the NHS*, Centre for Primary Care Research and Department of General Practice, University of Manchester, Manchester.

E Williams *et al*. (1992), 'NHS distribution of funds unfair', *British Medical Journal*, 304, p 643.

O E Williamson (1975), *Markets and Hierarchies: Analysis and Antitrust Implications*, The Free Press, New York.

O E Williamson (1985), *The Economic Institutions of Capitalism*, The Free Press, New York.

P Williamson (1989), 'Second thoughts on the white paper', *King's Fund Newsletter*, 12, p 7.

F Winkler (1987), 'Consumerism in health care: beyond the supermarket model', *Policy and Politics*, 15, pp 1–8.

F Winkler (1989), *Post the review: community/consumer representation in the NHS with specific reference to Community Health Councils*, GLACHC, London.

I Wisely (1993), 'GP fundholding: experience in Grampian', *British Medical Journal*, 306, pp 695–7.

J Workman and D Turnbull (1993), 'Preparing for pay negotiations in an NHS Trust', *Trust Network*, 20.

J Wright (1993), 'Fundholding practices get preference', *British Medical Journal*, 304, p 845.

INDEX

accessibility of services, older patients 153
    community services 131–2, 153
accountability
    aims of reforms 3, 21, 22, 31
    medical audit 157, 158–9, 167–70, 173
    trusts 55
activity, patient
    GP fundholding 90
    trusts 59–61
acute sector 60
administration
    GP fundholding costs 101, 250
    trusts 69; costs 61
appointment systems 137, 144
audit, clinical 173
    see also medical audit
availability of services, older patients
    131–2

back problems, patients with 95
balance sheet, GP fundholding 98–105
bankruptcies, and trusts 59
bargaining leverage 35–6
bathroom facilities, hospitals 147, 148
Bevan, Aneurin 210
block contracts
    GP fundholding 92, 93, 94
    managed competition 38, 40–1
    trusts 56; cream-skimming 64
blood pressure checks 140, 141, 145

break even requirement 55–6, 58
budgets
    GP fundholding: control 96–8; coverage
        76; equity 222–3; freedom 83, 85;
        setting 86–91; volatility 78
    non-acute health care 235–7
    trusts 59

Caines, Eric 184, 119–200
capital
    trusts 55
    Working for Patients 19
capitation benchmark
    GP fundholding 90–1
    resource allocation 229–30
carers of older patients 136
Caring for People 232, 234, 237, 238
case notes, medical audit 163
cataract operations 60
chiropodists 141, 142
choice, user
    elective surgery referral: GPs' views
        122–6; patients' views 117–19
    evaluation 246; direct research 250–1
    older patients: community services
        131–2, 153; hospitals 146, 153
    trusts 63–4
clarification of reforms 34
Clarke, Kenneth
    GP fundholding 75

monitoring of reforms 1
objectives of reforms 20–1
cleanliness, hospitals 147, 148
clinical audit 173
   see also medical audit
clinical service quality 248
commercial entrepreneurial organisations
   66–7
commercial mutual organisations 66
commitment, corporate 34–5
communication
   hospital-GP fundholders 218
   hospital-patient 146, 153
   of reforms 34
community care 230
Community Health Councils 109
community services
   GP fundholding: contracting 95–6;
      inefficiency 77–8
   older patients 131–2, 133–5, 136–45,
      151–3; non-acute health care
      entitlements 232–3, 239
competition
   aims of reforms 21–2
   equity considerations 211–12
   evaluation 253–5
   managed 48–49
   measurement 43
   role 36
   trusts 63, 64
competitive tendering 15
computers
   GP fundholding 83; allowances 223;
      costs 101–2; equity 102–3; upgrading
      90
   medical audit 163–4
confidence in reforms 32
consultants, hospital
   elective surgery referral 118–19
   equity 218, 224, 240
   GP fundholding: contracting 93–5;
      equity 218, 224; non-emergency cases
      77
   medical audit 161, 163, 165, 168–70
   mobility, London 204

Working for Patients 19
consultative mechanisms 35
consumer research 35
consumerism 108–14, 128–9
contestable markets 26, 50
continuing care 231–9
contracting
   competition 26, 36–45, 46–9
   consultants 19
   equity implications 214, 222, 240
   GP fundholding 91–6, 222; efficiency
      100; elective surgery referral 113
   information 256
   policy development 15
   trusts 56
corporate commitment to reforms 34–5
corporate issues, personnel function 201
cost-and-volume contracts
   GP fundholding 94
   trusts 56
cost-per-case contracts
   GP fundholding 94
   trusts 56
costing systems 19
costs
   audit of 164
   GP fundholding 101–2
   labour 183–4, 187, 188; *see also* pay
   trusts 61–3, 72–3
cream-skimming
   GP fundholding 78, 103–5, 213,
      251–2
   trusts 64
criteria-based audit 162–5

databases 164
day cases
   older patients 142
   trusts 60
decision-making
   information for 51–2, 255–7
   by patients 111–12
   trusts 68–9
dental charges 211
Department of Health

GP fundholding 81–2; budget
    setting 87–8
    trusts 55
deprivation payments 230–1
diabetic patients 147
diagnostic tests 76
direct access services 218
directly managed units (DMUs)
    contracts 56
    health care assistants 184–5
    patient activity 60
    staff levels 186
discharge planning, older patients 135–6,
    147–50
    non-acute health care 235–7, 238–9
district general managers (DGMs)
    attitudes 31–3
    provider teams 37
    purchasing teams 37
district health authorities (DHAs)
    funding 4
    general practitioners 5
    integration 2, 5
    role 3, 4
district nurses 140, 142–3
domiciliary care 237–8, 239
donative entrepreneurial organisations
    66–7
donative mutual organisations 66
drugs see pharmaceuticals

East Anglia 16
economic policy 14
economies of scale 253
education and medical audit 170–1
efficiency
    aims of reforms 21
    evaluation 245–6; direct research
        249–50
    GP fundholding: balance sheet 100–2;
        catalysts 77–8
    internal market 26
    NHS working group 17
    organisational 14
    trusts 63–4

elderly people see older people
elective surgery referral 108–9, 128–9
    choices 251
    GPs' views 122–8
    patients' views 118–22
    research 114–17; methodology 117–18
    Working for Patients 110–14
employee relations 187–91, 197, 200
employee services 201
Enthoven, Professor 16, 18
entitlements, health care 209
entrepreneurialism 15
entry, market 26, 50
equity 208–11, 239–42
    advantages 214–15
    dangers 211–14
    entitlements 231–9
    evaluation 246, 251–3
    GP fundholding 78, 215–25; balance
        sheet 102–5
    needs assessment and resource allocation
        225–31
    trusts 63–4
ethical purchasing and providing 241
ex ante transaction costs 257–8
ex post transaction costs 257–8
exit threat, GP fundholding 92
expertise, contracting 37, 42
external financing limits (EFLs) 55–6, 58

Family Health Services Authorities
    (FHSAs)
    contracting 41
    GP fundholding 76, 82
    integration 2, 5
'feel-good factor' 210
finance function 205
financial performance, trusts 58–9
financial risks, pooling of 209
flexibility, contractual 93–4
flexible local pay supplements 192
food, hospital 147, 150
Fowler, Norman 14
free nature of services 209
    exceptions 211

fundholding GPs *see* general practice fundholders

funding
health services 4; crisis 16–17; managed competition 52; underfunding 32; *Working for Patients* 19
medical audit 171

general practice fundholders 74–107, 83–6
balance sheet 98–105
budgets; control 96–8; setting 86–91
competition 255
contracting 91–6
controls 22
decision-making 2–3
efficiency catalysts 77–8
elective surgery referral 113, 124–6
equity implications 212–13, 215–25, 230–1, 252
future 105–7
implementation of reforms 30, 81–2
information 256–7
motivation 259
older patients 136–7
policy development 18
quality 247–8
research 78–81
role 5
spread 86
general practitioners (GPs)
elective surgery referral 116–18, 122–8
older patients 137–8, 139–40, 141
role 5
general surgery 46–50
geographical distribution
GP fundholding 86, 87
health care services 209, 212
government borrowing 52
Griffiths, Sir Roy 14, 157, 180–1

Hawthorne effect 250
trusts 61
Health and Medicines Act (1988) 15
health care assistants (HCAs) 184–5

health checks, older patients 139, 140, 144, 153
health gain 226
evaluation 248
purchasing for 226–8
health maintenance organisations (HMOs) 75
budget control 96
budget volatility 78
health promotion strategies 214, 226
health visitors 139, 140–2, 143

heart by-pass operations 60
hip replacement operations 60
Hirschman-Herfindahl index (HHI) 45–50
home visits 138–9
human costs and benefits, distribution 241

implementation of reforms 29–30
incentive structures
GP fundholding 101
medical audit 176–7
trusts 69, 70
income generation schemes 14–15
inefficiency *see* efficiency
information
contracting 37
for decision-making 51–2, 255–7
for patients; hospitals 146, 150–1; practice leaflets 137, 138, 143–4
for trusts 63, 64
Working for Patients 19
inpatients
GP fundholding 76
trusts 60
insurance-based NHS proposals 17

Jenkin, Patrick 14
job security, personnel function 199
junior doctors, medical audit 161, 165, 166, 169–70

laboratory services 92
labour costs 183–4, 187, 188
see also pay

labour-managed firms 66, 67, 70
labour market intelligence units 202–4
Labour Party 106
lavatories, hospital 147, 148
learning-by-doing strategy 35
local aspects of reforms 31–6
    GP fundholding 91
    pay determination 191, 194–5
local audit committees 168, 169
London, personnel function 204
long-term policy implications 242

managed competition 24–5
    changes 25–6
    contracting 36–45
    future prospects 50–3
    local factors 31–6
    monitoring 26–9, 45–50; methodology
        29–31
management, health services 4
    GP fundholding 78
    medical audit 156–7, 169
    personnel function 178
    trusts 68–9
management allowances 90, 101
    equity 223
Management Executive Outposts, NHS 3
managerialism
    policy development 14
    Working for Patients 19
manpower utilisation, personnel function
    201
market signals, response to 63, 64
market structure 253–5
market testing see competitive tendering
maximisation approach, trust theory 67–9
Maynard, Alan 74–5
means tests 235, 237
medical audit 155–9
    accountability 167–70
    education 170–1
    future 171–4
    implications 175–7; equity 214
    as information source 256
    in practice 160–7

quality evaluation 248–9
    research 159–60
    Working for Patients 19
medication see pharmaceuticals
Mellor, David
    general practice fundholders 18
    objectives of reforms 21
monopolies
    and competition 25, 253–4, 255
    Hirschman-Herfindahl index 49, 50
Moore, John
    insurance-based NHS proposals 17
    NHS review 16
morale, personnel function 199–200
motivation, purchasers and providers
    258–9

National Health Service and Community
    Care Act (1990) 2, 13, 24
    expectations 24
    reforms 2
national pay determination 191–3
need, clinical 210
needs assessment 35
    contracting 40
    equity 225–31, 240–1; non-acute health
        care 235, 237, 239
negotiation of contracts 39
Netherlands 16
New Zealand 16
non-acute health care, entitlements 231–9
non-distribution constraint 65, 66
non-emergency cases 77
non-exploitation ethos 210
non-profit organisations 65–70
notice of hospital admissions 145–6, 150
nurses
    hospitals: medical audit 162; pay
        determination 193; skill mix 184,
        185, 186
    practice 137, 139, 141, 144

occupational therapy 62
older people
    health service changes 130–1, 151–4;

community study 131–2, 133–5, 136–45; hospital study 132–3, 135–6, 145–51; quality, service 247; research methods 133–6
non-acute health care entitlements 232–9
operations
  GP fundholding 76
  trusts 60
optional extras, hospitals 147
organisation of medical audit 160–2
organisational development, personnel function 201
out-of-hours visits 138, 144
outcomes of audit 166–7
outpatients
  GP fundholding 76, 77
  older people 143
  trusts 60
overspending 96
ownership structure, nonprofits 65–6

patient activity
  GP fundholding 90
  trusts 59–61
patient-focused care 186–7
Patient's Charter
  awareness of 119
  pay determination 192
  quality aspects 112
  resource allocation 228
pay
  determination 191–5, 196, 200, 202–4
  skill mix 183–4
Pay Review Bodies 191, 200
peer accountability, medical audit 167–8, 169
performance pay schemes 192, 193–4
personnel function 178–9
  changes 195–206
  effectiveness 206
  efficiency 249–50
  employee relations 187–91
  future 206–7
  pay determination 191–5
  post-reform 181–2

pre-reform 179–81
  staffing levels and mix 182–7
pharmaceuticals
  GP fundholding 76; budget setting 88, 90; efficiency 77, 100–1; equity 219–20, 221
  older patients 140, 142, 145
physiotherapists 95
policy options, assessment 242
postgraduate education 171
practice staff
  GP fundholding 76; budget setting 88, 90
  nurses 137, 139, 141, 144
prescription charges 211
presentation of audits 172
prioritisation of reforms 34
privacy, hospital 147
private health care 67
  GP fundholding 219
  older patients 233–4
  private rooms 147
private sector 14
privatisation policy 24
pro-active authorities 33–5
productivity, trusts 61
profits
  equity considerations 211–12
  maximisation, trusts 67–8
Project 2000   186
property rights, nonprofits 65–6
provider–purchaser relationships 38
provider teams 37, 41–5
psychiatrists 95
public sector 14
purchaser teams 37, 41–5
purchasing decisions, influencing factors 42

quality, service 36
  contracting 38
  elective surgery referral 112
  evaluation 245, 247–9
  GP fundholding 83, 84–5, 93
  medical audit 156

older patients 132, 153
  skill mix 185
quality management 158

RAWP formula 229, 230
reactive authorities 33–5
receptionists 137, 139, 140
recession, economic
  pay determination 195
  skill shortages 198
referrals
  budget setting 88, 90
  fears 78
  equity 102, 219–20, 221
  freedom 83, 85
  see also elective surgery referral
regional health authorities (RHAs) 5
regional pay units 202–4
regional rewards, personnel function 201
remuneration levels, trusts 55
resource allocation
  audit of 164–5
  equity 225–31, 240, 252–3
  pre-election 244
Resource Management Initiative 157
responsiveness
  evaluation 246; direct research 251
  trusts 63–4
return on assets 55, 58, 59

sample sizes, medical audit 163, 165
satisfaction, patient
  audit of 164
  elective surgery referral 118
  older patients 130; GPs 139–40;
    hospitals 145–9
satisficing approach, trust theory 69–70
Secretary of State for Health
  competition, control 21–2
  NHS trusts, accountability 3
self-governing hospitals see trusts
self-selection effect, trusts 60, 62–3
service development, GP fundholding 83
service maximisation, trusts 68
simplification of reforms 34

skill mix 183–4
social deprivation 91
social inequalities 226
social policy 13–14
social security payments 233, 234–5
Social Service Departments 2
staff
  levels 183, 184, 185–7, 196
  mix 183–4, 185, 186–7
  practice: GP fundholding 76, 88, 90;
    nurses 137, 139, 141, 44
  trusts 55
strategic issues, personnel function 201
strategic purchasing 35
supermarket model of consumerism
  128
surpluses, financial 56, 59
syndicalism 68–9

telephone advice 138, 144
Thatcher, Margaret
  philosophy 13–14
  Working for Patients 1; competition 22
  working group 16, 17
timetable of reforms 38
trades unions
  employee relations 189–91
  pay determination 195
training and development 201
transaction costs
  competition 26
  evaluation 257–8
  GP fundholding 222
  trusts 63, 64
travel for treatment
  competition 254
  elective surgery referral 113–14,
    119–22, 126–7, 128
  trusts 213–14
trusts 55–7
  accountability 3
  aims of reforms 21
  efficiency 249
  equity implications 213–14
  implementation of reforms 29–30

21.95

performance 54–5, 71; direct research
    57–63
indirect research 57, 63–5
personnel function; employee relations
    189–90; pay determination 192
policy development 18
responsibilities 3
restrictions 22
theory of 65–70
trustworthiness of doctors 210
turnover, patient 185
two-tier services 102–3, 213, 215–25, 252
underfunding 32
under-referral 78
underspending 98
under-treatment 78
unit general managers 32–3
United States of America
    health maintenance organisations
        (HMOs) 75; budget control 96; budget
        volatility 78
    Hirschman–Herfindahl' index 49
    medical audit 173
    patient focused care 186–7
    trustworthiness of doctors 210

wages see pay
waiting lists

attitudes towards 32
elective surgery referral 128; GPs' views
    125; patients' views 119
GP fundholding: budget control 96;
    equity 218, 220; non-emergency cases
    77
older patients 142, 145, 150,
    151; non-acute health care 237
trusts 60
waiting times 137, 140
Waldegrave, William 23
ward costs 61
West Midlands 27
    managed competition 48, 49; block
        contracts 38
Whitley Councils 183, 187–9, 192, 200
Working for Patients
    and Caring for People 232, 238
    consumerism 110–14
    contents 18–19
    evaluation 245–6
    expectations 24
    medical audit 155
    objectives 19–22
    personnel function 181
    publication 13, 18
    self-governing hospitals 18
    Thatcher, Margaret 1